The Free Mind through the Ages

The Free Mind through the Ages

Edward L. Ericson

Frederick Ungar Publishing Co. / New York

Ericson, Edward L.
The free mind through the ages.

1. Liberty——History. 2. Political science——History.
3. Dissenters——History. I. Title.
JC571.E726 1985 323.44 09 84–28051
ISBN 0–8044–5358–6
ISBN 0–8044–6149–X (pbk.)

Printed and bound in Great Britain by
Biddles Ltd, Guildford and King's Lynn

Contents

Preface / *1*

1 The Future of the Free Mind / *3*

2 Evolution's Orpheus: **Lucretius** / *13*

3 Emperor-Philosopher: **Marcus Aurelius** / *25*

4 Persian Agnostic: **Omar Khayyam** / *37*

5 Martyr of Free Inquiry: **Giordano Bruno** / *49*

6 Eternal Nature Is God: **Benedict Spinoza** / *65*

7 Joyous Infidel: **Voltaire** / *75*

8 Prophet of Reason: **Thomas Paine** / *91*

9 Freethinker in the White House: **Thomas Jefferson** / *105*

10 Imperative Thinker: **Immanuel Kant** / *121*

11 Patriot of Humanity: **Friedrich Schiller** / *133*

12 The Inner Eye at Large: **Ralph Waldo Emerson** / *149*

13 Ear Trumpet and Ram's Horn: **Harriet Martineau** / *165*

14 Pilot of a Brooding Heart: **Mark Twain** / *183*

15 First Citizen of the Cosmos: **Albert Einstein** / *195*

16 A Lord Unsanctified: **Bertrand Russell** / *207*

17 Prisoner of Conscience: **Andrei Sakharov** / *225*

Author's Preface

After an introductory glance toward the future, this book sketches the intellectual and moral profiles of fifteen men and one woman (no "token," she!) who have contributed strikingly to humanity's most glorious passage: the ageless venture to make the mind free. They include skeptics, agnostics, freethinkers, spiritual nonconformists and rebels against every expression of religious or ideological repression. A period of more than two thousand years separates the first of them–the Roman Poet Lucretius–from the last–the Soviet nuclear physicist and humanist, Andrei Sakharov–who still lives, although in perilous circumstances, even as I write. All are joined by the thread of a spiritual saga we shall endeavor to trace, although of necessity in barest outline.

Some facts and issues dealt with earlier had to be touched upon again in later chapters, so that each profile is accessible to the selective reader.

This study does not presume to be a systematic history of Western liberal thought. Many of the greatest minds of our civilization are absent. Those portrayed stand as *representative* of a much larger fellowship of the human spirit. It is the author's hope that they are, or will become, spiritual heroes for every reader who cherishes our most precious legacy.

I wish to thank members of the staff of the New York Society for Ethical Culture who typed portions of the manuscript, Professor Joseph L. Blau of Columbia University who advised me on several points of philosophical history and interpretation, and especially my publisher, Frederick Ungar, who invited me to undertake this book and has given many hours of helpful review, suggestion, and encouragement.

Frederick Ungar Publishing Co. has generously given permission to quote extensively from the James H. Mantinband translation of Lucretius' *On the Nature of the Universe*, and *Friedrich Schiller, An Anthology*, translated and edited by Frederick Ungar. They have also consented to inclusion of the chapter on Emerson which I wrote originally as an introduction to a volume of Emerson's writings, scheduled to be published by Frederick Ungar Publishing Co.

1

The Future of the Free Mind

In the history of the Western world, the free mind has brightened the horizon with two magnificent bursts of enlightenment. Each blazed like a nova, making all previous knowledge seem a distant star by comparison. Physicists tell us that novae rapidly exhaust their energies and are quickly extinguished. Will it be so with the human mind? Or will free thought continue to light the way for the future?

The first great burst of the free mind lasted for a thousand years and then faded into an era which, with unjustified exaggeration, has been called the Dark Ages. While not totally dark, and indeed fruitful of much science and culture, the middle period of Western civilization was not equal in intellectual daring and humanistic imagination to the age that began about the century of Isaiah and faded shortly after Marcus Aurelius–its climax extending at most from Democritus to Lucretius and the early Caesars.

After well over a thousand years had passed, a second great explosion of intellectual vigor occurred; it is by this aura that our present age is illuminated. If we date its appearance from the revival of the ancient learning in the Renaissance, the present era is already more than six centuries old and its beginning at least a century older. Will this burst of intelligence be exterminated by an act of political folly? Or will it slowly fade, its furnaces of thought exhausted? Will it, like the black holes of radio astronomy, collapse under its own accumulated weight, with the excessive mass of ideology and bureaucracy permitting no ray of critical reason or spontaneous imagination to emerge? Or will it continue, to be followed by even greater bursts of unfettered thought?

These are urgent questions with no certain answers. But despite the historical brevity of philosophy and science as we know them, we are perhaps justified in drawing certain tentative conclusions about the nature and future of the free mind. Without claiming that history repeats itself, or that two cycles of freethinking philosophy and flourishing science establish a pattern, we might discern certain parallels and recurrences that may be useful as guides to the future.

First we might emphasize that a creative age involves the forceful and often violent stripping away of old certitudes and inherited folkways. The ancient Greeks began to reason about the causes and meaning of life when the old gods could no longer be believed. The Greeks were shaped by their commerce and that of their neighbors–the Egyptians, Phoenicians, and Persians–as well as of the earlier civilizations they had conquered. With commerce had come knowledge of a broader and more complex world. The stay-at-home gods were no longer considered all-wise. When Greek travelers discovered a world that their gods back home had never known, they espoused new religions and bold skeptical theories.

Determined skepticism seldom if ever overturns old beliefs without long preparation and a wealth of evidence that cannot be refuted. Old beliefs are themselves subject to the influences of a new age and in time take on an altered appearance and meaning. Christianity is an example of this process. For the educated twentieth-century believer Christianity bears only a remote relationship to the intellectual creed of the cultivated believer of fourth- or fifth-century Alexandria or Athens. Old bottles *do* hold new wine; we often fail to recognize changed and novel ways of thinking and believing because they bear old labels. Radical ideas in philosophy and culture often wear the sacred vestments of ancient cults and rituals. Yet the converse of this is also true: outdated forms of thinking, regressions, and frozen orthodoxies in science and philosophy frequently comport themselves as revolutionary and scientific.

This was exemplified a few years ago in a "dialogue" between a panel of Communist intellectuals in Moscow and a visiting group of American religious scholars and representatives of many faiths. Our Soviet hosts at the Institute of Scientific Atheism made a determined, if clumsy, effort to champion the "progressive" position of the Soviet ideology toward religion, arguing the fallacy and superstitious nature of all religion. This totally biased position offered no ground for a meeting of minds, and the discussion was a near disaster.

During the following reception, I decided to forgo diplomatic nicety and told the director of the Institute that he and his colleagues had wasted a great opportunity for fruitful communication and that he had only reinforced old sterotypes about both believers and nonbelievers. These American religious leaders and scholars, I contended, were astute, critically minded men and women, well versed in contemporary philosophy, including the philosophy of science. Had our Soviet hosts taken their guests' perspectives seriously, they would have learned that much of contemporary religious thinking is far removed from the naive supernaturalism and popular superstition that they assumed.

As the socializing continued, the leaders of the Soviet Institute murmured among themselves and returned to say: "We have considered your criticism and would like to invite the American group to return for a second session." In the changed atmosphere of the second meeting, honest discussion took place with a minimum of pat speeches and dogmatic posturing. If our conversation produced nothing more, it taught at least one small group of Soviet intellectuals to lay aside, even if only momentarily, an untenable and outmoded caricature of Western religious philosophy, and we from the

West gained a clearer understanding of the roots of anticlericalism in the Soviet Union.

We tend to forget that Soviet hostility to organized religion did not develop without good cause. Anyone unfamiliar with the cruelty, oppressiveness, and superstitiousness of the state church in Czarist Russia should read Tolstoy's accounts of the suppressions and persecutions sanctioned by the religious authorities. Neither Soviets nor Americans can approach the other fairly, or even intelligently, without understanding each other's history. This does not mean that we can for a moment acquiesce in acceptance of political or intellectual repression.

Why is antireligious and especially anticlerical feeling so dominant in Russian history, and in French and Latin American history as well? And why is anticlericalism of so little consequence in the United States? Even our Western European friends marvel at the continuing strength of organized religion in the United States and are puzzled to understand the grip of religious belief on American culture. Why should religious vitality be a distinguishing trait of secular, pluralistic America?

Three reasons stand out as probably determining both the strength and the prevailing conservatism of religion in America. The first is the relative weakness of any historic religious establishment in America. Although some of the colonies had state churches, others did not. Rhode Island, New York, New Jersey, and Pennsylvania were conspicuous havens of religious tolerance. The southern colonies had established churches, but their authority was limited from the beginning and progressively diminished. Only in parts of New England did a governing orthodoxy hold impressive power; but even there, the Calvinist supremacy was overthrown by the rise of revolutionary liberalism and Unitarian rationalism. Without a persecuting state church to fear, Americans have no historic memory to equal the experience of the Russians or the French under the iron law of cross and crown. Similarly, these countries are not aware of the role of dissenting and reforming religious movements in giving birth to the progressive and liberal traditions of the English-speaking world (and the Dutch)–from the Lollards of medieval England and the "levelers" and "diggers" of Cromwell's revolution, through the antislavery, labor, peace, civil-rights, and women's movements of more recent times.

In the light of this complex history, the terms "religious," "antireligious," and "secular" acquire an ambiguous meaning. "Religious" humanists, "nonreligious" Christians, and "secular" Jews adopt labels that express a mixture of attitudes and approaches that are often not really understandable to outsiders. Half a world apart, an atheist Marxist and a devout Baptist preacher may lead parallel movements for black liberation–the one reflecting the ethos of colonial Africa, the other the black experience of the American South.

We always write our social compacts and constitutions in the life blood of particular histories, a fact which, once recognized, underscores both the folly and the stubborn persistency of ideological conflict. We cannot be other than what we are; but neither can our antagonists. In the realm of the eternal, purity may be a higher value than tolerance, but tolerance and accommodation offer greater survival value in time, and time is life's ultimate resource and ground for hope.

The second reason for the strength of religion in America is tribal or familial. Since the introduction of Christianity, the most completely theological of religions, Westerners under its influence have been blinded into equating religion with a theory of Being or a doctrine of God. This drastically narrows and intellectualizes religion. Primitive societies were wiser. An aboriginal tribesman is said to have asked an anthropologist: "What religion do you dance?" In preliterate cultures your religion is what you dance–what you express–what you feel and experience of the world that envelops you. You are not even aware of "being religious." The original and continuing function of religion is community. A people's religion is their pattern of socialization. Theologizing comes later. The search for social solidarity is primary and perennial. Lacking the security of fixed, extended kinship groups, contemporary men and women turn to the fraternity of ideologies and sects to give structure to their relationships. Closed, totalitarian movements are thrown into competition with open, more fluid groupings. Except for a few extreme nonjoiners, most human beings gravitate toward voluntary communities, churches, lodges, and parties that give personal and social coherence to their lives. The urgency of this need in a fluid contemporary society such as the United States is obvious. The strength of organized religious bodies in America reflects the magnitude of the "identity crisis" in our mobile society and the urgency that many people feel to resolve a lack of spiritual definition.

A third reason for the strength of religious life in America owes something to both reasons just cited, but makes another demand of its own. Having only a weak sense of established social order, the American seeks to impose an individual stamp on the design of the world, to give it a special thrust. This impulse is at least as old as Emerson, Thoreau, and Whitman–our distinctively American triad–in whom it was a controlling characteristic. The world does not exist simply as an *is*; it is not merely a fact. It is also the crucible of an *ought*, a receptacle for the reality that *deserves to be*, which individual will and effort can help bring about.

The religious mind in America is thus closely woven in with the reforming, perfecting, utopian strands of our national character, linked to everything that the ideas of progress and justice express so forcefully in our experience as a people. But it will be seen that this impulse is often at odds with one other force propelling the spiritual life of Americans: the hunger for enduring social institutions and the related demand for a spiritual identity that is secure. Conservative and innovative impulses are thus joined in the American psyche, and the boisterous collision of conflicting elements is assured. When the backward-looking, rigid elements prevail, the free mind in America loses ground; the extremes of fundamentalism and authoritarian religion harden into a force for cultural retardation, a state of mindless conformism, which many observers, both here and abroad, regard with increasing anxiety.

On the other hand, a living society requires at least a certain minimum of responsible conservative traits to give it internal coherence and the stability necessary to survive. This conserving, nurturing role is played particularly by religion in a pluralistic culture caught up in rapid, unpredictable change. Even groups and organizations that call themselves liberal or progressive play this conserving function in a society that is in transition. The Bill of Rights, for example, is an instrument that guarantees the freedom to introduce change, heterodoxy, and innovation. But this very instrument of change acts as a conservative shield against forces that would overwhelm or devour freedom. Thus the concept of liberty itself is necessarily bound up with a history; freedom is a tradition in its own right, and in defending its historic institutions and conventions, we are in fact playing a conservative role against outbreaks of the authoritarian obsession. A free and open society requires the interaction of both conservative and innovative factors, and when the balance swings too far in either direction, the process of freedom is endangered. Once we understand this, we learn to approach political, ideological, and even religious controversies in a new light and to pursue the resolution of our differences with appropriate humility. To disrupt or punish any element whose survival depends on the freedom of the open society tends to undercut and weaken all other elements that depend on the freedom of the open society to survive.

Institutions must be understood and evaluated by the part they play in particular histories. The Roman Catholic Church was an oppressive regime in pre-Revolutionary France, but it has served as a vehicle for the preservation of the Irish and Polish peoples in their periods of servitude. The black Protestant church in the South, on the very eve of Martin Luther King's civil-rights movement, was written off by many as an escapist institution which diverted feelings of injustice with pie-in-the-sky consolation. Yet, when the moment came, the black church was ready, and more than any other institution enabled blacks to mount an irresistible moral and social struggle for racial justice. That transformation did not happen overnight. The alleged escapist character of black religion was largely a misreading by outsiders who failed to see the part that the black church had played for generations in nurturing the dream of freedom and providing the spiritual resources for the survival of its people.

It was all-important simply because it was the only major social institution that blacks themselves controlled and which could express their yearning for justice. We should note this fact carefully and draw the correct inference from it: a people deprived of participation in the established instruments of power will use whatever institutions are in their hands. All oppressed nations and minorities have done so, and for this reason, princes and kings historically allowed no such institutions to exist; to control the church was as necessary in the eyes of the sovereign as it was to control the army. Heretics and sectarians were put to the sword, and Jews, who almost alone retained their own spiritual institutions and practices, were viewed with suspicion and periodically exiled or abused.

Twentieth-century totalitarianism has revived this medieval principle of forbidding any institution to exist that offers empowerment to the dispossessed. Even in democratic societies a constant alertness on the part of nonconformists and civil libertarians is needed to resist pressures to subordinate all institutions that shape the human spirit and to place them under the control of those who want to dominate the social order.

Although there are profound differences between the extent of personal freedom within the Western democracies and within the one-party Communist societies–and those distinctions ought never to be minimized–it is nevertheless true that the future of the free mind is threatened by the growth of converging forces in both of these rival systems. In the Communist states and the Western nations technological structures and bureaucracy instill in the individual citizen a feeling of helplessness and hopeless passivity.

While each world system likes to accuse the other of drifting toward fascism or of already being fascist under a liberal or

Marxist façade, there are indeed grounds to fear that both social systems are advancing toward corporate structures that efface individuality and freedom of expression. Both are managerial societies which tend to equate virtue with conformity, pliability, and administrative efficency. Even religious leaders and other teachers of ethics are reduced to functionaries controlled by a corporate mentality concerned most of all with "success" as measured in quantitative terms.

If the experience of the past twenty-five hundred years contains a lesson to be learned, it is this: To maintain one's freedom of mind is always an individual, sometimes even a quixotic accomplishment. The appeal of the freethinker, the skeptic, the liberator, the discoverer of new truth, is always *against* established patterns and presumptions. As the founders of the American Constitution understood, a free and open society is one that inhibits the power of institutions, and especially of the state, from interfering with the life of the mind.

A society of heretics is an uncomfortable and unstable community. Yet that is what true spiritual democracy represents. It is an extremely difficult form of social organization to bring about, as the dismal failure to establish democracy in historically unprepared cultures demonstrates. The free mind creates the free society, not the other way around. Freedom is not mandated; it is cultivated through experience.

The future of the free mind depends upon forces in modern culture strong enough to sustain its intellectual fire. Bertrand Russell recognized that free thought is an intellectual tradition that can be passed from teacher to student, if, but only if, the teacher, like the artist or thinker acts, as Russell expressed it, from "an inner creative impulse, and [is] not dominated and fettered by an outside authority. If the world is not to lose the benefit to be derived from its best minds, it will have to find some method of allowing them scope and liberty."

While we can have no guarantee that the free spirit will flourish in the future, the benefit that the world can derive from creative thinking provides freedom with the best chance to survive. Those societies that encourage the free mind are rewarded by superior vitality, increasing knowledge, and a more resilient and dynamic spirit.

For heirs of the liberal, humanistic tradition, there is no stronger spiritual resource than this realization. The passion to achieve our promise as human beings, strengthened by the gains won through the ages, encourages us to believe that freedom to think, and the disposition to do so, continue to gain historic momentum. To be human is to think; and to think affirmatively about life's possibilities is to become more satisfyingly human. No religion or ideology that ignores this need can gain the lasting assent of the human mind and heart.

2

Evolution's Orpheus:

Lucretius

(c. 96–55 B.C.)

Born a century before the time of Christ, the Roman poet Lucretius died while still young, leaving behind a long philosophical poem on the origins of the universe and all living things. *De Rerum Natura (On the Nature of Things)* is still celebrated as a moving description of cosmic and biological evolution as visualized by early Greek science and materialistic philosophy. Lucretius's philosophy expresses the thoughts of Epicurus (c. 342–270 B.C.) founder of the philosophical school bearing his name. He was also a proponent of the pre-Socratic materialists of Greek Ionia and especially of Leucippus and Democritus who are remembered for their early versions of the atomic theory of matter.

Epicureanism, which denied the intervention of the gods in human life or nature, strongly opposed popular religions of the time as mere superstitions and recommended a life of reason, moderation, and the cultivation of inner tranquility. After Lucretius, Epicureanism rapidly lost influence. This opening portrait in the dramatic story of the free mind presents the thought and artistry of Epicureanism's most appealing representative.

One of the supreme literary achievements of the free mind in its ageless quest for enlightenment was accomplished by a young Roman poet more than a hundred years before the earliest books of the Christian bible were written. His name was Titus Lucretius Carus, remembered simply as Lucretius. In mature wisdom and spiritual composure his philosophical poem compares favorably with any of the world's great scriptures. As a work of uncompromising intellectual honesty, humane moral passion, and a courage free from illusion, it has rarely been equalled. If the spirit of freedom had a bible, surely Lucretius's masterwork, *De Rerum Natura*, commonly known throughout the English-speaking world by its title *Of the Nature of Things*, would occupy a place as the free mind's book of Genesis, Job, and Psalms. Of course, the searching mind can view no book as final or infallible, but continually draws insight and enlightenment from many sources.

Lucretius's poem on the nature of the universe and the place of human affairs within the order of things occupies in ordinary print several hundred pages. Because of its length, comparatively few have read it through, although excerpts of this classic are often included in anthologies. It is impossible to survey the history of ideas, especially the theory of evolution in terms of its development from ancient Greek and Roman sources, without reference to the dazzling description of the origin of the universe written by this Roman poet more than twenty centuries ago.

Following the atomic theory of the Greek philosopher Democritus (of the fifth century B.C.) Lucretius describes how the heavens and earth took shape from swirling primitive atoms combining in space, and how all living forms gradually emerged from unguided, random combinations of material particles occurring over the immensity of time, all without divine purpose or design:

> For surely,
> the atoms did not take their places by volition
> nor did they place themselves by sharp intelligence,
> nor did they agree what movements to produce;
> but many elements in many different ways,

bombarded with blows and carried along by their own weight,
from time immemorial, have been wont to move and meet
in various ways, and try out all the permutations
that they were able to produce by coming together.

And so it happens, after being dispersed for ages,
attempting every sort of motion and conjunction,
at last those atoms come together whose combination
can form the first-beginnings of all great things we know;
the earth, the sea, the sky, and the races of living creatures.

This brief passage is representative of many equally startling descriptions of the evolution of the cosmos and the beginnings of life. It is based on the conception of a naturalistic universe of matter and space, working out the composition of all living forms by its own dynamic process and not as a result of supernatural creation or guidance. In terms of human desires and values, the cosmos offers no guarantee of perfection, as the atoms pursue their ever-changing permutations:

But even if I knew nothing at all about the atoms
still I would insist from the heavenly bodies themselves,
confirming it with evidence from other sources,
that the universe was certainly not made for us
by divine power, for it is too full of faults.

For all its beauty, the world is an arena of disease and terror and all living things are set at risk:

Why do the changing seasons
bring pestilence? Why does untimely death roam the world?
Then again, an infant, like a shipwrecked sailor,
cast up by the cruel sea, lies naked on the ground,
speechless and helpless, when Nature first has thrown him forth
with painful birth from his mother's womb into the sunlit world;
he fills the air with pitiful cries, and rightly, too,
seeing how much trouble life holds in store for him.

Since life did not spring perfected from the hand of an all-wise Maker, its very creation was a blind process of false starts and violent terminations, from which the abler and fitter survived to reproduce themselves. Thus Lucretius, with uncanny prescience, anticipates Darwinian natural selection by nineteen centuries:

> Many monsters the earth attempted to create:
> ones with fantastic shapes, grotesque in their appearance;
> the hermaphrodite, neither man nor woman, but partly both,
> and creatures with no feet, and some without any hands;
> and some were mute without a mouth; some blind with no face;
> and some with all their limbs adhering to their bodies, . . .
> So with all the monsters and grotesque things she made,
> it was in vain: for Nature did not let them grow,
> they could not reach the flower of maturity,
> they could not find their food nor join in the arts of Venus.
> For we know that living things need many factors
> in conjunction, to reproduce their several species.

Thus says Lucretius, "many kinds of creatures have become extinct, unable to propagate . . . their species." Others, he tells us, have been preserved by human intervention, "because they are useful to us." He enumerates these as,

> the alert, intelligent, and faithful dog
> and all the animals that we call beasts of burden,
> the fleecy sheep and all the hornèd breeds of cattle.

The human species itself was not exempt from this rough treatment at Nature's hand. Unlike other ancient schools of religion and philosophy, the Epicureans refused to imagine a lost paradise or Eden where human life had once existed in pristine joy. On the contrary, human beginnings shared the rough origins of the animal kingdom:

> The human beings that lived in those days in the fields
> were a tougher sort of people as the tough earth has made them so.
> They lived for many revolutions of the sun,
> roaming far and wide in the manner of wild beasts.
> They were not sturdy farmers who turned the curvèd plowshare,
> for they did not know how to work the land with iron,
> nor had they learned to plant the new shoots in the ground
> or how to prune dead branches from the trees with a sickle.
> What the sun and rain bestowed, and what the earth
> produced of her own accord, this was enough for them.

From this primitive origin, civilization gradually evolved; the arts and sciences developed and life became richer and more refined:

> Ships and agriculture, fortresses and laws,
> weapons, clothing, roads, and all else of this sort,
> and all the amenities and pleasures of this life,
> music and pictures and statues carved by the artist's genius–
> all were learned by usage and experience,
> little by little, as men have groped with faltering steps.
> So time brings by slow degrees each separate thing,
> and reason ushers it into the light of day.

Lucretius explains the celestial motions "by the hallowed authority of Democritus." To guide one's understanding "by reason" is to "find great wealth in a modest livelihood by peace of mind." This also is true reverence: "For piety does not consist of veiling the head before a graven image, . . . and sprinkling blood on altars. . . . True piety consists of contemplating the universe with peaceful mind."

For all of its luminescence, this treasure of ancient scientific speculation was lost for many centuries. After Lucretius was rediscovered early in the fifteenth century with the finding of but one surviving manuscript, his work almost immediately inspired painters, musicians, and poets–as well as natural philosophers and free thinking moralists. Botticelli's celebrated painting, *La Primavera* (The Spring), is said to have been prompted by Lucretius's description of the procession of the seasons. Adults now in middle age will recall from childhood Walt Disney's animation *Fantasia*, which followed the visual music of the dawning and unfolding of life as celebrated in the verses of Lucretius. *The Faerie Queen*, an English classic composed by Spenser in Shakespeare's generation, paraphrases Lucretius. The young Shelley regarded Lucretius as his favorite ancient author, along with Benjamin Franklin, his favorite modern. One doesn't wonder, with models like these, that as a schoolboy the audacious Shelley was expelled for writing a treatise that he titled, "On the Necessity of Atheism."

Lucretius was admired by a seemingly endless list of artistic and intellectual greats, including Giordano Bruno who would die at the stake sixteen centuries after the time of Lucretius for daring to publish similar views; by Voltaire, Diderot, Goethe, Elizabeth Barrett Browning, Gladstone, Matthew Arnold, Victor Hugo, Keats, James Joyce, and earlier by Shakespeare and Milton.

Albert Einstein was fond enough of Lucretius to contribute an introduction to a German translation of the Roman poet's masterpiece. Walt Whitman was deeply influenced by the moral philosophy of Lucretius, commending both his view of death as containing nothing to be feared and his sensitive rapport with the world of nature, characteristic of Whitman and Lucretius alike.

When we come to love and revere this exceptional treasure which Lucretius left to posterity, our awe is deepened when we reflect how close the world came to losing this prize of the human imagination and spirit. In that melancholy age following Lucretius, when Christian orthodoxy closed upon ancient Western culture like a steel vise, much of ancient science and wisdom was crushed. Except for the survival of a small fraction of the works of Greek and Roman thinkers, largely preserved and trasmitted back to Europe by Islamic scholars, Western civilization would have lost forever virtually the whole world that was Greece.

Even so, most was lost in such pious villainies as the sacking of the great library at Alexandria, in the bonfires and pogroms that snuffed out ancient knowledge and art–the excesses of a primitive fundamentalism that almost succeeded in effacing every memory of secular science and humanistic philosophy. Of the three hundred books of Epicurus, the philosophical heir of Democritus and also the principal source for the science and ethics of Lucretius, not a single book–not one out of three hundred–escaped the flames. Only a few personal letters addressed to friends and a handful of other fragments survive. Yet these are enough to show that Epicurus was a generous, moderate, and sympathetic man, a wise teacher and counselor who taught modesty, quiet courage, and a life free from excess and extravagance–the very opposite of the slanders circulated about his habits and doctrines.

But why this scandal-mongering and book-burning, a campaign of vilification that succeeded so completely that even our language still reflects the ancient bigotry in the very meaning of the world "epicurean"? Epicurus, said his enemies, was an atheist. And that seems to have justified the slander they circulated. Even before Christianity came upon the scene, the same sort of zealots and conformists who had condemned Socrates to death displayed unremitting hostility to Epicurus and to the earlier philosophers of science who were his precursors.

In fact, Epicurus was not an avowed atheist. He understood well enough the intolerance of the multitudes and the treachery of the cult leaders who manipulated prejudices and popular passions. The course he took was the same compromise that most enlightened figures have taken down to Thomas Jefferson and the present. They have nominally accepted the ceremonial practices and symbols of the prevailing creed while opposing its intent to restrict freedom of thought. Yet fanatics have never been satisfied with anything less than abject submission to their spiritual dictatorship.

In the perplexing world of a declining civilization, Epicurus counseled prudence. Educated Romans, adopting Greek religion and culture, followed the same tolerant but skeptical practice during the period of the late Republic, the time of Lucretius.

Epicurus had taught that the world was not made or directed by the gods. He did not deny their existence but held that they were totally removed from this world of strife and change and that they in no way impinge upon his nature. His view had something in common with our science fiction or science fantasy which frequently plays upon the theme of radically different cosmic orders existing beyond time and space, upon universes so fundamentally different from the reality we know that even in principle we cannot determine whether or not they exist; and we are equally beyond the reach of their perception or interest. The gods exist, said Epicurus, but eternally at peace on their happy isles, unaware of our quite different world.

Was this compromise only a disguised atheism, a clever ruse to banish the gods to an eternally unknowable paradise? Thinkers have argued the issue for the twenty-three hundred years since Epicurus. Because atheism is such an opprobrious term in most cultures, many people will stretch every point to avoid the charge of being atheistic. Yet we pay a high price for this lack of forthrightness. Atheism is a perfectly honest and honorable intellectual position, one which throughout history has been held by many admirable, courageous thinkers.

In a nonprejudiced context, we may conclude that Epicurus did not believe in the supernatural. The gods, whatever and wherever they are, have nothing to do with our universe, human affairs, or our destinies. We are completely on our own. The gods did not create the world nor are they concerned with its existence. Indeed, they know as little of us as we know of them. So Epicurus bent his knee to the civil religion of his age but kept his mind independent; the supernatural was not part of the world of ideas and values by which he shaped his philosophy.

While this tradition was based on the concept of nature as a self-contained material order free from divine plan or intervention, the real point of Epicurean philosophy was not theoretical knowledge but practical ethics, the art of living. If we ask how to live a moral life Epicurus answers that moral life is based on the rational examination of human conduct for happiness and peace of mind according to nature. We must look not to the gods but to human experience as the source of moral wisdom. Ethics thus became independent of theology. The key term is the word *human*. To ask what is right, how we should live, is but to inquire in disguised form: if I cherish human existence, if I consider myself, you, and all others as human, what then must I do to promote the well-being of the life I reverence as identical with my own?

This question contains all that ethics is, all that practical morality and civilized conduct can mean. Anything beyond this is imposition. We note that even earlier than Democritus, in far away India, the Buddha had reached a similar conclusion. He did not deny the gods. He said they simply had no bearing on the conduct of life; they existed apart, and we human beings must work out our own salvation, unaided by supernatural beings. When Lucretius wrote his great poem, which James Mantinband recently translated into modern English under the title, *On the Nature of the Universe* (a translation I recommend for its clarity and grace), the Latin poet followed Epicurus in regarding science and the understanding of nature primarily as a resource for moral living. The understanding of nature liberates us from superstition. If humanity were emancipated from fear of the supernatural, and particularly from the fear of death exaggerated by the supernatural, we would become free to know and to live true morality. Many readers express surprise that Lucretius and his teacher Epicurus regarded belief in the supernatural not as a comfort but as a source of delusion and terror while most people look to supernatural beliefs and to the hope of a life after death as a source of consolation and strength.

If we examine closely the beliefs of most religions, particularly those of the West, we find that almost without exception they teach a doctrine of divine retribution holding a destiny of terror and torment for most of the human race. In Calvinism, this doctrine is even elevated to the view that an angry God chose those to be condemned at the beginning of time: individuals can do nothing to change their fate. Parallel doctrines prevailed among the ancients, particularly in the age of Greek civilization riddled by superstition and already in decline.

The Epicureans, who were in many respects the foremost rationalists and freethinkers of their age, cut through these irrational fears. We have no reason to fear death, Epicurus taught. Death is nonbeing; it is unknowing, and when we thoroughly grasp this fact, the termination of life holds no terrors. In truth, we never actually experience death. We may know pain and fear in the anticipation of death, but death is a release from all pain and fear. Thus when death comes, we are not actually there to receive it. Thus, no man or woman, no conscious mind, ever has or ever will experience death, for experience always belongs to the living. Let this thought penetrate your consciousness, percolate through the layers of your mind, said Epicurus, and you will be purged of the fear of death. You will be free to live every moment of your life joyfully without superstition or dread. This is what is joyful in Epicurean philosophy–the pleasure of a sane and rational life, free from dread. The pleasure principle is a rational principle, not–as slander has it–a life of lust and gluttony, which Epicurus taught can lead only to misery.

Throughout all the ages prior to your conception and birth, you knew no sense of dread, no knowledge of your nonexistence. The world had taken form, the dinosaurs had come and gone. Ages passed. The billions of years and eons of ages to come, after you cease to be, will mean no more to you than the ages before you existed. They hold no cause for fear or self-pity. Life is now. We inhabit the "now" as long as we exist. We are completely contained within the circumference of consciousness and shall be for as long as we are. Nearly two thousand years after Lucretius, the same thought appeared in a passage by Thomas Henry Huxley, the celebrated champion of Darwin. Huxley was characteristically succinct. A hundred years from now, he declared, I shall no more exist that I did a hundred years ago, and the time after my existence shall concern me as little as the time that came before me.

The soul is mortal, wrote Lucretius; the mind and living body are composed and dissolve together; and as paradoxical as it may seem, in recognizing our mortality we find freedom and moral dignity.

For a new age of humanism and free thought, Lucretius raised the lamp of freedom as he sang:

> Often men for fear of death are seized by hatred
> of life itself. . . .
> For just as children tremble, afraid of everything
> in blinding darkness, so we sometimes in broad daylight
> have fears as groundless as the ones that frighten children–

imaginary terrors lurking in dark corners.
This terror of the mind, these shadows must be dispelled
not by the sun's bright shafts nor by the brilliant daylight,
but by an understanding of the laws of Nature.

3

Emperor-Philosopher:

Marcus Aurelius

(121–180 A.D.)

While the Epicurean philosophy produced no important exponent after Lucretius, its popular rival, Stoicism, continued to exert wide influence for more than two centuries. Marcus Aurelius, the Roman emperor who ruled from 161 A.D. until his death nineteen years later, was Stoicism's most celebrated champion, as well as its last major advocate.

Before Epicureanism went into decline, these two schools of thought competed for the allegiance of cultivated Greeks and Romans who disdained the popular mystery religions and vulgar superstitions of the masses. While the more academic philosophies of Plato, Aristotle, and their successors prevailed in the formal schools, Epicureanism and Stoicism–especially the latter–provided inspiration and practical guidance to the cultured classes of Rome. Deploring alike omens, miracles, and divination as regrettable superstitions, these philosophies differed in basic assumptions about God and nature. While Stoics usually scorned the nonreligious Epicureans, it is characteristic of the generous Marcus Aurelius that he spoke of Epicurus with respect.

Seldom are the emperors of ancient Rome thought of as philosophers, but the name of one will live in the annals of thought as long as civilization survives.

One admires the Stoics for their celebration of courage and endurance. Yet too often the popular image of their philosophy is painted in dark carbon tones. They are pictured as impassive, melancholy figures, accepting suffering and weariness as a destined fate. Regrettably, that is what the words "stoic" and "stoical" have come to mean. Only the name of the Cynics, an admirable school of ancient Greek philosophers, has suffered greater abuse. But while there are many passages in the literature of Stoicism to support the popular somber view, others are open to wider interpretation.

The one-sidedness of the common stoic stereotype denies one the knowledge of a philosophy of life that remains as valuable in this day as in ancient times. Those who see Marcus Aurelius as a noble but dour figure should meet him as he rises expectantly from his bed to meet the duties and challenges of the day. Anticipating daily routine, he is teeming with the imaginative powers of the artist and builder. His insight into the psychology of self-actualization is quite modern as he writes of the reward of creative work.

"At daybreak, when you rise unwillingly," he advises, "have this thought in your mind: *I am rising to the work of a human being.*" If this thought does not fill you with delight, [he says,] something in your life is amiss. The villain, he explains, is self-hate. All living things need and enjoy demanding activity, work that is natural to their being. If this is not the case, Marcus says, "The answer is that you do not love your own self, for if you did, you would love both your nature and its purpose." Those who are in harmony with their creative powers will even go without food or sleep to pursue their craft or art.

This is hardly the doctrine of a soul despairing of life, a spirit weary of work and turning away from the world. As Walter Lippmann observed half a century ago, every philosophy of maturity involves renunciation; the life-affirming humanism that Lippman propounded requires setting aside inferior purposes and pleasures for the sake of deeper, more lasting satisfactions and goals. Stoicism goes further than most philosophies in renouncing external possessions and indulgences for the sake of perfecting an inward satisfaction and contentment; this Marcus Aurelius finds most of all in expressing our creative and altruistic impulses.

Obedience to the divine spark within each human soul–surrender to the inner light of one's nature, a rational principle which nature has placed in each individual–provides, according to the Stoic teaching, peace and happiness. Each living being is a fragment of the universal whole; by service and benevolence one becomes secure in the knowledge of the highest good that is given to human beings.

> If you find in human life anything better than justice, truth, temperance, fortitude, and, in a word, anything better than your own mind's self-satisfaction in the things which it enables you to do according to right reason, . . . and in the condition that is assigned to you without your own choice; if, I say, you see anything better than this, turn to it with all your soul and enjoy that which you have found to be the best. But if nothing appears to be better than the deity [the rational principle] which is planted within you, which has subjected to itself all your appetites, if you find everything else smaller and of less value than this, give place to nothing else.

Marcus does not propose that we mortify the flesh from a misguided sense of guilt or self-hate, as religious asceticism would want us to do; he simply challenges us to select the best. He is confident that if we act according to right reason we shall choose a life of socially useful service or creative work–activities that serve human needs. We must do this not to win praise or favor from our fellow men, a motive that Marcus disparages, but for the satisfaction of knowing that we have accomplished our best.

If this seems to grant too little allowance for human frailty, Marcus counsels: "Be not ashamed to be helped." One is like a soldier whose duty is to storm a town. "How then," he asks, "if being lame, you cannot mount up on the battlements alone, but with the help of another it becomes possible?" We are made for one another. If we help one another, we shall be strong. We are all of one nature and destiny, and all our fellow men enjoy the same divine nature and dignity. Stoicism proclaimed the equality of all human beings and the brotherhood of all nations and races; it taught these moral truths long before the introduction of Christianity, which often claims to have first given them to the world.

Born among the Greeks three centuries before the beginning of the Christian era, Stoicism represented the high-water mark of ancient ethics. In many respects it has never been surpassed as a system of practical humanism. Although its founder and principal teachers do not enjoy the intellectual reputations of Socrates, Plato, and Aristotle–the commanding figures of Greek philosophy–they were far superior to these giants in their moral thinking. The idea of equality was alien to Plato. He disdained the common folk and also all non-Greeks and countenanced a policy of deliberate deception to propagate the myth of a superior governing caste. Work would dishonor the noble class and should be done by those of lesser rank.

The Stoics would have none of this. Adopting the teaching of a school of philosophers known as the Cynics, who refused to be awed by wealth or pretensions of kingly power, they rejected Plato's doctrine of a superior class, holding the slave to be the moral equal of the master–a congenial doctrine for a philosophy that included slaves among its greatest teachers.

In its flexibility Stoicism was able to develop through the centuries. Unlike its rival, Epicureanism, which never deviated from the original teaching of Epicurus, the Stoic doctrine assumed a variety of forms as it progressed from its founder, Zeno of Cyprus, who taught in the early third century, B.C., to its consummation in the meditations of Marcus Aurelius, nearly five hundred years later. Some Stoic philosophers believed for example that the soul survives the death of the body; others denied this doctrine, insisting that the soul is simply the animating principle of the organism and can have no separate existence. Epictetus, a slave regarded as the greatest of the Stoic philosophers, taught this latter view. While Marcus is less dogmatic than Epictetus on this and other doctrines, he inclines to the opinion that the personality does not survive the death of the body. This concept concerns him little, since he feels there is no consciousness of loss or despair where there is no existence.

Stoics tended toward a materialistic metaphysics, although on this point also there was considerable disparity of thought. In general, they were pantheists, equating God with nature or maintaining that deity is a rational, animating principle that inheres solely in material nature. What is not material is nothing, one of their great teachers said. "God flows through the universe as honey flows through the honeycomb," became one of their celebrated proverbs. Thus they rejected Plato's concept of ideas as eternal, immaterial forms. On the contrary, whatever is real is of material substance, including deity, which is only a finer manifestation of matter. Zeno borrowed this idea from the Cynic philosophers, Diogenes and others. They had derived their view of materialism from the pre-Socratic materialists of Iona, modified by Heraclitus; he related fire to spirit and saw all reality as restless, ever-changing energy.

From Socrates the Stoics developed a philosophy that was chiefly concerned with ethics, with logic and metaphysics holding only secondary positions and of interest only as they relate to the theory of ethics. Their view of the cosmos supported the idea that all existing bodies, from stars and planets to living plants and animals, had evolved from relations of the original fire; in time, they thought, the universe will again be absorbed into a single, incandescent sphere that will explode into a new universe, a process that will never cease. Thus each eon of time is the result of the pulsation of an eternal substance, each cosmic cycle beginning and ending in universal conflagration. The extent to which this cosmology resembles modern theories in physics is noteworthy; it is also strikingly similar to myths of creation which are as widespread as the Hindu and the Native American. A Cherokee myth, for example, accounts for the creation of the earth as condensation of water and mud from the same ancient cosmic fire.

This view of creation is important to Stoic ethics in supporting a belief in the unity of all things. Nature and deity are one. Human beings are sparks of the divine whole. The gods and goddesses are only aspects or particular manifestations of an all-encompassing reality. All human beings are from one source and share one nature. For ethical considerations, the significance of this idea is noteworthy. The faithful Roman emperor who took seriously his Stoic philosophy labored tirelessly for the well-being of his subjects. Marcus recognized that insofar as he was a human being–even if an emperor–the meanest slave was his equal. He wore himself out performing his public duties, and when he died of fever in March, 180 A.D. after a reign of nineteen years, he lay in a military camp on a troubled frontier, where he had led his legions in the service of his country.

Marcus Aurelius Antoninus was not born to the purple. He had been adopted by the previous emperor, Antoninus Pius, who himself had been adopted by Hadrian, one of the most effective and enlightened of all Roman rulers.

In an earlier transfer of power, Hadrian, the adopted son of Trajan, had been preferred to the emperor's own sons as his successor. And still earlier, Trajan, a renowned soldier, had been adopted by a distinguished Roman statesman, Nerva, who had become emperor during a period of constitutional reform. Recognizing the need for a strong military leader to control a rebellious army, Nerva had abdicated in favor of Trajan. Thus Nerva put in place a system of succession through adoption that lasted for more than eighty years, giving Rome five of its most effective and enlightened rulers. It is to the discredit of Marcus that he chose as his successor an unworthy son, Commodus, who brought Nerva's era of good government to an end. Thus, while Marcus was the most saintly of this distinguished line, he proved to be a poor judge of character, giving credence to the popular opinion that saints are blind to the motives of less worthy men.

Writing of the long and brilliant administration of five successive emperors, beginning with Nerva and ending with the death of Marcus Aurelius, the historian Edward Gibbon, in *The Decline and Fall of the Roman Empire*, declared:

> If a man were called upon to fix the period in the history of the world, during which the condition of the human race was most happy and prosperous, he would, without hesitation, name that which elapsed from the death of Domitian to the accession of Commodus. The vast extent of the Roman empire was governed by absolute power, under the guidance of virtue and wisdom. The armies were restrained by the firm and gentle hand of four successive emperors, whose characters and authority commanded involuntary respect. The forms of the civil administration were carefully preserved by Nerva, Trajan, Hadrian, and the Antonines, who delighted in the image of liberty, and were pleased with considering themselves as the accountable ministers of the laws.

The age of the benevolent emperors that Gibbon describes stands in stark contrast to the madness and tyranny of the century that came before them:

> The golden age of Trajan and the Antonines had been preceded by an age of iron. It is almost superfluous to enumerate the unworthy successors of Augustus. Their unparalleled vices, and the splendid theatre on which they acted, have saved them from oblivion. The dark, unrelenting Tiberius, the furious Caligula, the feeble Claudius, the profligate and cruel Nero, the beastly Vitellius, and the timid, inhuman Domitian, are condemned to an everlasting infamy.

Only the brief reign of Vespasian afforded uncertain relief from this brutal and corrupt succession that lasted eighty years. Following the able Augustus, who ruled at the very beginning of the Christian era, the history of Rome may be summarized as eighty years of imperial insanity and treachery, followed by eighty years of leadership as capable and enlightened as the ancient world ever saw, and then a long decline casting its shadow over centuries. Speaking of Marcus Aurelius and his adoptive father, Antoninus Pius, Gibbon wrote in sentences as celebrated as any in historical literature, "The two Antonines . . . governed the Roman world forty-two years. . . . Their united reigns are possibly the only period in the history of the world during which the happiness of a great people was the sole object of government."

The moral philosophy that prepared the young Marcus for his arduous duties and then sustained him through the emotional and physical rigors of leading a sprawling empire while having to control a restive and conspiratorial army was the gift of wise teachers chosen by his great-grandfather. In acknowledging his ethical roots, Marcus notes his moral obligation to his great-grandfather, "not to have frequented public schools, to have had good teachers at home and to know that on such things a man should spend liberally." To his teacher, Diogenetus, he expressed gratitude for the counsel "not to busy myself about trifling things and not to give credence to what was said by miracle workers and jugglers about incantations and the driving away of daemons and such things; and . . . to endure freedom of speech; and to become intimate with philosophy."

The reference to miracle workers who claim the power to exorcise evil spirits is thought to be a reference to Christians who claimed the power to cast out devils. Marcus was opposed to the doctrines of the Christians, as to all other cults then springing up throughout the empire with claims of special revelations and possession of the keys to salvation. To Stoic philosophers who regarded all such creeds as superstitious, the proper cure for religious fanaticism was the full use of reason–not an abstract, purely intellectual reason, but the still small voice of conscience guided by the inner light of a rational soul. To use reason for the proper conduct of life was the Stoic ideal. To venerate temples and sacred places where God or gods were said to dwell and there to be propitiated by holy rites was contrary to the Stoic conviction that such practices were not only worthless but demeaning. But as a concession to popular piety, the Stoic emperors followed common practice in observing the official cults and in deifying their illustrious predecessors as custom required.

The Stoic disclaimed religious enthusiasm as delusions. Although Christians were persecuted in south Gaul during his reign, recent historians have questioned the claim that Marcus was such a persecutor. He was generally tolerant and mild in his administration of the laws. Yet there can be no question that he looked with foreboding on this new cult of fanatics who breathed contempt for every religion other than their own and enthusiastically proclaimed the imminent end of the world.

With their doctrine of a divinity within nature that is a finer but nevertheless material substance, the Stoics occupied a middle position between the Epicureans, who were both materialists and atheists, and the followers of Plato, who regarded the material universe as a corrupt lower realm, greatly inferior to a totally transcendent and incorruptible sphere of pure mind or spirit. The gnostics and Christians occupied an extreme position on the spectrum with their doctrine of divine messengers, a resurrected god, and salvation in the hereafter.

While Zeno the Cyprian had modified the materialism of the pre-Socratics to allow for a rational principle, a divine fire at the heart of nature, the Stoic founder and his successors never departed from the method or temper of the early Greek materialists. They sought not salvation but enlightenment; not purification from above but betterment from within. Stoic ethics followed Socrates to the extent of making right living and the pursuit of right reason more important than either pure speculation about the nature of things or faith in revelations claimed to come from the gods. To live courageously and nobly, remaining always faithful to one's work without expectation of reward here or hereafter–that is the moral ideal that guided Marcus through his life.

Strictly speaking, he was not a philosopher; at least he appears not to have intended to be a teacher of a philosophical system. Most historians believe that he never expected the little volume of meditations he wrote to be read by others. It is actually a spiritual diary, the record of a monologue directed to himself. All his counsel is addressed to himself. He is continuing within himself what had once been a dialogue with his teachers. Many passages appear to have been composed in military camps far from Rome. This most peaceful man, who saw himself as a citizen of the world and a brother of every human being, was fated to live extended periods of his life in the rigorous and violent role of a soldier, a commander leading troops. In fact, it was in camp that he contracted disease and where he died. For all his love of philosophy and a life of solitude, the role for which he had trained from childhood–the Stoic sense of obligation to serve–did not permit him to retire or to command his armies from the safety of a Roman palace.

Always his philosophy permitted no easy consolation. The Christian might be a martyr at the stake anticipating the reward of heaven. In centuries to come the Muslim would eagerly throw himself into battle, eager for the joys of paradise which were reserved for those who died defending Islam. As a Stoic, Marcus rejected all such indulgences as both untrue and unworthy. As the much maligned Cynics before them had taught, the Stoics believed that virtue is its own reward. And the only sure reward of a virtuous character *is* a virtuous character. Without either heaven or hell to anticipate or fear, the Stoic was dedicated to the virtuous life, believing that all other pleasures and possessions were of lesser worth. Knowing that we have fulfilled our purpose as social beings who have responsibilities to others gives us greater contentment–and greater spiritual freedom and courage–than any other way of living. For this we are made, and only by so living can we find the inner resources to live in contentment and to die at peace with ourselves.

Why should we believe this to be so? It is so, according to Stoic metaphysics and ethics, because we are part of one another, part of the great stream of animate nature, part of the grand procession that proceeds from nature and returns to the nature that gave it being. All are one; and the whole is present in every part.This is the heart of Stoic ethics. Beginning with the self-reliance and solitary courage of the Cynics, the Stoics produced an ethical humanism that was universal in scope, unbounded by racial pride, religious narrowness, or class arrogance.

In summarizing Marcus's character, the historian Gibbon wrote:

> War he detested as a disgrace and calamity of human nature; but when the necessity of a just defense called upon him to take up arms, he readily exposed his person to eight winter campaigns, on the frozen banks of the Danube, the severity of which was at last fatal to the weakness of his constitution. His memory was revered by a grateful posterity, and above a century after his death, many persons preserved the image of Marcus [Aurelius] Antoninus among those of their household gods.

It was a fitting memory of an emperor of the Western world who had lived by the thought: "We are made for cooperation, like feet, like hands. . . . And inasmuch as I am . . . intimately related to the parts which are of the same kind with myself . . . I shall turn all my efforts to the common good."

4

Persian Agnostic:

Omar Khayyam

(Died c. 1123 A.D.)

With Christian orthodoxy triumphant by the early sixth century, the last surviving schools of pre-Christian philosophy were effectively suppressed in the Roman Empire. Even eminent Christian bishops who were found not to be wholly orthodox, as judged by developing church doctrine, were forced to take refuge beyond the borders of the Empire. As a result, independent Christian communities, like the Nestorian and Monophysite branches of the faith holding opposing views on the nature of Christ, were established in Syria and Zoroastrian Persia. There the knowledge of Greek science and philosophy, especially Aristotelian or neo-Platonist works attributed to Aristotle, was welcomed and preserved. This learning was later disseminated to the Islamic world with the Moslem conquest of the Near East in the seventh century. Brilliant schools of skeptical philosophy developed from these studies, producing such luminous thinkers as the agnostic and hedonistic poet, Omar Khayyam.

As we shall trace, the free speculations of Arabic students of Greek philosophy sparked the Renaissance, thus restoring Greek humanism and science to Europe.

Many know him only as the legendary author of quaintly romantic, hedonistic rhymes or, as some contend, a very minor versifier of adolescent effusions about destiny and death. Others have denied that he was the composer of the poems at all but simply the fictional source of many old Persian drinking songs too blasphemous for the actual authors to claim.

Yet Omar was no fiction. One of the most accomplished astronomers and mathematicians of his age, he was one of eight learned astronomers chosen by the Sultan Malik Shah to reform the calendar. Their achievement gave to the eleventh-century Islamic world a calendar that according to historian Edward Gibbon surpassed the Julian and approached the Gregorian in accuracy. Omar also wrote a book on algebra still cited for its contributions to that branch of knowledge. Along with his achievements in science, he was a student of Greek philosophy as it had been transmitted to the Islamic world. His poetry, while admittedly daring and blasphemous from the standpoint of Moslem orthodoxy, was much more than a collection of drinking songs. Verse provided the dress for Omar's religious free thought and skepticism, giving voice to a deterministic philosophy that had its roots in Greek physics as well as Oriental fatalism.

Discoveries in our lifetime of early manuscripts containing extensive selections of his poetry have reversed a half century of doubt about the genuineness of the verses ascribed to Omar. Again he has come to enjoy the critical recognition that he first received in the English-speaking world more than a century ago following Edward FitzGerald's free translation of a small selection of his quatrains titled, "The Rubaiyat of Omar Khayyam." Few translations have ever equaled FitzGerald's version in making famous throughout the world both poet and translator, the latter proving to be a distinguished poet in his own right. At the height of his reputation in the closing years of the nineteenth century, popular acclaim of Omar's verse in FitzGerald's translation reached the extravagance of a cult. Young ladies packed romantically illustrated volumes of the *Rubaiyat* in picnic baskets, to be recited to their beaux on spring meadows along the banks of the Thames, on the glades of Boston Common, or among the arbors of Central Park:

And this reviving Herb whose tender Green
Fledges the River-Lip on which we lean–
  Ah, lean upon it lightly! for who knows
From what once lovely Lip it springs unseen.

No matter how ecstatic the present moment of youth and spring, Omar keeps before us the knowledge that life passes quickly and that the living are but a morning's frost on the glistening hills. Life must be drunk quickly like wine from the glass.

Come, fill the Cup, and in the Fire of Spring
  The Winter garment of Repentance fling:
The Bird of Time has but a little way
  To fly–and Lo! the Bird is on the Wing.

Look to the Rose that blows about us–"Lo
Laughing," she says, "into the World I blow:
  At once the silken Tassel of my Purse
Tear, and its Treasure on the Garden throw."

But while it would lead us astray to read Omar literally as a celebrated tippler knocking at the tavern door at dawn, demanding to be admitted early to begin another day of dedicated wine-drinking–he hardly would have become the accomplished scholar and poet had he imbibed at that pace–it is important to recognize that wine was an accepted symbol of cultural protest in Persia following the Moslem conquest. Wine expressed the civility of Persian culture which the proud heirs of an ancient civilization enjoyed flaunting in the faces of their upstart desert conquerors. Mohammed prohibited intoxicating drink, but the old Zoroastrian religion of Persia had permitted its use. Even though most Persians had converted to Islam long before Omar's time–at least nominally, if only to avoid paying the tribute required of the surviving communities of Jews, Zoroastrians, and Christians–the tolerant Islamic court and upper-class Persians ignored Mohammed's stern commandments and lived and thought much as they pleased. At least they did when they dared. Periods of fanaticism and persecution alternated with eras of religious indifference and unbelief, reflecting the whims and beliefs of the current ruler. One of the distinctive features of Islamic civilization throughout the centuries that were called the Middle Ages in the West was this alternation between periods of enlightened skepticism and of savage religious zeal. The explanation lies in Islam's lack of a central religious hierarchy–such as controlled Christendom from Rome or Constantinople–thus allowing the tides of religious conformity in Islam to rise or fall with each changing of the guard in Baghdad and its provincial capitals.

But if wine in Omar's poetry is a deliberate symbol of protest against Moslem orthodoxy, it is even more a timeless and universal token of the blood of life itself. Ancient religious cults considered drinking the blood of the grape a ritual expression of union with the god, a concept preserved in the Christian communion. Certainly Omar understood this. In the imagery of his poetry the blood of the wine becomes the embodiment of life's precious but fragile beauty which he celebrates in one of the most tender and compassionate affirmations of life ever written.

His philosophy has been called hedonistic and also pessimistic. But while hedonism and pessimism are often opposite faces of the same coin, both are prominent elements of Omar's thinking. His vision of life suggests a deeper sympathy for all that lives, for the long procession of present, past, and future life. Some have even seen in him a mystic philosopher perceiving the Eternal One in everything. Professor A. J. Arberry of Cambridge, an authority on Omar and the culture of his time, as well as a recent translator of the *Rubaiyat*, denies that Omar was inclined to mysticism. He credits FitzGerald with interpreting Omar correctly on this point. In many of his quatrains Omar ridicules the extravagent claims to divine knowledge of the Sufi mystics–a wayward Moslem sect–as mercilessly as he attacks the stupidities of the orthodox. He was a skeptic and ultimately an agnostic who refused to step beyond human experience. A few of his verses, a mere handful out of many more than a thousand attributed to him, ask for God's acceptance of his doubt, providing an opening to those who claim a late conversion of Omar to the Moslem faith. But stories of his deathbed repentance are as improbable as those told of other noted freethinkers. On inspection, Omar's verses of repentance can be summed up as variations on the familiar agnostic's prayer, "O God, if there be a God, forgive my doubt"–a sentiment entirely consistent with the assumptions of agnosticism.

But if Omar's thought stops short of a claim to mystical enlightenment and rejects orthodox revelation, it is nevertheless a more sympathetic and deeper philosophy of life than mere hedonism or pessimism. Omar evokes a passionate caring for life as the frail but supreme florescence of beauty. No philosopher or poet has ever excelled Omar in celebrating the loveliness of life, the joyfulness of the present moment that goes beyond hedonism to sing of reverence and mercy for all that is and that, however fleeting its existence, shares the destiny of the vine and the rose. The *red* rose, the *red* orb of the sun hurling skyward in the morning, the *red* lips of beauties now gone but remembered, the song bird pleading for the pale rose to rouge her bloom in wine, the *red* blood of fallen heroes and departed princesses, and always the *ruby* of the wine itself–all these are constant images of life that can never be internalized, but must cast themselves upon the garden of life and by so doing produce a timeless song of beauty.

There is a boundless cheerfulness in Omar that belies the description of his philosophy as defeatist. Pessimist he may be in refusing to drug himself with false hopes which deny the tragic shadow that oppresses life. But this tragic vision surmounts despair and affirms the priceless worth of living, even as it consoles. Because Omar can laugh at himself and other wise men, knowing that the sum of philosophy and wisdom is always less than the savor of the grape or the redness of the rose, he escapes the self-pity of those despairing philosophers and saints whose metaphysics can never save them.

Myself when young did eagerly frequent
Doctor and Saint, and heard great Argument
About it and about: but evermore
Came out by the same Door as in I went.

Why, all the Saints and Sages who discuss'd
Of the Two Worlds so learnedly, are thrust
Like foolish Prophets forth: their Words to Scorn
Are scatter'd, and their Mouths are stopt with Dust.

Omar will not accept the crutch of a promised world to come, for he recognizes that no prophet or sage can describe or know it. Instead, he embraces his life, without closing to it any portion of his heart, viewing it with fully open eyes, touching it with totally alert fingers; and like Goethe's Faust, having lived the fulfilling moment, he can let go of vain illusion, finding the contentment of those at peace with themselves.

Omar's *rubaiyat*–a word meaning simply "verses"–are most fully understandable as poems of the acceptance and celebration of life within the limits of mortal existence. Omar rejects the false promises of supernatural religion that coax human beings into exchanging the true miracle and mystery of existence for the delusion of dogma and speculation. Remembering that wine is the recurring metaphor for life, Omar's affirmation of this world becomes clear in FitzGerald's rendering.

I often wonder what the Vintners buy
One half so precious as the Goods they sell.

We sell our life blood to buy . . . what? That is the question Omar repeatedly asks. And he answers: we exchange the precious blood, the wine of our being, for all manner of shoddy and useless goods–and, yes, for no goods at all, for illusion, self-deception, extravagant pretense and a slavish piety that leaves life sear and dry. Omar will not exchange his vintage for such as these. Turn from fable to fact, from magic-lantern shows at midnight to the reality of the dawn of morning, he entreats. Life's beauty and joy lie about us, ready to be received to restore us to youth and contentment, so different from the lifeless consolations of deceiving revelations of faith and the barren speculations of reason.

> You know, my Friends, how long since in my House
> For a new Marriage I did make Carouse:
> Divorced old barren Reason from my Bed
> And took the Daughter of the Vine to Spouse.

To give a more exact rendering of Omar's thought than is provided by FitzGerald's paraphrase, Professor Arberry, in his less known translation, includes faith as well as reason as a source of barrenness against which is counterposed the freshness of life in its flowering. Omar's philosophy is not an appeal to irrationalism; on the contrary, he stands near the close of a period of several centuries of brilliant Islamic freethinkers who, glorying in the life of the mind, took their stand resolutely (and often dangerously) against the intolerance and superstition of the Koran and its rival scriptures of Christian and Jew. Islamic eagerness for Greek philosophy and science, which provided the historical bridge enabling much of this ancient knowledge to escape destruction and come down to us through Moslem Spain and other Arabic centers of civilization, was motivated by a desire to understand rationally the nature of the world and our place within it.

If we picture in imagination a great bridge of rationalism and free thought spanning the centuries from the age of ancient Greek philosophy to the modern age, Omar's place and that of his fellow Persian-and Arabic-speaking freethinkers is at the center of the span, both chronologically and in terms of cultural transmission. Other paths existed through which fragments of the ancient science and learning survived and were transmitted, but no causeway rivals the great bridge of medieval Islamic science as it spans the chasm of comparative darkness between ancient and modern times.

Born in the mid-eleventh century according to the Western calendar, Omar stands chronologically almost exactly at the midpoint between the forced closing of the ancient Greek philosophical schools in the Christian West, and the explosion of modern science represented in the work of Galileo and

Sir Isaac Newton. We are forever in debt to the philosophers of the Near East who transmitted to the West the science that sparked the modern age. It was Greek science that interested the Islamic thinkers most of all. By the time of Omar's birth, Persian and Arab philosophers had acquired and interpreted much of what was still available of Greek mathematics, philosophy, astronomy, and medicine–especially whatever had found its way into the encyclopedic work of Aristotle or was attributed to him. Meanwhile in the West, Arisotle and other Greek scientific and medical writers were mostly forgotten while the ancient Christian theologians preferred Plato whom they revised and abridged to suit their purposes.

Omar was born into the rich and varied culture of old Persia, and so an heir to the high Islamic civilization that radiated from the Abbasid dynasty at Baghdad which had come to power over the Moslem East largely because of Persian influence. It was steeped in the philosophy of Athens and Alexandria as it had been brought to the East by heretic Nestorian and Monophysite Christians who found sanctuary in Zoroastrian Persia before the Moslem conquest. Thus Omar was the beneficiary of the broadest and most liberal learning of his age, or of any previous era since the golden age of Greece. But his erudition confirmed his skepticism and his belief in the transitoriness of all that is:

> Alas, that Spring should vanish with the Rose!
> That youth's sweet-scented Manuscript should close!
> The Nightingale that in the Branches sang,
> Ah, whence, and whither flown again, who knows!

Like many profound thinkers from Democritus down to Spinoza, Omar could not believe that the fates or gods could justly punish mortal beings for what we can neither understand nor control. His philosophy is wholly deterministic, and whether one accepts this philosophic concept or not, one must admire the strength with which Omar puts forth his case. In the fifth and final version of FitzGerald's free rendering of Omar's thought, a number of quatrains meditate about human dependence on fate or necessity. Where there is no free will or even knowledge, there can be no responsibility, Omar reasons. God consequently has no ground to punish his creatures for their imperfection. Human beings are hurtled about the field like balls in a game of polo:

The Ball no question makes of Ayes or Noes,
But Here or There as strikes the Player goes:
  And He that toss'd you down into the Field,
He knows about it all–HE knows–HE knows.

But the "He" in this verse is not a benevolent personal deity but simply unknowable fate. All that exists or ever will exist, hurled about by the relentless motion of atoms was determined at the creation of the world as the materialist and determinist Democritus would have reasoned, driving and compelling all to a predictable conclusion:

With Earth's first Clay They did the Last Man knead,
And there of the Last Harvest sow'd the Seed:
  And the first Morning of Creation wrote
What the Last Dawn of Reckoning shall read.

Can the potter punish the pot for the deformity that the maker himself has made? Omar's is the ageless protest against blaming the created for the creator's fault. Omar imagines himself standing in a potter's shop, listening to the conversation of the clay vessels as they debate their fates:

Said one of them–"Surely not in vain
My substance of the common Earth was Ta'en
  And to this Figure molded, to be broke
Or trampled back to shapeless Earth again."
"Why," said another, "Some there are who tell
Of one who theatens he will toss to Hell
  The luckless pots he marred in making."

The misshapen pot thinks this nonsense, the maker is good, and all will be well. A more skeptical goblet, speaking perhaps for Omar himself, answers jestingly in this gallery of loquacious crockery:

"Well," murmuring one, "Let whoso make or buy,
My Clay with long Oblivion is gone dry:
  But fill me with the old familiar Juice,
Methinks I might recover by and by."

To all this vain speculation, Omar provides his now familiar response. The only answer to death is life; the only rebuttal to "evermore" is now. Be part of life in its present moment; in ages to come you will be the very clay that nurtures future life:

Ah, with the Grape my fading life provide,
And wash the Body whence the Life has died,
And lay me, shrouded in the living leaf,
By some not unfrequented Garden-side.

In his effort to render Omar's meaning more exactly than FitzGerald's paraphrase conveys, Professor Arberry substitutes for FitzGerald's line, "lay me, shrouded in some living leaf," the words, "lay me in a coffin cut from the wood of the vine."

This raises the question of how faithful to the original is the century-old FitzGerald translation. Critical opinion over the past hundred years has varied widely, from extreme adulation to scornful dismissal. But in recent years FitzGerald has been vindicated. The discovery in 1950 of two very early manuscripts offered two independent verifications of Omar's verses; both are selections, one containing 252 quatrains, the other 172. These compare favorably with the 158 quatrains of the much later manuscript in the Bodleian library at Oxford that FitzGerald had available. Roughly half of the quatrains that FitzGerald paraphrased in his final edition of the *Rubaiyat* are authenticated by these earliest known manuscripts, the first of which was compiled within seventy-five years of Omar's death. Since both of these early manuscripts are clearly identified as only selections from the much larger volume of Omar's poetic works, the authenticity of many others, if not all of the verses ascribed to Omar, is strongly supported. Thus Omar emerges from the shadows of controversy and doubt as a major voice of Islamic free thought at its summit.

As for FitzGerald's handling of the limited material that he had available in the 1860s and 1870s, we can now appreciate the genius of his accomplishment. No one will pretend that he produced a very faithful translation. He substituted images that were familiar to English readers. Yet a comparison of his free translation with recent ones closer to the original shows how loyal he was to the spirit of his material in transforming Omar's thought into a lucid masterpiece of English verse. As one distinguished critic, Hugh Walker, observed, FitzGerald's translation stands with only a select few that will survive as long as the English tongue itself. Walker points to the Authorized Version of the Bible, the translations of Homer by Chapman and Pope, and Jowett's Plato, as alone comparing with FitzGerald's *Rubaiyat* as timeless; all are inspired free paraphrases.

Omar thus stands at the center of the Islamic bridge spanning the ancient and modern worlds, a middle figure between Lucretius and Voltaire, and for good reason he has been dubbed "the Voltaire of the East." He prefigures the Mark Twain who wrote *The Mysterious Stranger* and *Letters from the Earth,* but without Twain's anger or despair. It is the good temper of this cheerful agnostic of the East that calls us back again and again to verses that refill our cup of life, that rekindle the ruby sun of spring.

5

Martyr of Free Inquiry:

Giordano Bruno

(c. 1548–1600 A.D.)

The revival of classical learning and ancient humanism brought about by the Renaissance did not diminish the determination of religious orthodoxy to control the gates to heaven and hell—and the minds of men and women while on earth. The challenge to papal authority and Catholic doctrine embodied in the Protestant Reformation only heightened repressive and persecuting passions on both sides. Witch hunts and religious wars exposed the worst in human behavior.

Giordano Bruno, an ordained Italian monk with an audacious hunger for forbidden knowledge and a blasphemous devotion to the pursuit of truth, fell under the condemnation of both Catholic and Protestant censors and heresy-hunters. He died at the stake in Rome, equaling if not surpassing Socrates' example of moral heroism and unflinching intellectual courage.

The year was 1600; the place, Rome. The exceptional event was the celebration of a jubilee year; the commonplace incident, the burning of a man at the stake.

Pilgrims from all over Europe flocked to Rome in that year. Fifty of the cardinals of the church assembled there. The rich, the sophisticated, and the scholarly came to explore the treasures of the Eternal City. The pious, the cripple, and the repentant came to worship at the center of Western Christianity. Merchants were there to sell their wares. A year of jubilee was also a year of carnival. Gamblers and harlots came in from the provinces, and kings and ambassadors arrived to celebrate the feast days of the church.

It was an intolerant age. No mercy was shown to any who offended the sacred doctrines of the Mother Church.

So it was that the most famous heretic of the age walked through the streets of Rome early on that February morning of 1600. After eight years in the dark, solitary dungeons of the Holy Inquisition, the heretic, accompanied by a procession of priests, walked with bare feet over the tufa pavement to a terrifying freedom–the release of a man from a dread life. Within a few hours only a warm heap of ashes attested to the recent existence of one of the most gifted speculative philosophers of all time. And out from Rome through the cities and universities of Europe went the news that Dr. Giordano Bruno had perished at the stake. The date of the execution was Thursday, February 17th.

The life that ended in the flames of an execution pyre of Rome had begun only fifty-two years earlier in a little hamlet just outside the walls of Nola in southern Italy. At that time Nola was part of the Kingdom of Naples, a province under the rule of the Spanish throne and subject to Spain's unforgiving Holy Inquisition.

Bruno's boyhood homeland has been described as a "generous and beautiful countryside." The plain around Nola is a fertile land, lavish with vineyards. It is called by its inhabitants "the happy fields." The sky and air are what travelers have come to associate with southern Italy and Naples, and westward from the plain rises a range of hills dominated by Monte Somma. Except for those hills, an inhabitant of Nola would be able to look out upon Mount Vesuvius.

As a boy Phillip Bruno was precocious. His restless, brilliant, turbulent mentality was to lead him far from his native Nola. It would win for him distinction as a scholar and a place among the great teachers of Europe; but there would be few honors, a fatal renown, ostracism, exile, persecution, and finally death. His interests read like the catalogue of a university curriculum: theology, metaphysics, mathematics, logic, the psychology of memory, literature, drama, astronomy, physics, politics, and mysticism. He made significant contributions in several of these fields; he proved to be utterly wrong or fanciful in others. Restless, brilliant, turbulent–those three words were the keys to his character. They were a fatal combination, dangerous in most ages and particularly deadly in Bruno's times. The mind that pondered the deceit of the senses drove him who possessed it over most of Europe.

Bruno began his adulthood as a student for the Catholic priesthood, a novice in the monastic Order of St. Dominic. Even then his questioning mind placed him under the suspicion of his superiors, and later, at the heresy trial which cost him his life, he admitted that at the age of eighteen he had begun to doubt the doctrine of the "three distinct persons" of the Trinity. As a theological student, he came under the censure of his master for having given away the images of St. Catherine and St. Anthony and for advising a fellow student to read "suspect" books instead of those prescribed for instruction and edification.

Still, he seems to have been recognized as a student of exceptional gifts. It was here that he received the monastic name Giordano by which he is known to the world. The name was taken in honor of the River Jordan. No one knows why this name was selected for Phillip Bruno, but it is known that the name was reserved for monks of the highest promise. Although he was a problem for his superiors, he was at the same time their pride. In 1572, at the age of twenty-four, Bruno chanted his first mass as a priest of the church. For two years he continued, wearing the habit of the Dominican order and celebrating the holy offices.

Arianism, a form of unitarianism and a doctrine that

denied the deity of Christ, had become a popular heresy in the south of Italy. Socinianism, a more radical form of anti-trinitarian heresy, was already rising in other parts of Europe, representative of the theological "left wing" of the Reformation, a movement that went far beyond the reforms of Luther and Calvin in preparing the way for skepticism and free thought. Bruno claimed that he did not accept Arian theology, but he did not believe it to be such a dangerous doctrine as was supposed, and he argued at his heresy trial that he had defended Arianism only to clarify its concepts.

As the young priest knelt before the high altar and raised his eyes to the bright candles burning above him, he was struck with the thought that all these rites and rituals that he loved represented no literal truths but addressed the conscience of man in a symbolic way. The Eucharist, for example, asked the question: does this bread really become the flesh of Christ? Bruno rather supposed that this doctrine expressed the love of one's fellow man. He gave similar symbolic interpretations to other teachings and rituals of the Church. Long after leaving the priesthood as a fugitive, he would continue to prefer the Catholic religion to all others for beauty and spiritual richness, although challenging a strict interpretation of its doctrines.

Giordano was a priest now, no longer under the discipline and protection of his teachers. As a student, he had escaped opprobrium for his unconventional views, a mere threat sufficient to bring him back into line. Now that he was a priest, he was susceptible to conviction for heresy. As Giordano chanted the mass, lit the candles of the high altar, and elevated the host that accomplished the miracle of transubstantiation, his mind worked feverishly, interpreting these acts to make them conform to a rational system. He has been called the first modernist.

But energy of mind was only one of Bruno's attributes. A spirit of irrepressible speculation would not allow him to remain long under the roof of a sheltering orthodoxy. Only two years after ordination, the disciplines of monastic life were already unsettling him, when–because of his spirited defense of the Arians–the Provincial of the Ordear drew up a process against him. Fearing imprisonment if found guilty, Giordano Bruno made the decision to go into exile. He first sought refuge in the Papal States, where oddly enough, he believed a more cosmopolitan spirit prevailed. Italy, he reasoned, even under the Popes was not Spain. He left Naples and went to Rome, thus beginning sixteen years of wandering through Europe, often with the threat of arrest for heresy hanging over his head.

It was common in his day for monks to move from place to place, seeking hospitality at the monasteries of their brotherhood and even in private homes. There was so little organization between provinces that with reasonable safety Bruno could claim hospitality at Dominican monasteries even though he was an exile from that order in Naples. In Rome he boldly claimed hospitality at the very headquarters of his order, but soon learned that the forbidden books he had used in secret at Naples had been discovered. This increased the seriousness of the charges against him, and he considered it prudent to depart.

Yet prior to leaving Rome, he appeared before the Pope himself, demonstrating a system he had developed, now called the art of mnemonics. This skill brought Bruno his first touch of fame. Throughout his subsequent European wanderings he gave much of his time to perfecting his techniques of artificial memory, astounding people with prodigious feats of recollection.

Early in his career he began to advocate the astronomical theories of Nicolaus Copernicus, who had died only five years before Bruno's birth. The Copernican theory that the earth and the planets revolve around the sun was still denied by both Catholics and Calvinists as inconsistent with Christian doctrine. Aristotle, regarded by the Church as the supreme authority in natural philosophy, had taught otherwise, and Catholic thinkers, particularly Thomas Aquinas, had constructed a harmony between theology and philosophy that rested on Aristotle's cosmology.

Anything that weakened Aristotle's authority threatened

orthodox thought. Disregarding the theological scholars, Bruno despised the Aristotelian system with its earth-centered universe. Aristotle had divided the cosmos into concentric spheres, the celestial regions above and the terrestrial below, a scheme harmonizing with the biblical conception of a heaven above and an earth below. Bruno would have none of this. He was particularly impatient with Aristotle's idea of a universe arranged like the layers of an onion with the terrestrial regions at its core.

Copernicus had limited himself to reviving the ancient hypothesis of Aristarchus that the planets, including the earth, revolve around the sun. Even this limited concept seemed to the orthodox to shake their whole system. But if Copernicus shook it, Bruno overran it, reasoning that if the earth and the other planets revolve around the sun, it was also reasonable to believe that the most distant visible stars and their planets are similarly arranged. Thus every star visible to man, and many more invisible, are suns like our sun with planets of their own. By a great speculative leap, Bruno then asserted that an infinite deity would manifest his power in an infinite universe filled with an infinite number of stars and planets.

This concept outraged the Church, which taught that only God is infinite. Adding to this heresy, Bruno suggested that the universe was eternal as well as infinite–not the changing cosmos–but the substance of which the worlds were made. As the "body" of God, the cosmos had always existed. God was an impersonal force or mind "within" and "above" nature, rather than a personal being external to nature. This amounted to pantheism, a doctrine the church held to be heretical. Bruno's God was the indwelling spirit of the universe. In that speculation, he was the precursor of Benedict Spinoza, a philosopher considered greater than Bruno. His idea of God as the spirit of the whole "infusing" the whole, or oversoul, also makes him something of a forerunner of Emerson and the transcendentalists.

Probably his greatest ideas were the concepts of the orderliness of nature and his insistence upon empiricism, the direct observation of nature, rather than reliance upon traditional authority. It is upon this foundation that science is built. Here Bruno stands with Galileo and Bacon and the other fathers of modern scientific thought. His speculation of stars beyond our sight was later to be verified by Galileo's invention of the telescope. The general outlines of his view of gravity were confirmed by the laws of Isaac Newton. Bruno denied that there was such a thing as absolute weight, reasoning that what we call weight results from the tendency of objects to attract. He denied also that there is such a thing as absolute measurement for either space or time. As for the latter, Bruno contended, we measure not time itself but the movement of objects in space.

Many of his other speculations about natural phenomena were uncanny in their prescience and have been substantiated by later research. He maintained that the sun had an outer atmosphere whose luminescence radiated her light. He also suggested that the particles of the stars are in constant motion, that they decay and in time give rise to new formations. He proposed his own crude theory of the transmission of energy, foreshadowing the modern concept of radioactivity. He believed in a rational monistic universe, arguing that nature constitutes a whole, rather than a mere collection; the cosmos is not a collection, he said, but an "infusion."

He also gave much thought to the origin and nature of ethics. In Bruno's time, natural reason, sentiment, and feeling were regarded as valueless in the formulation of an ethical system. It was held, and is still held by many, that there can be no morality without the sanction of supernatural authority. But Bruno is said to have been the first to ignore this explanation and to treat moral conduct as a natural development, an impulse growing out of human experience and serving the social usefulness of binding communities together.

He was interested in the study now called "comparative religion." While he valued Christianity above all faiths, conceiving it as the gospel of love, he did not regard other religions as without value. In some respects, he said, paganism was superior to Christianity. It was "more tolerant, nearer to nature" and had a more profound metaphysical basis. Greek metaphysical thought, and Aristotle in particular, had deprived civilization of the primordial religion of nature found in Egypt. This Egyptian nature religion, he said, will be recovered in the future. Only by understanding our animal nature, by respecting instinct and feeling, can we regain spiritual health.

Above all, Bruno stood for religious and intellectual freedom and criticized Catholic and Protestant authorities alike for enforcing dogmas they did not understand. The value of religion lies in its practical application and should not be hindered by subtle, valueless theological baggage.

He looked at the Bible through modern eyes, accepting as factual neither the recorded creation of man nor the story of the universal flood. He rejected the idea that Providence intervenes in the operation of nature. What are called miracles can be explained in terms of natural laws, if we but understand all the facts. This faith in relentless, immutable natural law made him a patron saint of the deists more than a century after his death. John Toland, a pioneer of deistic "natural religion," a school of thought that we shall explore further in the philosophy of Thomas Paine and Jefferson, deeply venerated Bruno's memory and translated one of his works into English.

Bruno's knowledge of both philosophy and esoteric literature was prodigious, and there is in him a confluence of ideas drawn from the entire world of thought, a mixture of ancient, medieval, and renaissance themes and conceptions. In challenging Aristotelian metaphysics and cosmology, he borrowed from the still suppressed Copernicus the denial of an earth-centered universe; and not content to stop there, he blended the concept of a heliocentric solar system with far-reaching speculations that have their origin in eastern mysticism, neo-platonist philosophy, and the occult wisdom of Egypt and the Orient. He even explored the literature of magic, which for ages had served as a depository for suppressed science, although at his heresy trial he claimed to despise necromancy and denied having practiced the magical arts.

Several of his leading ideas show an affinity with Hindu thought, which, infiltrating the Near East in the wake of Alexander's conquests, left its deposit in gnostic and neoplatonist speculations that a thousand years of Christian orthodoxy was unable to obliterate. We have already seen these influences in Bruno's pantheistic tendencies, his conception of nature as the "body" of an infinite, impersonal divine being that "infuses" material reality. The infinite universe was not created *ex nihilo* ("out of nothing") as orthodox Jewish and Christian theology maintained, but expresses an underlying, permeating divine substance.

In Bruno's thought an "eternal incorporeal substance" supports an "eternal corporeal substance," a distinction that intellectual historians have regarded as a source of Spinoza's somewhat parallel distinction between *natura naturans* and *natura naturata*. The incorporeal nature is changeless but nevertheless enters into the tangible universe as its "efficient and formative principle." This obliteration of the impassable gulf between the essence of the Creator and the "creation" was regarded with particular aversion by Catholic orthodoxy, which over the centuries had bestowed several of its most conspicuous orgies of persecutions on sects accused of "pantheism"–in the eyes of the Church representing atheism in a particularly blasphemous disguise. In contrast, Hindu philosophy from the time of the Upanishads had conceived God as eternal, impersonal reality, within which the material universe is only a transient "breath" or appearance, a link in an infinite chain of decaying and recreated worlds.

The spirit of Hindu philosophy is also manifest in Bruno's view that all doctrines contain an element of truth. This logical and ethical principle is common to pantheistic systems of religion and philosophy, just as monotheistic systems, in contrast, tend toward exclusiveness and intolerance. Bruno viewed creativity as expressing the interactions of "contraries" in nature, a thought owed to the fifteenth-century thinker, Nicholaus of Cusa. Bruno states that "the birth, growth, and perfection of all that we see come from contraries through contraries into contraries to contraries" in apparently endless cycles.

Bruno did not take these themes directly from Indian philosophy; any influence from this source was indirect by way of ancient schools already mentioned and from similar doctrines derived from the pre-Socratics, especially Pythagoras. Following the Pythagoreans, he believed in the transmigration of the soul through many incarnations. Condemned by the Church as contrary to the teaching of the reunion of the soul with a resurrected body, destined to dwell in eternal bliss or torment, the doctrine of transmigration had been espoused by many ancient schools of occult wisdom and had, for a considerable time, even invaded the early Church.

The third-century churchman, Origen, for example, widely regarded as the greatest theologian before Augustine, had believed in transmigration, at least for the perfecting of souls for salvation. Such a belief was consistent with his doctrine that all lost souls would eventually be saved, a view that other early church fathers had promulgated, including Origen's great teacher, Clement of Alexandria, who had taught that Christ's mission was to extinguish all sin and redeem the whole of creation. Thus would be fulfilled the words of St. Paul that God would be "all in all." This doctrine of universal salvation–providing the basis for the eventual rise of the Universalist Church in post-Reformation times–continued throughout the ages to shoot forth fresh branches from the stump of Christian charity, evidence of an enduring belief in a God of infinite mercy and goodness, which the axe of orthodoxy could truncate, but never extirpate.

Bruno also seems to reflect another aspect of Origen's philosophy: his method of biblical interpretation. In common with many other ancient interpreters of scripture, Origen had sought to make Christianity intellectually coherent by interpreting its teachings allegorically. The literal meaning gave way to a higher significance, conveyed through an understanding of image and symbol. Teachings that offended a sense of decency or that involved logical or historical absurdities were reconstructed as types or masks concealing more profound meanings. Thus the uninitiated and simple-minded might accept Christianity as literally represented in the scriptures, but the more sophisticated would detect deeper truths. Condemnation of this approach by the Church proved as futile as other efforts to suppress unorthodox speculation.

In his brilliant, if somewhat idiosyncratic, reconception of Catholic doctrine, Bruno developed an elaborate system of allegorical interpretation. He readily admitted that it was necessary for a philosopher to use "language of accommodation"–to express himself in veiled terms familiar to the world in which he lived. Thus instead of denying the Trinity, a capital offense, he attempted to invest the concept with new meaning. The triune Godhead, he maintained, is a symbolic way of treating the three primary aspects of deity; the Father is substance; the Son, intellect; and the Holy Spirit, love. This explanation, however, was not to satisfy the Inquisition, which, upon capturing Bruno after his foolhardy return to Italy, formally condemned him for denying the orthodox doctrine of the Trinity.

Before this occurred, Bruno spent sixteen years wandering over Europe, finding security nowhere and enjoying only brief respites in which to teach and to write his prolific works. Upon learning in 1576 that the Neapolitan Inquisition had discovered among his effects several proscribed books of Erasmus–thus increasing the seriousness of the charges against him–Bruno had hastily departed from Rome and moved in rapid succession through Genoa, Turin, Savoni, and Noli to Venice where he arrived in 1577 and published his first work (now lost). Unable to find employment, he traveled to Padua where he was persuaded by Dominican brothers that it would be prudent to wear the habit of his order, which he had laid aside for secular dress in his flight from Rome. After sojourns in Brescia and Bergamo, he traveled to Milan, where he first learned of the works of Sir Philip Sidney who would in later years become an influential friend in England.

Thinking that he might find greater security and opportunity in Lyons, he was en route there when warned that he would not be welcomed. Turning instead toward Geneva, he encountered in the city of Calvin a religious dictatorship equal to any that he had known in Catholic Italy. Denounced, arrested, and forced to destroy a pamphlet he had written attacking the ideas of an Aristotelian professor of philosophy–and then to apologize–Bruno departed from Geneva, embittered for life against Calvinists and "pedants." As a result, his animus for Aristotle's philosophy was much reinforced.

He traveled to Lyons, but finding that city as inhospitable as had been foretold, he proceeded to Toulouse, then a Huguenot stronghold. Here he took a doctorate in theology and received appointment to a chair in philosophy. This interlude, 1579–81, ended abruptly when an outbreak of war against the Protestants prompted him to seek refuge in Paris. Again Bruno was able to make a place for himself, brilliantly exhibiting his system of memory–based on principles of mnemonics derived from Ramon Lull–and winning applause among scholars for his series of lectures on Thomas Aquinas's thirty attributes of God. Learning of his display of memory, King Henry III of France called him to a royal audience and became a steadfast admirer, a patronage that was vital when rising religious tensions threatened new warfare between Catholics and Protestants and induced Bruno to seek safety in England.

A letter of introduction from King Henry secured an invitation from the French ambassador in London, Michel de Castelnau, who became a warm and supportive host. Except for a misadventure of three months at Oxford, where Bruno again united the reigning Aristotelians in opposition to him, he accepted the hospitality of Castelnau, an intellectual, tolerant Catholic who was apparently cut from the cloth of Thomas More and Erasmus. He lived at his house for nearly all of his two and a half years in England. Castelnau took Bruno under his wing, allowing him to accompany him on numerous audiences with Queen Elizabeth, who like many of her subjects had a keen interest in Italian culture. Through the French ambassador Bruno met many of the leading intellectual lights of the international community of scholars living in London, including John Florio, Sir Fulke Greenville,

Albergio Gentile and Sir Philip Sidney (to whom Bruno would later dedicate two of his works including his celebrated satire on orthodoxy, *Spaccio de la bestia trionfante*).

This happy period, which nevertheless involved the bitter personal quarrels that seem to have been inevitable in Bruno's relationships, ended when his host was recalled to Paris. Following him there, Bruno soon fled France and its religious wars for Germany. Living in several German university towns, and for a time in Prague, Bruno continued to write and publish, finding himself well received by the Lutherans but rejected by the Calvinists, where first in Wittenberg and then again in Helmsteadt this intolerant religious party was displacing the more accommodating followers of Luther.

In 1590 Bruno took the step that destroyed him. He had never regarded himself as anything but a Roman Catholic, and his great hope was to be reconciled with the Church and with his own order. He belonged to that group of liberal reforming Catholic scholars who believed that the Church would finally adopt a more open view of philosophy and science, thus allowing freedom of thought to become untrammeled. At last came the opportunity that he thought would return him to Italy and his Church. Signor Giovanni Mocenigo, a patrician of Venice, had chanced upon a copy of a work of Bruno in which he noted the art of mnemonics. He invited Bruno at once to come to Venice to live in his house as his teacher.

With the incredible innocence that links great minds to childlike credulousness, Giordano Bruno – the man who could solve the mysteries of the heavens and describe the behavior of atoms – walked into a trap that anyone of even modest foresight and prudence would have anticipated and avoided. Not only did he teach his pupil the system of memory but, as he had done many times before in his years of wandering, he soon confided his heresies. Within a few weeks Mocenigo had gathered the evidence that would lead Bruno to the stake. Even then he was so confident of his ability to explain everything acceptably that he treated his first appearance before the tribunal as a joke. The charge could not possibly be anything but the spurious claim of a half-wit – as he could easily demonstrate to the court. When he realized his grave mistake, he threw himself on its mercy, hoping for leniency that at least his life would be spared, and that he had reason to think this would be the case. Had not more than fifteen hundred been tried by the Venetian Inquisition and only five been put to death? But his calculations failed to include the determination of the incumbent pope, Clement VIII who on mounting the throne of St. Peter had promised to ferret out heretics without mercy. Bruno's writings were too well known for him to escape notice, and the Roman Holy Office would not rest until the Republic of Venice agreed to Bruno's extradition.

After months of maneuvering, the Venetian court turned Bruno over to Rome, and on February 27, 1593 he was cast into the dungeons of the Roman Inquisition. At that point, shadows conceal the life of Giordano Bruno. What happened during his long, solitary imprisonment of seven years remains unknown. We know only that unrepentant heretics were generally disposed of in a matter of weeks.

When the veil lifted, the barefoot, emaciated figure of a tortured man stepped out into the twilight streets of Rome. It was the morning of February 17, 1600. The order of execution had been given by the Holy Office–the Inquisition–and like all executions of heretics the sentence provided, in the pious language of the church, that the deed should be done "without the shedding of blood."

It was a time of festival in Rome, a day in the year of jubilee. Outside of Rome is a plain called the Field of Flowers, the place of Bruno's execution. Bruno was accompanied that February morning by a band of monks, brothers of his own Dominican order, Jesuits, and others, all pleading for his repentance. As a biographer described the scene: "He was chained at the neck and wore a sheet emblazoned at the corners with the cross of St. Andrew and illuminated here and there with devils and red flames."

The procession arrived at the place prepared for the execution. The prisoner was stripped and bound to a stake. An image of Jesus was presented before him, but disdainfully he averted his eyes. His last words–expressing his unorthodox faith–offended his executioners, and so he was gagged. The torches were applied; the prisoner received the full measure of the sentence–"without the shedding of blood."

6

Eternal Nature Is God:

Benedict Spinoza

(1632–1677)

The dissemination to Europe of Greek philosophy and science via Jewish scholars in Islamic lands had begun more than three centuries before the Jews were expelled from Spain. That was in 1492, when Ferdinand and Isabella conquered Moorish Granada. The Moslem thinker, Averroës (c. 1126–1198), had been a pivotal figure in redirecting the course of Jewish and Christian philosophy and especially in influencing the precursors of Thomas Aquinas (c. 1225–1274), the Italian scholastic philosopher who gave Aristotle preëminence in subsequent Catholic theology.

Spanish and Portuguese Jewry continued to maintain a remarkable tradition of learning, which they carried with them in their quest for refuge to various parts of North Africa, the Near East, and the Netherlands. They constituted a major branch of Jewish culture–the Sephardim, so designated after the placename Sepharad, found in the biblical book of Obadiah and identified with Iberia by early commentators. Afterward the term came to be applied to all Arabic as well as Iberian Jews, in contrast to the Ashkenazim of German and Slavic lands. The Sephardim of seven-

teenth-century Amsterdam, while only half as numerous as their Ashkenazi neighbors, had achieved far greater wealth and influence, perhaps helping to make this community of respectable burghers severely intolerant of heresy in their own ranks, especially when it involved political radicalism that risked the reprisal of conservative Christians. More than one young Jewish iconoclast suffered orthodox condemnation. None is more illustrious in intellectual and religious history than Baruch (Benedict) de Spinoza.

Rarely does there arise in human history an intellectual genius of the first rank who is at the same time a moral and spiritual giant. Perhaps in the entire record of the human race one can count such figures on the fingers of one's hands. Gautama, the founder of Buddhism, was such a man; Socrates is commonly considered another. Since there are substantial reasons to support such a view, many would place Spinoza in this select circle.

Ernest Renan considered Spinoza "the greatest Jew in modern times" despite his excommunication from the synagogue. Will Durant acclaimed him the greatest of modern philosophers, with a lasting influence that may come in the future to rival Plato's in its impact on civilization. Others have admired him equally for his intellectural achievements and for the courage and purity of his life. For his nobility of character and exalted vision he has been called a saint without a church.

Like Gautama the Buddha Spinoza owed much of his power of thought and feeling to a profound understanding of human psychology, carefully considered over many years of reflection. He anticipated Freud's discovery of hidden and dreaded specters that lurk beneath the surface of consciousness.

Spinoza reasons that mental maturity is preferable to a state of innocence, and that acceptance of reality is a greater safeguard to emotional health and security than comforting illusions and self-deceptions. Every mature life finds its way to inner peace through acceptance of life's unavoidable limitations and setbacks.

It is not a philosophy for everyone. Although Spinoza believed in democracy and was an earnest advocate of intellectual and religious liberty, he was the first to acknowledge that men and women in the mass are not prepared to accept a philosophy that requires surrendering comforting mythologies and popular deceptions. Many will follow spiritual concepts that offer escape from responsibility. He addressed his teaching to those few who are unable or unwilling to base their lives on fables and pretenses, and to those who choose to look the facts of life in the face and still find the spiritual resources in themselves to view life as of value.

Baruch Spinoza was born in 1632 into a community of Spanish and Portuguese Jews who had found refuge in Holland, there escaping the forced conversion and terror of the Holy Inquisition that had destroyed an incredibly rich and creative Jewish culture. In Spinoza's time the Netherlands was a sanctuary for many other refugee groups, including a band of English separatists who only twelve years before Spinoza's birth had departed from Leyden on the first leg of a voyage to the frigid coast of Massachusetts.

Although religious toleration in Holland flourished to a degree rare for that age, Jews and other minorities were always conscious of the danger of provoking the majority. This fear, reinforced by the natural inclination of any orthodoxy to punish members who question sacred truths, prompted the synagogue to expel Spinoza at the age of twenty-four for heretical opinions concerning the nature of God, the existence of angels, and for pointing out the Old Testament's lack of support for the doctrine of immortality.

His excommunication deprived him of the support or sympathy of any member of the religious community. He was forced to earn his living by grinding lenses, which however was considered an appropriate occupation for a self-supporting intellectual. He earned no more than what was essential for a meager existence, and reserved as much time as possible for his philosophical studies. He boarded with a family of

Mennonites, themselves a recently persecuted sect. This family respected his integrity and simplicity of living. Like Henry David Thoreau at Walden Pond two centuries later, Spinoza embraced the simple life in order to disentangle himself from the tyranny of material involvement–not from ascetic self-hate or contempt for the body, but because simplicity of living meant independence and freedom.

Yet he did not remain unnoticed or without being honored. As scandalized as many were with his views–he was widely denounced as an atheist and corruptor of morals–Spinoza acquired considerable fame, even during his lifetime, with philosophers and scientists as well as royalty. Through it all he kept his serenity. He died quietly at the age of forty-five with only his faithful physician in attendance. He had been afflicted by tuberculosis for many years, apparently complicated by silicosis, the result of breathing the dust of lens-grinding.

What is the legacy that this man left to humanity, and why should we value his philosophy today? Of all the thinkers of past and present, Spinoza is our perennially contemporary philosopher–contemporary because timeless in his profound comprehension of human nature and destiny. The problems he treats are always with us and his resolution of those problems is perpetually relevant. This fact may be questioned by those who regard Spinoza as a transitional figure between the old world of medieval Catholic scholastics and the new world of scientific positivists and pragmatists. But if we look beyond Spinoza's stylized geometrical proofs and avoid becoming ensnared in a terminology and form of argument that the geometrical method imposes, if we focus on his moral and intellectual conclusions and the vitality of his cosmic vision, we reach a quite different assessment. Spinoza used old-style language and logic to support a new world view. After him, there was no going back to ancient and medieval conceptions of reality and of human life. The medieval Christian age viewed the cosmos through the lenses of theology; the lenses that Spinoza ground enabled a new age to view the cosmos in terms of mathematical physics. That frame of reference, making allowance for the astonishing advances of mathematics and physics since Spinoza's day, is still capable of assimilating today's discoveries in astronomy or genetics.

Spinoza pursued a radically different path, viewing the universe in terms of mathematics, a concept that he had borrowed from scholars and dreamers of the Renaissance. It was the special goal of his genius to organize this new learning into a unified intellectual and moral world view, a conception of Nature and of the place of intelligent, purposeful human life within that order.

What remains undiminished in Spinoza's philosophy is his unique way of conceiving the freedom of the moral life and of the human spirit. It is a liberating philosophy, as Spinoza consistently reminds us, yet one that can be attained only by the courage to face the limitations of life and give up cherished illusions. What, we ask, was Spinoza's insight that caused him to be expelled from the religion of his people, to be slandered as a godless, lawless corrupter of the innocent and, at the same time, to construct a new foundation for human dignity and freedom?

Most frequently Spinoza's teaching is reduced to a simple equation: God is Nature; Nature is God. There is no God except Nature viewed as a self-contained, creative whole, "under the aspect of eternity." Many people who know nothing else about Spinoza are familiar with this formula. But such a simplified equation can lead us astray unless the ideas of God and Nature are carefully construed in accordance with Spinoza's distinctive concepts.

Spinoza was no materialist. Mind and matter, he believed, are only two aspects or modes of an underlying reality having an infinite number of other aspects, unknowable to us as finite beings. Mind cannot be reduced to matter, nor matter to mind. Yet mind and matter do not pertain to independent, parallel worlds, the one regarded as natural and the other as supernatural. Mind and matter are two modes of an infinitely greater, unified order of reality. Spinoza's technical term for this comprehensive reality was "substance." In Spinoza's interpretation, substance retains an earlier meaning, from the Latin, signifying that which stands below, literally, the reality that supports or contains the world we experience.

It would perhaps be more profitable to approach Spinoza in terms of his practical moral philosophy, rather than head first as a metaphysical thinker. The essence of Spinoza's psychology and moral philosophy can be expressed in terms of two related principles. First, he endeavors to show that there are no cosmic purposes in Nature, and then, as he proceeds to argue, that freedom for any being is based on its ability to act in accord with its own nature, not to be forced to act contrary to it. Strictly speaking, there is no "free will." Given its nature, every creature acts at any moment as it must.

Nature as a whole, or as an infinite, eternal system has no purpose; God or Nature seeks to fulfill no goals. From our human perspective we imagine that God is of our own likeness and that he shares human desires and goals. We torment ourselves needlessly and cannot understand why bad fortune, illness, and death befall us. We fancy that Providence must have some inscrutable purpose in mind to afflict us so, or that we are being punished, often unreasonably and savagely, for real or imagined sins. Yet the hurricane that crushes the squirrel under the falling tree does not have the sins or virtues of the squirrel in mind; the hurricane has no motives or intentions. These are facts of mindless nature, its power flowing from the necessity of things.

When we give up the fallacy of believing in a purposeful God, in a nature that gives special protection, guidance, or punishment, we are free to recognize the truth about our moral and spiritual situation and to understand the human origin of nature's imagined purposes. Facing the reality of our situation, we are delivered from pointless superstitious fears about the future.

Spinoza's second principle follows from his belief that Nature as a whole has no purpose and from his conception of universal necessity. All events are determined, he believed, and the behavior of human beings is equally determined. Doesn't this notion of natural determinism deprive human beings of moral freedom and reduce us to automatons? Not so, says Spinoza. Every human being acts in accord with his or her nature. Our desires, fears, purposes and ideals make up our nature. Our powers of reason, our ability to foresee consequences and to weigh alternatives are also factors that help determine how we shall act under given circumstances.

Thus understood, Spinoza's insistence that human behavior is determined and necessary according to our natures does not deny moral responsibility. On the contrary, he argues, the principles of childrearing and education are based on the assumption that good behavior is learnable, that good habits can be induced, and that socially desirable behavior is the expected outcome of loving relationships and worthy examples. His theory of moral education is entirely up to date. When we act according to reason, we punish criminals not to exact revenge but to reform them. Spinoza would have understood rehabilitation and education as the desirable goal of the criminal justice system, a system that still brutalizes and dehumanizes.

Here are all the elements of a philosophy of emotional and moral maturity. We must stress the emotional factor because Spinoza is often misunderstood as a purely cerebral philosopher. His life no less than his principal writings belie such a portrayal. He was a deeply feeling man, passionate in his love of truth and his attachment to human liberty. In his person he paid an excessive price to attain the freedom to pursue truth that he valued more than life itself–and for which he was in danger of assassination or lynching at least twice in his lifetime.

Denounced in his own time as a hater of religion, Spinoza was seen as a "God-intoxicated man" by subsequent generations. With heroic courage he rejected ideas of God or infinite reality that he regarded as a hindrance to a truer and deeper conception of being. He was acutely aware of the high cost of rigid and tyrannical systems of "revealed" religion which hold men and women in a stunted, childish dependency. He opposed oppressive and delusional ideas and opened the way for a clearer vision of reality and of human freedom.

He identified Nature and God not to dishonor either concept but to stretch human understanding and to show a unity of being that would expand our vision of the cosmos and affirm its transcendant sufficiency. So from first to last, his moral philosophy and intellectual vision merged into a religious conception that has never been surpassed and seldom equaled. His philosophy has the grandeur and beauty of a great poem.

When Einstein was asked to summarize his religious views, he said simply: "I believe in Spinoza's God." Like his great predecessor of three centuries ago, Einstein sought a unified concept of the cosmos, a unification still best expressed in the language of mathematical physics. Like Spinoza, Einstein saw the delusion of trying to find our human purposes in the cosmos at large. True religion, born of spiritual maturity, is based on accepting the finiteness of our existence, on living our portion of time with courage and serenity, and of lifting our eyes to the great heavens beyond our galaxy to find in the silences of the stellar archipelagos a splendor that, by its reflected light, makes us not paltry or insignificant, but incomparably greater than we could ever be apart from our place in nature.

Spinoza's eyes were not fixed solely on the heavens. A republican against monarchy and oligarchy in his theory of government and an advocate of human rights, he belonged to the liberal political party of his day. It was no mere happenstance that, following his banishment from Jewish society, he found sanctuary among the Mennonites, who were representative of the political democrats as well as religious radicals of the period; they were pacifist survivors of the recent Anabaptist revolutionary movement, the "left-wing" of the Reformation that Luther, Calvin, and other conservative Protestant leaders had conspired with the civil authorities to destroy.

For more than a century, the Netherlands had been a center of religious dissent, a refuge for Europe's religious minorities and nonconformists, for Portuguese and Spanish Jews, Huguenots fleeing from France, and Anabaptists and Socinians driven from Poland, Germany, and other European countries. Holland itself had been a hotbed of revolutionary Anabaptist agitation, suppressed by the bloody measures freely used by both Catholic and Protestant powers to extinguish religious and social dissent. Yet Protestant Holland owed its independence from Spain to the bravery of these Anabaptist revolutionaries. It was estimated that three-fourths of the Dutch freedom fighters were of this forbidden sect.

Anabaptist doctrine and organization differed markedly in their many manifestations, but in the main Anabaptism represented a mass movement for religious, political, and economic transformation that wanted to go far beyond the reforms contemplated by conservative Protestant leaders. Many Anabaptists boldly proclaimed the right of armed rebellion. Christ Himself was typically depicted as the avenging liberator of the downtrodden, leading his soldiers of righteousness by fire and sword into a utopian society where all should be equal. The abolition of hereditary privileges, the holding of all property in common, and the elimination of all priestly rank and authority were familiar demands of this radical wing of the Reformation. Those more moderate Anabaptists who stopped short of equating the gospel of Christ with pure communism were insistent on far-reaching reforms that usually included republican government and complete liberty of conscience.

While the back of the Anabaptist revolution had been broken before Spinoza's time, the old ideals of the "left-wing Reformation" still survived in the democratic and egalitarian doctrines of such minority sects as the Mennonites on the continent, and the Quakers and similar dissidents in Britain. A small number of radical Quakers also became established in Holland and, like the Mennonites, influenced Spinoza's religious and political outlook.

During the same period that English republicans under the leadership of Oliver Cromwell were overthrowing the Stuart crown, the Dutch disowned the royal House of Orange and established a republic that lasted for twenty years under the guidance of Spinoza's friend, Jan de Witt. Finally, after defeat in European wars, de Witt was expelled from office in 1672 and shortly afterward was lynched by a mob–a savage and ironic fate for one of the most illustrious champions of democracy of all time. Spinoza himself was endangered by this turn of events, which occurred only five years before his premature death.

Spinoza harbored no illusions about the imperfections of human beings, nor was he blind to the risks of democratic government. But he grasped the evils of autocracy and recognized the menace to freedom represented by the rule of the clergy. Spinoza's appreciation of balanced and moderate politics, avoiding all excesses and extremes, clearly prefigures the ideal of constitutional liberalism as it has evolved in the three centuries since his time.

7

Joyous Infidel:

Voltaire

(1694–1778)

That a supreme Intelligence created Nature, set it on its course and left it without further intervention, subject only to natural laws that can be discovered through scientific investigation, is an opinion that has been widely held for three centuries. Known as "Natural Religion" or "deism," this school of thought generally discounts miracle and special revelation as delusion or fraud and tends to be opposed to Christianity.

The three thinkers to be presented next exemplify this perspective. Although there are shades of difference in the religious philosophies of Voltaire, Thomas Paine, and Thomas Jefferson, these men hold virtually identical views on most essentials of their beliefs. This is not surprising when we consider that deism was a strong intellectual movement in the late seventeenth and eighteenth centuries. Born and developed in Britain, it came to great influence throughout Europe—especially in France—and in British North America. Lord Herbert of Cherbury (1583–1648) is regarded as the precursor of the movement which in the following century became increasingly bold in its attacks on

Christian doctrine and ecclesiastical power. John Toland, Anthony Collins, and Matthew Tindal wrote popular deistic works between 1696 and 1730 and laid down the principles of deistic free thought that Voltaire, Paine, and Jefferson expressed with incisive trenchancy.

On October 13, 1761, while his parents and brother, Pierre, were entertaining an unexpected dinner guest, Marc-Antoine Calas slipped unnoticed into the shop below and hanged himself from the cupboard doors. His body, swinging from a cord attached to a timber placed over the open doors, was discovered at about ten o'clock that evening by Pierre as he was leading the visitor, Gaubert Lavaysse, to the guest room downstairs.

The shouts of Pierre and Lavaysse brought the father, Jean, to the scene. Stunned, he released the cord and lowered his son's body to the floor. He immediately sent Pierre for the family doctor, while Madame Calas, attended by the maid, Jeanne Viguier, tried unsuccessfully to resuscitate her son. When the physician arrived, he pronounced Marc-Antoine dead.

Suicide in Catholic France in 1761 was an unspeakable crime. The law prescribed that the suicide's body should be stripped naked and dragged face downward through the streets to be stoned and defiled by the crowds and finally hanged on the scaffold. Any property of the deceased was to be confiscated.

Jean Calas begged his family and their guest to conceal the suicide and spare his dead son this final ignominy. But recognizing the seriousness of the situation, Lavaysse reported the facts to the authorities.

While the father's efforts to protect his son's body was understandable, the consequence to himself and his family exceeded all imagining. What made the situation so volatile was the fact that the sixty-three-year-old Calas, a merchant and a gentle, peaceable and devout citizen, was a Protestant.

It was known that his son Marc-Antoine had been disqualified from pursuing his dream of becoming a lawyer because he was not Catholic. Suffering severe depression, the youth began frequenting taverns where he recited morose poetry on suicide, including the familiar soliloquy from *Hamlet*.

The court, prevented from learning the truth by Calas's adamant refusal to admit his son's suicide, concluded that Calas himself had killed him–in order to prevent Marc-Antoine's conversion from Protestantism to Catholicism! There was no indication of any kind that Marc-Antoine had even considered conversion to Catholicism; nor was there a shred of evidence to indict his father for murder.

Yet Jean Calas, protesting his innocence to the end, was condemned to be broken on the wheel–this medieval torture to be protracted over many hours "to last as long as God would let him breathe."

As if this penalty was not enough, the sentence directed that breaking on the wheel was to be preceded by what was called "ordinary and extraordinary torture." Georg Brandes, a biographer and historian of the era, outlines the ordeal:

> The ordinary and extraordinary torture consisted partly of forced drinking of water, at the ordinary torture eight cans of water, at the extraordinary torture sixteen cans, and partly of the Spanish shoe, which meant that the leg of the tortured victim was put between two boards which were screwed together as firmly as possible, after which wedges were driven between them with heavy blows of the hammer. As a rule the bones were crushed during the process. Here, too, were two degrees: These were four or eight wedges driven in. Jean Calas underwent the ordinary as well as the extraordinary torture. In the sixteenth and eighteenth century the feet and hands were twisted out of their sockets. This torture was practiced in France outside of Paris until 1788.

The day after sentence was passed both the torture and the execution were carried out. If the Calas family had not belonged to the despised and persecuted Huguenots, followers of John Calvin, the suicide of Marc-Antoine would have remained a private misfortune; but as it was, it became one of the most notorious examples of judicial barbarism and religious animus in Bourbon France. Not only was Jean Calas cruelly dismembered and destroyed, but the original indictment called for similar treatment of his wife, whose only offense had been a mother's desperate attempt to breathe life into her dead son. Even their devoted maid, Jeanne Viguier, although a strict Catholic, was implicated in the alleged conspiracy to commit "murder." Only Jean Calas's refusal to render the expected confession implicating others spared their lives. After his execution the maid, the unexpected guest, Gaubert Lavaysse (who had stayed over only because a post-horse could not be rented until the following day), Madame Calas, their two daughters and their son Pierre were released.

The rationale for this strange verdict is to be found in the religious situation of pre-revolutionary France. Everyone in Catholic France "knew" that Protestant teaching, laid down by Calvin, obligated parents to murder their children to prevent their turning Catholic. Public wisdom had "known" since the Middle Ages that Jews were directed by the Talmud to kidnap Christian infants whose blood was a necessary ingredient for the Jews' Easter bread. These two slanders, accepted by the gullible population as uncontrovertible fact, inspired the massacre of untold thousands.

In the case of the Calas family, an older son had already embraced the Catholic religion without interference from his father. Jean Calas was a peaceful and respected merchant who maintained friendly relations with both Catholics and Protestants. The family was served by a Catholic maid whose zeal for her church was unquestioned. And on the night of the supposed murder, they were entertaining a guest: a strange occasion on which to carry out murder in their home. But the facts of the case did not matter when, hours after the son's death, an unfriendly crowd began to gather and someone made the inevitable accusation. From that moment Jean Calas was as good as dead.

Like thousands upon thousands of similar cases of religious outrage before it, the judicial murder of Jean Calas would have been soon forgotten but for the indignation of a most remarkable Frenchman. Francois Marie Arouet, who had become famous as the philosopher, dramatist, historian and essayist Voltaire, was outraged by this fresh exhibition of religious ignorance and vindictiveness. For three years Voltaire made exposure of the Calas case his principal concern, gathering evidence to impeach a corrupt and brutalized legal system, demanding a reopening of the trial and spreading far and wide his brilliantly written exposures of the judicial atrocity, and finally showing its relation to a record replete with torture and slaughter in the name of holy Catholic France.

Voltaire's uncontrollable indignation has been pointed up by the biographer and literary critic, Georg Brandes, who observed that in the century preceding Voltaire only one French intellectual of note, La Bruyère, had raised his voice to protest the barbarity of the criminal law. The lives of ordinary people counted but little, and those of heretics not at all. The young Chevalier de La Barre was broken on the wheel for the insolence of walking past a religious procession of monks without removing his hat or making the sign of the cross; at his trial he admitted having sung, at a private gathering, bawdy songs showing disrespect for the Virgin.

In attacking these monstrosities of law, Voltaire and his few allies found themselves immediately confronting the power of the clergy and the objections of Christian piety: Efforts to abolish torture were condemned as impious affronts to God's law. Divine justice required that heretics and blasphemers be put to death by the severest torment. Anything less subverted the authority of Christian faith and government. Later generations of Christians, reared in a more humane civilization, were to discover in disbelief that the struggle to abolish what the American Constitution calls "cruel and unusual punishment" was begun by avowed infidels and freethinkers over the protests of Christian moralists and theologians who insisted on punishments more heinous than the Roman crucifixion. The Sermon on the Mount had yielded to the ominous maxim: "I come to bring not peace, but a sword." These medieval practices, sanctified in the name of Christ and the Virgin Mary, persisted in France until the collapse of clerical power on the eve of the French Revolution.

From the torture and execution of Calas in 1761 until his own death in 1778, Voltaire became a one-man league for the defense of human rights and religious tolerance. The Sirven family was accused of the same crime as the Calas–in this instance, the murder of a daughter, Elizabeth, a mentally handicapped child. Through his legal acumen, Voltaire was able to establish the innocence of the Sirvens and overturn the draconian verdict, a struggle that continued on for seven years. But this happy outcome owed nothing to French justice under the Bourbons. Only the timely flight of the Sirvens to Swiss territory saved their lives, where after months of separation in hiding and furtive wandering they were finally reunited; they had been condemned in absentia to death, with the torture and execution tediously inflicted on effigies, after the images of the condemned had dutifully done penance for their sins. The flight of the Sirvens proved their guilt in the eyes of the French court, but Voltaire's retort was to the point: "You wretch! Did you perhaps imagine they would remain and let you work your insane fury upon them?"

With the defendants secure in Switzerland, Voltaire was able to turn French public opinion around and compel the courts to recognize that Pierre Paul Sirven, a prominent surveyor of Castres, could not have murdered his mentally handicapped daughter to forestall her conversion to Catholicism. On the fateful night of her disappearance Pierre Paul was many miles from home on an assignment for his employer. Distinguished witnesses had been his hosts and provided him with an unimpeachable alibi. When the body of the unfortunate Elizabeth was discovered at the bottom of a well where she had apparently fallen during a typical nocturnal wandering, the familiar accusation was made with no supporting evidence. Influenced by a Catholic friend, Elizabeth had indeed flirted with the idea of conversion from Protestanism to Catholicism. Her parents had acceded to her wish to live under the care of a nunnery; later on, tiring of the sequestered life, Elizabeth herself had made the decision to return home. As Voltaire was to prove, at no time had her family acted cruelly toward the troubled girl. Although the family was eventually acquitted, Madame Sirven died in her Swiss refuge, grieving over the loss of her daughter and her family's affliction.

Through cases similar to those of Calas and Sirven, Voltaire and his supporters–most notably the encyclopedist Jean le Rond d'Alembert–were able to educate a generation of French intellectuals to the enormity of French "justice." Thousands of peasants, living on church lands that had been fraudulently obtained through forged "grants," were reduced to slavery by the religious orders. Even a freeman who married a serf became feudal property himself and saw his descendants born into perpetual bondage. The religious orders were as rich and powerful as they were degenerate.

The bloodletting of the Jacobin terror, which swept king and clergy before it in a sanguinary riptide of reprisal, had its origin in the humiliation of a long-suffering people that under Christian kings and ecclesiastical masters endured a torment equal to any recorded in history. The total number of victims massacred, burned at the stake, broken on the wheel, or pulled limb from limb between tugging horses, ran into hundreds of thousands. Victims of witchcraft trials, heresy hunts, and convictions for blasphemy were liquidated by the Christian monarchs of Europe in numbers there were not to be exceeded until the twentieth century auto da fé of Hitler and Stalin; indeed in terms of the total populations subject to their control, it is not likely that the great madmen of our era, even with their advanced instruments of repression and control, claimed a greater percentage of victims than many of the sainted patrons of Christian benevolence.

"Crush the infamy!" Voltaire repeated the slogan until it became as much a motto for his age as the cry of Cato against Carthage had been for the Roman Republic; Voltaire himself made the comparison. The power of the Church, and the superstition that supported and secured its control, were the constant goads of Voltaire's indignation. He did not separate the abuses of Christianity from the religion itself. The "infamy" was too pervasive, too insidious, and too rampant to allow compromise. Christianity *was* the abuse, and Voltaire was determined to break its hold over the human mind. He passionately believed that Christianity was not basically a good or harmless religion only occasionally tainted by corruption. Christianity *itself* was the taint, the moving spirit of superstition and tyranny. Founded on fraud, kept alive by moral cowardice and gullibility, and expanded by fanaticism and treachery, the Christian system was through and through a doctrine of darkness and oppression. It preached love to disarm its slaves; but given power, it practiced hatred and tyranny. Mankind, said Voltaire, would not be free until the last priest was strangled with the entrails of the last knave.

Voltaire's fury at the continuing slavery and misery that he saw around him, together with his wit and love of farce made him the most effective publicist of anticlericalism that the world has ever known. If Voltaire had not set out on this crusade against priestcraft–by which he meant Protestant as well as Catholic religious control–he would be remembered as one of the greatest of French classical dramatists. His more than thirty tragedies earned him immortality on the French stage.

Yet the world remembers and loves him–or hates him–for the work he did primarily after these masterful plays were composed.

The seeds of his rebellion came early. The better part of his more than sixty years of adult life were spent in exile–either forced exile in England early in his career, or token exile near the Swiss-French border, in Switzerland itself, or for a period of voluntary expatriation at the Court of Frederick the Great, who idolized him. One of the truly exceptional facts in the career of this unequaled iconoclast and freethinker was the fascination he engendered in two of Europe's most powerful and resourceful sovereigns: Frederick of Prussia and Catherine of Russia. If Louis XV and his ill-starred successor had received Voltaire's ideas with even half the enthusiasm of Frederick and Catherine, the Bourbons might have loosened the thongs of their oppression, sooner and more gradually and thus saved their kingdom.

If Voltaire hated "the superstition," by which he meant the whole edifice of revealed religion–whether Christian, Jewish, or Moslem–his exile in England brought him into contact with one sect of Christians that he truly admired. They were the Quakers who proved, he said, that a plain people who lived without priesthood, sacraments, or creed, guided solely by the Inner Light, could be followers of Jesus without the claptrap of ecclesiastical pomp and power.

He marveled at a country where the established church had been deprived of most of its traditional authority, where more than thirty sects openly competed for converts and where the government permitted opponents to ridicule cabinet ministers in a manner that would have brought swift punishment in France. Although many French exiles lived in England for a lifetime although scorning the harsh Anglo-Saxon tongue as an abomination, Voltaire undertook the arduous task of mastering the language of his island sanctuary. Finding English pronunciation extremely difficult, he set about conquering the barbarous speech with the same industry that would make him an author whose collected works would run to seventy volumes. His technique for learning English was to sit day after day in the English theater with a borrowed script in hand, reading and listening until the written and spoken language were unified in his mind.

England gave Voltaire his philosophy and his mission. When he came, he was already a nonbeliever in the Christian religion; he was convinced that nature required a Supreme Architect, and in English deism he found the system already perfected that would guide his thinking and give content to his science.

Within a year of his arrival in 1726, Isaac Newton died. Voltaire saw the British nation in mourning as if it had lost a king. He watched a funeral procession that would have done honor to royalty, as a people and their government followed the bier of their great scientist to its place of rest in Westminster Abbey.

For Voltaire the funeral of Sir Isaac Newton was a parable on the virtues of English science and statecraft: The greatest intellect since Archimedes–perhaps the greatest since the dawn of civilization–had lived in freedom and honor for eighty-five years in the island kingdom; he had revealed more than men had ever known, or believed possible to know, about the forces that govern the movements of planets and the most distant stars. He had demolished the sacred assumptions of medieval science for which the scientists and philosophers of Europe, including Copernicus, Bruno, and Galileo, had suffered papal condemnation. Although a devout Christian, Newton doubted the doctrine of the trinity regarding Jesus as a messenger of God, but not God himself–the loathsome heresy for which Calvin had burned Michael Servetus and for which the followers of Faustus Socinus had been extirpated in Italy and Poland.

When the thirty-two-year-old Voltaire set foot on British soil, John Locke, the other stellar thinker of England, had been dead for only twenty-two years. With the zeal equal to his enthusiasm for Newton, Voltaire embraced Locke's empirical philosophy, his reliance on sensation and the association of ideas as the source of all knowledge. On Newton and Locke, these two pillars of thought, Voltaire erected his philosophy; and because of Voltaire's influence on a younger generation of philosophers, Diderot, d'Alembert and others, the French Enlightenment had its origins in English science and philosophy.

But as they developed, England and French free thought steadily diverged, the English variety remaining deistic while the French moved toward atheism. Part of the reason for this difference lay in the gulf separating English and French culture and institutions; part, perhaps in temperamental differences deeply imbued in the French and English psyche. For centuries the English have displayed an aversion to master systems, to neat syllogisms, and rigorous logical constructions. English philosophy and religion resemble

English gardens and hedgerows–rambling, uncultivated, with thickets hospitable for badgers and foxes. English thinkers, one might argue plausibly, have been mostly badgers, with a few foxes.

French philosophy, in contrast, seems made to complement the formal courtyards of Versailles and Fountainbleau. French intellectuals had minds like polished marble. Their thoughts, however energetic and original, moved like the clockworks of Paris or dazzled the eye with a logical tracery as intricate as Chartre.

Voltaire, this unabashed Anglophile who admired the plain English Quaker and adored even more the plain English philosophy, was extravagantly, quintessentially French. Pursued in the streets of London by a rock-throwing mob during a period of French-British tension, Voltaire suddenly turned and addressed his tormenters in excellent English: "Is it not a sufficient misfortune for me not to be English by birth? Why do you add to this misfortune?" Overwhelmed to find a French gentleman of quality who addressed them so eloquently in their native tongue, the mob's hostility melted at once, and they escorted the charming foreigner to his quarters.

It took equal parts of Gallic wit and agility for a dissenter of Voltaire's views to survive under the regime of the last Bourbon kings. His critics found him deceitful and sly; they condemned the ease with which Voltaire lied to protect himself and his causes. He confided that he did not intend to be burned at the stake, and so he turned to bluff and duplicity whenever prudence required it. But his critics forget that this political fox–this singular example of forest wisdom among the French philosophers–outsmarted and outmaneuvered all the agents and informers of an unprincipled and unpredictable despotism. Without question, there was ample ground to break him on the wheel for his acts of political and religious defiance, his lese-majesté, his persistent heresies, and assorted blasphemies. He wrote the script and set the stage for the high drama that a decade after his death brought down absolutism. But despite all he lived into his eighties, and after a final grand entry that took all of Paris by storm—even Marie Antoinette wanting to see him—he died peacefully in bed, virtually under the disapproving nose of Louis XVI. If covert resistance to a tyrant is immoral, blameworthy because such resistance necessarily involved concealment and deception, then Voltaire cannot be justified. But he used his tricks not to advance himself in the world—fame and luxury were his already—but to free the hapless partridges of France caught in the Bourbon net.

Most of Voltaire's deception involved ruses to conceal his authorship of forbidden pamphlets, but in covering his tracks, he did no more than do most authors of forbidden tracts. Voltaire was unusual only because the magnitude of his fame as a poet and dramatist increased the difficulty of remaining anonymous.

His elaborate denials were in effect licenses to publish. As long as he denied authorship of a work known almost beyond dispute to be from his quill, the authorities could pretend to accept the pretense. Arresting a nation's most celebrated and widely admired author is no welcome assignment even for an oppressive government. Had Voltaire declared his responsibility, his admission would have represented defiance, and the regime would have had little choice but to accept the challenge. Voltaire's survival, uneasy as it was—requiring him to live far from Paris on the Swiss frontier—is lasting evidence of his skill as well as his good fortune in taking the measure of the government.

What other French subject could have maintained, even under the disguise of pseudonymity, such an unrelenting barrage against his church and king? Assuming the identity of his old English friend, Lord Bolingbroke, who had recently died, Voltaire penned an indictment of all theological pretension:

> A theologian, a factional man, wishes to conquer like a prince; and there are many more sects in the world than kingdoms. To whom shall I submit my soul? Shall I be a Christian, just because I come from London or Madrid? Shall I be a Muslim simply because I was born in Turkey? I ought to think only for

> myself; the choice of a religion is my greatest interest. You adore God through Muhammed; or through the Grand Lama; or through the Pope. How unfortunate! Adore God for your own reasons!

For Voltaire, as for deists generally, adoring God "for your own reasons" meant basing one's belief entirely on reason and experience, unsupported by any priesthood, scripture, or revelation. The reader comparing these passages with the later statements of Paine and Jefferson will find remarkable similarities–similarities owing their origin not simply to Voltaire's influence on these later deists, which was a factor, but because of the widespread agreement of eighteenth-century English rationalists on the principles of "natural religion." In his unwavering deism–which he called theism–Voltaire remained decidedly the English type of freethinker rather than joining the later and more militant French variety. Indeed, a subsequent generation of French philosophers, nurtured on the atheism of Holbach, already regarded Voltaire as timid and conservative, one firebrand exclaiming scornfully: "*Voltaire est bigot, il est deiste.*"

While Voltaire believed that individual atheists might be people of integrity and gentleness–Epicurus and Spinoza coming to his mind as examples–he feared that if atheism as a system ever came to power, it would prove to be as tyrannical as the Christian "superstition." Deism, he asserted, represented a middle way of reason between two fanaticisms. His theory was never put to a test and probably never can be. The Jacobin regime of Revolutionary France included both deists and atheists; and Robespierre, the arch terrorist, was a zealous believer in a Supreme Being and a merciless executioner of his atheist rivals.

Once, when his guests at dinner began to argue for atheism, Voltaire excused the servants, explaining after their departure, that he did not propose to be murdered by his charges. While his gestures may have been a joke to tease his company or an act of prudence to spare the servants' religious sensibilities–and, incidentally, to avoid the risk of being denounced to the Catholic authorities–Voltaire was entirely serious in regarding belief in God as an aid, indeed a necessity, of social peace. His oft-quoted remark, that if God did not exist, it would be necessary to invent Him, was more than a logical deduction. Above all, it expressed a sociological and political judgment.

Voltaire lived in the style of the grand seigneur and would have been comfortable as a high Whig of the British model. Never a democrat in the extreme sense of either Rousseau or Marat, he always distrusted the extravagance of radical utopianism. The type of open aristocracy that produced the constitutional parliamentarianism of Britain, so much admired by Voltaire, never took root in France. The natural aristocrat would have been at home with Burke or Lafayette, or perhaps even with Washington or John Adams, but not with Tom Paine or William Cobbett.

John Morley, a Victorian who wrote a distinguished biography of Voltaire, drew a parallel between deism's concept of a Supreme Being who rules the world solely through natural law and the constitutional monarch of Britain who after the settlement of 1688 reigned but did not govern. Morley observed:

> English deism, . . . was only a particular way of repudiating Christianity. There was as little of God in it as could well be. . . . The Being who set the reason of each individual on a kind of judicial bench within the forum of his own conscience and left him and it together to settle belief and conduct between them was a tolerably remote and unreal sort of personage. His spiritual force, according to such a doctrine, became very much as if it had no existence.

This compromise, predicated on an absentee and barely existent God, Morley notes, ended in Britain in the evangelical revival, "terrible and inevitable, which has so deeply colored religious feeling and warped intellectual growth in England ever since." In contrast, the forward movement in France continued unabated:

> In France, thought took a very different and much simpler turn. Or perhaps it would be more correct to say that it took no turn at all but carried the godless deism of the English school to its fair

> conclusion and dismissed a deity who only reigned and did not govern. . . . Voltaire, who carried the English way of thinking about the supernatural power into France, lived to see a band of trenchant and energetic disciples develop principles which he had planted into a system of dogmatic atheism.

But can we agree that the deism of Voltaire and his English precursors was the short-lived affair that Morley implies; or has its spirit survived, perhaps in a different guise? Although very few religious liberals, and no professional philosophers of note, wear the deistic label today, the religion of Voltaire, shorn of its militancy, is probably the prevailing belief of millions of nominal Protestants and Jews, and of many Catholics too, especially in the English-speaking world. Continental Europeans, especially in France and Northern Europe, even now are far more likely to profess the atheism that became the fashion during the reign of Louis XVI.

We fail to appreciate the scope of the deistic movement unless we understand its imprint on the forms of religious belief now prevailing. Most enlightened Jews and Christians, the fundamentalists and ultraorthodox aside, view the Bible and Christian origin in terms much closer to Voltaire's conception than to the dogmas that prevailed from early Christian times until the eighteenth century. Almost no one explains illness as a divine curse, few accept a literal belief in miracles, and even fewer tremble at the appearance of every comet or eclipse as an omen of heavenly wrath. While the orthodox churches still formally profess to believe that Jesus of Nazareth is God and Savior, millions regard him without mystery as a wise teacher or noble idealist whose life came to be shrouded in legend. Even the nonspecialist in history is well aware of the growth of mystery and myth around the lives of celebrated figures, especially those who existed long ago in far-away lands.

But if deism acted, and still acts as a voice of reason in Christian and Jewish modernism, it also continues in more secular dress as the ancestor of contemporary humanism and scientific naturalism. A century after John Morley made his observation that deism contained "as little of God in it as could well be," we are prompted to agree. Humanists, rationalists, agnostics, and atheists, rather than Christians or observant Jews, have been chiefly responsible in recent times for keeping green the shrines of Voltaire, Paine, and Jefferson–the three great apostles of the gospel of deistic free thought.

In the chapters that follow we shall trace the thought and work of the latter two of these exponents, whose spiritual likeness to Voltaire, despite their temperamental differences, is a tribute to the cogency and clarity of Enlightenment philosophy, and particularly of the deistic consensus.

8

Prophet of Reason:

Thomas Paine

(1737–1809)

Lacking Voltaire's wealth and worldly sophistication, Tom Paine, the impoverished son of a Quaker corsetmaker, left Great Britain—and a failed marriage—for America on the eve of the Revolution. Soon a revolutionary hero for his militant pamphlets urging independence and resistance to continued British occupation, Paine later became calumniated as an infidel because of his plainly written appeal for reason in religion—and for deism as a true system fit to replace a fraudulent and tyrannical Christianity. Scorned and vilified, he was abandoned at his death, even his bones disappeared from the country he helped liberate after an admirer undertook to transport them back to England.

"A filthy little atheist," Theodore Roosevelt remarked of Tom Paine a century after his death. Yet this epithet was as inexcusable as it was unoriginal. As a historian, Roosevelt should have known better; and knowing better, as he almost certainly did, he should have exhibited a higher regard for the truth, if not for the man.

Nevertheless Roosevelt's scorn had popular opinion to support it. The memory of no figure in American history, including Benedict Arnold and John Wilkes Booth, was so maligned as that of Tom Paine. The very sound of his name malevolently intoned, summoned forth visions of the direst infidel. During the last years of his life Paine had been heckled, spat at, refused transport by stagecoach, and denied the franchise in New Rochelle, his home precinct, on the spurious ground that his religious beliefs had forfeited his rights of citizenship granted by the state of New York for service to the nation.

Yet the repudiated and ostracized patriot, the harbinger of American independence, had been recommended to Congress in 1782 by no less that Washington, Robert Morris, and Robert Livingstone for a stipend of eight hundred dollars per annum (then a respectable sum) in recognition of his "considerable utility to the common cause." His sponsors argued that this provision might enable Paine to continue to inform the people and rouse them "to action," as his wartime pamphlets by common acknowledgement had rallied the Continental cause during its most desperate days.

Fall from universal acclaim to nearly ubiquitous condemnation followed publication of a work that Paine had thought would be his last public act on earth–testimonial of principles of religion and morality that had guided his public life and fired his revolutionary passion for liberty. As he awaited arrest in revolutionary France, where only recently he had been welcomed as a hero of liberation, Paine was nearly certain that he would be executed. He believed that his spiritual testament, published when he could have no impure, self-serving interest, might continue beyond his lifetime to be an influence for enlightenment and liberation. In the rising Jacobin terror, designed to counter plots to restore the Bourbon kings, Paine feared for the destruction of pure religion and republican government. The two fanaticisms, both tending toward absolutism, between them would crush spiritual and political liberty. He wrote *The Age of Reason* in the short time left to him.

In common with his friend Jefferson, who from his post as

Secretary of State in George Washington's cabinet had followed with interest Paine's recent career in France, like another great friend in America, the late Dr. Benjamin Franklin, Paine was an avowed deist; he summarized his creed in a single sentence: "I believe in one God, and no more." With Jefferson, he viewed atheism as a destructive reaction to the spiritual depotism and superstition of priestcraft. But while Jefferson for the most part managed to keep his religious opinions within a circumference bounded by friendship, Paine proclaimed his unpopular beliefs before an intolerant and vengeful world.

Having expressed belief in a Creator and "hope for a life beyond this life," Paine made it clear that the heart of his creed was purely ethical: "I believe that religious duties consist in doing justice, loving mercy, and endeavoring to make our fellow creatures happy." Unwilling to accept established creeds, Paine threw down the gauntlet:

> But, lest it should be supposed that I believe many other things in addition to these, I . . . declare the things I do not believe, and my reasons for not believing them.
>
> I do not believe in the creed professed by the Jewish Church, by the Roman Church, by the Greek Church, by the Turkish Church, by the Protestant Church, or by any church that I know of. My own mind is my own church.
>
> All national institutions of churches, whether Jewish, Christian, or Turkish, appear to me no other than human inventions, set up to terrify and enslave mankind and monopolize power and profit.

Having declared himself so uncompromisingly, Paine hastened to affirm his support of the religious freedom of all those holding contrary views: "They have the same right to their belief as I have to mine. But it is necessary to the happiness of man that he be mentally faithful to himself. Infidelity . . . consists in professing to believe what he does not believe."

Paine charged that "mental lying" had done incalculable harm to society and attributed this to the "trade of the priest" who began "with a perjury" for professional gain. Such dishonesty was more destructive than anything else one could conceive. Paine saw a relationship between political liberty and spiritual emancipation. "Soon after I had published the pamphlet 'Common Sense,' in America, I saw the exceeding probability that a revolution in the system of government would be followed by a revolution in the system of religion."

The Age of Reason–written in two parts separated by the two years of Paine's incarceration in the Luxembourg Prison at Robespierre's behest–consists of two intertwining threads: an indictment of "revealed" religion in general and of Christianity in particular as fraudulent and inimical to true morality; and on the constructive side an argument for deistic religion as a rational and satisfying alternative.

Paine endeavors to show that deism is preferable to Christianity on every count, each point argued with wit, caustic irony, and passion–especially passion–throughout both parts of Paine's religious testament. The deist accepts, on grounds of reason and observation alone, the necessity for a Supreme Being. This Being is one and eternal, the infinite Intelligence that created nature and nature's laws. These laws are constant, uniform, and visible in the harmonious workings of the universe, from the fixed stars keeping their places in the ordered heavens to microscopic organisms exhibiting unsuspected design and purpose. Among the laws of nature are those of mercy and justice, indelibly inscribed by the Creator upon the human heart. The only scripture is the Book of Nature itself, read in the light of reason and conscience. There is no need–indeed no possible place or justification–for special revelation, miracle, divine mediator, or priesthood. Every claim for these is based on human credulity and priestly avarice.

Like Jefferson, whose deistic convictions were virtually identical with his own, Paine rejected the idea of Christ as a supernatural figure or incarnation of God. The man Jesus was not to be confused with the invention of the Christian Church and had no part in the deception attached to his name. In the first part of *The Age of Reason* Paine set forth his estimate of the great Jewish reformer:

> Nothing that is here said can apply, even with the most distant disrespect, to the real character of Jesus Christ. He was a

> virtuous and an amiable man. The morality that he preached and practiced was of the most benevolent kind; and though similar systems of morality had been preached by Confucius and by some of the Greek philosophers, many years before; by the Quakers since; and by many good men in all ages; it has not been exceeded by any.

More than a decade in the future, Jefferson would sit late in the evening before the fireplace in his White House study, clipping and pasting in his scrapbook testament the sayings of Jesus, excerpting from the gospels the authentic words of the great teacher, which he believed gleamed as brightly as "jewels in a dungheap." While Paine, energetically pressing his case against religious forgery and imposture, would concentrate more upon the dungheap than upon the jewels of the master teacher, he prefaced his indictment by distinguishing the two:

> Jesus Christ wrote no account of himself, of his birth, parentage, or any thing else; not a line of what is called the New Testament is of his own writing. The history of him is altogether the work of other people; and as to the account given of his resurrection and ascension, it was the necessary counterpart to the story of his birth. His historians, having brought him into the world in a supernatural manner, were obliged to take him out again in the same manner, or the first part of the story must have fallen to the ground.

This fabulous account deserved no credence and could not even claim the distinction of originality. It was a mere retelling of the tiresome fables of the ancients. "Almost all of the extraordinary men who lived under the heathen mythology were reputed to be the sons of some of their gods. It was not a new thing at that time," he wrote, "to believe a man to have been celestially begotten." The Jews, loyal to the principle of one God and rejecting pagan mysteries, would have nothing to do with this strange story. Paine thought it "curious" that "the theory of what is called the Christian Church sprung out of the tale of the heathen mythology."

The Christian theology was not only fabulous; it was also monstrous. What greater evil could be inflicted upon the minds of children than to teach them that an all-wise Father had required the cruel execution of Jesus, an innocent son, before he would forgive his other children for an act of disobedience committed by Adam and Eve at the beginning of time?

Paine wrote with the painful and still vivid memory of his childhood exposure to this biblical doctrine. Within him burned the anger of having heard this savage account of the "atonement" while still a tender youth and the recollection of wandering out into the garden in his distress, sensing there the eerie contrast between the light and beauty of nature and the baneful shadows of theology. The experience never left him. Nothing, he said, that could shock the mind of a child should be taught as true of the character of the Creator. By violating the best in human conscience and planting irrational fears, Christianity has laid the foundations of atheism:

> The belief of a God is so weakened by being mixed with the strange fable of the Christian creed, and with the wild adventures related in the Bible, and of the obscenity and obscene nonsense of the Testament, that the mind of man is bewildered as in a fog. Viewing all these things in a confused mass, he confounds fact with fable; and as he cannot believe all, he feels a disposition to reject all.

Paine concludes the second part of *The Age of Reason* by reinforcing the argument that he had pressed from the first pages of the previous part against the doctrine of revelation.

> I totally disbelieve that the Almighty ever did communicate anything to man, by any mode of speech, in any language, or by any kind of vision or appearance . . . otherwise than by the universial display of Himself in the works of the creation, and by that repugnance we feel in ourselves to bad actions, and the dispositions to do good ones.
>
> The most detestable wickedness, the most horrid cruelties, and the greatest miseries that have afflicted the human race have had their origin in this thing called revelation, or revealed religion. It has been the most dishonorable belief against the character of the Divinity, the most destructive to morality and the peace and happiness of man that was ever propagated since man began to exist.

Paine briefly traces the atrocities in the stories in the Bible attributed to the guidance of God who commanded his chosen to invade the land of unoffending peoples and put them to death, sparing neither human being nor beast. "It is better, far better," Paine exclaims, "that we admitted, if it were possible a thousand devils to roam at large . . . than that we permitted one such imposter and monster as Moses, Joshua, Samuel and the Bible prophets to come with the pretended word of God in his mouth."

The whole history of this fraudulent revelation has been a curse from ancient to present times:

> Whence arose all the horrid assassinations of whole nations of men, women and infants, with which the Bible is filled, and the bloody persecutions and tortures unto death, and religious wars that since that time have laid Europe in blood and ashes–whence rose they but from this impious thing called revealed religion and this monstrous belief that God has spoken to man?

Turn from this system of deception, cruelty, and slaughter to a religion founded solely on reason and conscience, Paine counsels in his summation. That alternative "teaches us, without the possibility of being deceived, all that is necessary or proper to be known. The creation is the Bible of the deist." In the study of nature's laws we learn to read the will of the Maker and to recognize that "all other Bibles and Testaments are to him forgeries."

When Paine returned to the United States in October, 1802, disembarking from the U.S. navy's warship, *Maryland*, on which he had crossed the Atlantic as a guest of the nation by invitation of President Jefferson, he found his reputation completely altered from the adulation he had received on his departure from America more than fifteen years earlier. This reversal of fortune had been caused by the publication of his treatise on religion. Many of his detractors had grossly imperfect ideas of the content of the book and knew nothing of the author's motives. They had been told by their clergy and Federalist editors that *The Age of Reason* espoused atheistic principles and attacked Holy Scripture and the Christian faith.

We shall see in the next chapter how the clergy in 1800 abused Jefferson as an infidel and Jacobin when he campaigned for the presidency. Jefferson privately admitted his agreement with Paine's opinions and, costly as it could have been for him politically, he now refused to repudiate his old revolutionary comrade and fellow of the American Philosophical Society. But others were not so courageous or charitable. Dr. Benjamin Rush, who shared with Paine a Quaker origin and had known him as an associate in revolutionary politics and scientific investigation, refused to have anything more to do with him. Some esteemed former allies took the same position. Franklin, Washington, and other leaders of the Revolution had, while being deists, only a nominal connection with a church or none at all. Yet they had never experienced the opprobrium now suffered by honest, plainspoken Tom Paine.

His plainspokenness was at the heart of his genius as a master polemicist and defender of democratic causes. He was not given to mincing words and never to the indirection that enabled the more cautiously guarded to conceal their real views from those less perceptive. It was this very gift for stating simple truths simply that had made Paine's passionate leadership invaluable in igniting and fanning the fires for America's craving for independence. The sale of his pamphlet *Common Sense* had grown to half a million copies in a matter of weeks–igniting a conflagration that cast its glow upon virtually every manor and cabin in the thirteen colonies, quickly transforming colonial resistance into a firestorm for independence. To be sure, John Adams and a few others had earlier supported the idea of separation from Britain. But Paine's spark had transformed an insurgency into a revolution.

The same talent that could move a continent to nationhood would in time also bring about the whiplash of religious hatred that would becloud the memory of Thomas Paine for a century. His rehabilitation as one of the greatest of American patriots and freedom fighters required the intelligent toil of more than a generation of admirers, beginning late in the nineteenth century with the work of his first and finest biographer, Moncure Conway, himself a hero in the fight for Abolition and a noted literary critic as well.

Paine's "unforgivable" offense, apart from his plain speaking, was the choice of his audience. He had known poverty and toil, and he spoke the language of those of his own station. Were not deism and free thought the appropriate accoutrements of culture and privilege? Throughout the century gentlemen of breeding had been writing tomes of polite skepticism. But their enlightened doubt was tastefully and prudently addressed to other gentlemen of quality. Many of Britian's outstanding thinkers, including many members of the clergy, were either deists or unitarians, and many of the latter were essentially deists, even if their thinking were couched in Christian nomenclature.

Gibbon, the greatest English historian of his generation, and the greatest ever to recount the rise and fall of ancient Rome, was a deist and an outspoken critic of the Christian religion. And Hume, the greatest British philosopher of the century, went even beyond deism to become the most systematic and indefatigable skeptic since Diogenes. But Gibbon and Hume did not excite or incite the common folk. Their books were of considerable heft and not hawked for a halfpenny. Insurrectionary writings are not bound in vellum. With cheaply printed pamphlets sold at cost or given away by tens of thousands, the consequences were quite different. Half a century after the French Revolution, Marx and Engels would spark another revolution with a pamphlet, the *Communist Manifesto*. Had Marx written only *Das Kapital*, a scholarly voluminous work, the world would have safely disregarded his views.

Paine's major defense of popular representative government, *The Rights of Man*, like *The Age of Reason*, was written in two parts–the first in 1790, the second in 1792. The first was rapidly composed to reply to Edmund Burke's attack on the French Revolution and to defend the right of revolution generally. Burke had protested the rising republican sentiment in Britain on the ground that the social contract, once given in the Whig settlement of 1688, was irrevocable. Paine countered that such a doctrine made them living slaves to the dead and that, contrary to Burke, one generation cannot sign away the rights of its descendants. Paine dealt with his principles on society and government. But despite its length, its militant advocacy and journalistic style made the work unbelievably popular in both the old world and the United States, with a million and a half copies sold in Britain alone.

Such penetrating effect on the popular consciousness could not fail to alarm the authorities. The more expensively printed first edition of part one was tolerated, even if received with official disfavor. But part two brought prompt prosecution and conviction of both the writer and printer. Warned by the pro-revolutionary poet, painter, and engraver, William Blake that his arrest had to be feared, Paine fled to France, embarking at Dover for Calais just twenty minutes before officers arrived with a warrant for his arrest. His publisher, less agile, was imprisoned, while Paine was convicted in absentia.

Paine's undeviating commitment to independence of conscience and equality of rights came from two converging forces in his thought and character. The stubborn egalitarianism of his Quaker origin, a doctrine both spiritual and political, merged into an acquired faith in science and reason as assuring every human soul free and equal access to the mind of God. In recent times some scholars have questioned the degree of both influences, and have denied the importance attributed by Conway to Paine's Quaker roots and affinities. But, contrary to this view, no one steeped in the ethos of the Society of Friends, or who is aware of Quaker influence on the social history of Britain during the previous century, can fail to recognize the depth and intensity of Paine's secularized and naturalized version of Quakerism. No pacifist, Paine was not given to turning the other cheek, as "fighting Quakers" were not unknown on either side of the Atlantic; and even the nonviolent Friends had convulsed Britain with their adamant disobedience, defying every social convention that required one human being to submit to another. Even the urbane and aristocratically bred William Penn had sat through dinner with a leading citizen with his hat on–refusing on Quaker principle to remove the hat for anyone but God–and in consequence had never again been invited by his host to return. Quakers by the thousands were incarcerated in filthy dungeons, suffered savage beatings, and often met death rather than bend the knee to any pretended social better.

At the fall of the Commonwealth and the restoration of the Stuart monarchy, many social radicals and Christian communists of the Levelers' and Diggers' parties, including doughty reformers such as John Bellers, found their way into a receptive Society of Friends. While in the generation prior to Paine's birth the Society had moved into a period of isolation and quietism, the old fires of spiritually prompting civil disobedience never went out; moreover, the more vigorous spirits reared in this milieu moved out of the Society into the tumultuous world of rising free thought and egalitarian unrest.

Paine's parents were of different beliefs. His mother was of the Church of England, his father Quaker. But from his writings it is clear that the latter influence prevailed. Paine even suggested in the summation of *The Age of Reason* that Quakerism owed its virtues to its identity with deism:

> The only sect that has not persecuted are the Quakers, and the only reason that can be given for it is that they are rather Deists than Christians. They do not believe much about Jesus Christ, and they call the Scriptures a dead letter. Had they called them a worse name they had been nearer the truth.

To clinch his argument, Paine stretches his case–and the facts–beyond the breaking point. Deistic influence was, or was to become, apparent among several sects, including many Unitarians and Universalists, some Anglicans, and also some Quakers. But fundamentally, the teachings of the Friends were steeped in New Testament doctrine of immediate revelation of God within each human heart. Regarded from this perspective, Quakerism was the opposite of the doctrine of deism; instead of denying revealed religion, it represented the *democratization* of revelation. Not only was every believer a priest, but, quite literally, every sincere man or woman was a conduit of the divine wisdom. Divine guidance was thus immediate, individual, and personal. Moreover, the Spirit whispering its guidance to the silent receptive heart was not confined to professed Christians or even to those reared in a culture acquainted with the story of the historic Christ. The "Christ Within" or "Inner Light" was revealed preeminently in the life of Jesus of Nazareth, as orthodox Quakers affirmed his divine mission. But the Christ Within was an emanation from God that dwelled as a divine flame within every receptive man or woman regardless of religion. Quakers did not have the problem of other Christians who believed that redemption (and escape from everlasting hell) required accepting the preaching of the gospel. An American Indian, a Confucian, a Buddhist, a Polynesian worshiping his tribal gods in the South Seas, or even a pagan born centuries before Jesus, had according to Quaker belief, direct access to the Inner Light, whether or not known by that name. The Bible was respected as a testimony of the Light revealed in the historic Jesus in whom the Christ spirit was fully manifest, although written scriptures could not replace the living revelation, the immediate presence of the Inner Light.

One can thus see how Paine glossed over essential details that differentiated the Quaker construction of Christianity from his own militantly anti-Christian evangel. Yet Paine correctly sensed important likenesses. A religion that disbelieved in all revelation–except in the laws of nature–and a religion that saw revelation alive in every open heart were as one in rejecting the dogmatism and exclusiveness of Christian orthodoxy and the absurdities of bibliolatry. As Quakerism moved into the nineteenth century, it took on more and more the characteristics of a Christianized deism; Quakers in both England and America were prominent in science, and one separated branch of the Society in America, the Hicksite Quakers (named after Long Island preacher-farmer Elias Hicks), moved to a radical deemphasis of both the historic Christ and the Bible, making reliance on the Inner Light almost the whole of religion. Walt Whitman, another spirited rebel of Quaker upbringing, fondly celebrated his childhood recollection of Hicks and acknowledged his debt to a Society that he, like Paine before him, could not join despite his admiration because, as he explained, he could not live inside a fence.

Paine's utter detestation of slavery similarly manifested his Quaker egalitarianism and love of liberty. As the American Revolution moved towards a close, Paine, as clerk of the Pennsylvania Assembly, was able to gratify his anti-slavery convictions by writing the preamble to an act providing for gradual emancipation in that state, the first such enactment in America.

His deistic and democratic faith gave him an outlet for the social idealism inherited from his father, a struggling Quaker corset-maker who tutored his son in his principles as well as his trade. That liberated idealism changed the world.

Was Paine fair to the objects of his wrath? To the Tory Party in Britain or America? To the Christian religion and its practitioners? To those who took the conservative side in religion, politics, and custom?

No, he was not fair. Makers of revolutions never are. And Paine made, or mightily advanced, at least *four* revolutions: A political and social revolution in America; an even sharper and deeper revolution in France; the beginnings of a nonviolent but nonetheless profound democratic transformation in Great Britain; and finally, a revolution in religious thought. In effecting these revolutions Paine was inevitably partisan, occasionally unjust, and sometimes wrong-headed.

Among his charges against the British crown was the violation of rights of the American Indians. Yet Indian nations on the American frontier took up arms in defense of the Loyalist cause, recognizing monarchy as their strongest defender against colonial adventurers who saw independence as a license to ignore treaties and dispossess the Indians. Paine inveighed for revolution because of the slave trade, historically fostered by the British government; yet more than a generation before the convulsion of the American Civil War, Great Britain would emancipate slaves in her colonies by peaceful means. Neither scholar nor historian, Paine read the Old and New Testaments, finding therein the rich, turbulent, varied saga of an ancient people–but he read it as if through the eyes of fundamentalist zealots and heresy hunters. His reading reinforced an interpretation he hated. He was a man of strong passions, shrewd judgments, and remarkably wide–if sometimes uneven–learning, driven by a mission that inspired, yet sometimes blinded him.

Nevertheless, the crimes of tyranny, superstition, religious oppression, special privilege, and avarice were as pervasive and onerous as Paine understood them to be. The Bible *did* contain gross absurdities, deceptions, and cruelties–and Pain unblinkingly exposed them. And we are in his debt for his courage and incorruptibility. He set an age to thinking and that was good–and necessary. But he missed even more that was beautiful, profound, evocative, and liberating. He read his Bible and Testament not as a Quaker quickened in the Spirit, but as a victim of Christian dogma enmeshed in the letter. He never threw off the spell of the delusion he despised.

But the pure deism of Thomas Paine shines through his anger as the noble affirmation of a heroic figure; he was a titan among the giants of liberty. He summarized his creed in a sentence that will last as long as the free mind and the spirit of true humanism live: "The world is my country, and to do good is my religion."

9

Freethinker in the White House:

Thomas Jefferson

(1743–1826)

With a Randolph on his mother's side, a socially privileged student at Williamsburg's William and Mary College, and classmate of other scions of patrician Virginia, Thomas Jefferson ought to have been a stalwart defender of the Church of England's Thirty-nine Articles. He disappoints such expectations by his unwillingness to state his views on religion publicly. Jefferson's personal correspondence is a stumbling block to zealous believers who like to represent the Founding Fathers as men of "sound Christian doctrine" and orthodox piety. Even worse for their case, such religious partisans are confronted by evidence that Franklin, John Adams, Madison, and the Father of His Country–Washington himself–entertained serious reservations about the supernatural origins of Christianity, which other "loyal" Americans are assumed to accept on the basis of heredity, tradition, or instinct. Jesus, said Jefferson, was a good man, but he saw no reason to believe that the man from Nazareth claimed to be more than that.

The presidential campaign of 1800 produced an eruption of that recurring partisan distemper described as the "paranoid style" of American politics. Members of the electorate would have insisted that they were distempered for good reason–with Washington recently laid in his tomb and such scoundrels as Adams and Jefferson vying for the presidency! Patriots and Christians had every reason to expect the worst.

Especially for New England–Adams's country–the dreaded victory of Jefferson, the "Jacobin" democrat and "infidel," portended the anti-christ, heralding all the blasphemies, orgies, and terrors of revolutionary Paris and Robespierre. Was it not obvious, bellowed the Federalist press, that Jefferson was a man devoid of moral principle or sound religious faith–an atheist, anarchist, and voluptuary prepared to ride the horns of the mob to dictatorship? Jefferson's partisans returned the compliment: unless the despot Adams were turned out of office, the American Revolution would be rescinded and the tyrant who had presided over the Alien and Sedition Acts would annoint himself king.

The clergy, especially in Calvinist New England, was militant from rostrum and pulpit denouncing the Jacobin Jefferson. Then as always Jefferson refused to answer his accusers. But privately he confided his hostility toward a doctrinaire and domineering clerical establishment that, in the name of Christian piety, resorted to calumny and slander to discredit anyone whose commitment to liberty of conscience threatened their special privileges. In later years Jefferson shared with a correspondent his thoughts about these Calvinist and Federalist theocrats (Massachusetts still maintained tax-supported parishes) who pursued him even in retirement:

> I am not afraid of the priests. They have tried upon me all their various batteries, of pious whining, hypocritical canting, lying and slandering, without being able to give me one moment of pain. I have contemplated their order from the Magi of the East to the Saints of the West, and I have found no difference of character, but of more or less caution, in proportion to their information or ignorance of those on whom their interested duperies were to be plaid off. Their sway in New Eng-

> land is indeed formidable. No mind beyond mediocrity dares there to develop itself.

Sixteen years earlier, in the heat of the campaign of 1800, Jefferson confided in words that have since become immortal his vow to break the grip of clerical power. Writing to his friend and fellow philosopher, Dr. Benjamin Rush, Jefferson declared: "They believe that any portion of power confided to me will be exerted in opposition to their schemes. And they believe rightly: for I have sworn upon the altar of God eternal hostility against every form of tyranny over the mind of man."

For Jefferson the issue was unambiguous. There could be no uncorrupted expression of genuine religious feeling or belief so long as state emoluments and duress extorted conformity to a creed secretly despised by much of the public. State sponsorship reduced religion to the lowest level of pretended obeisance and hypocritical profession. Such false religiosity injures every true conviction.

"Millions of innocent men, women, and children, since the introduction of Christianity," he wrote, "have been burnt, tortured, fined, imprisoned; yet we have not advanced an inch toward uniformity. What has been the effect of coercion? To make one half the world fools, and the other half hypocrites. To support roguery and error all over the earth."

In his widely admired *Notes on Virginia* (quoted above), Jefferson pressed his argument against state regulation or favoritism in religion. Contemplating the religious variety to be observed over the face of the earth, he reasoned:

> Let us reflect that it is inhabited by a thousand millions of people. That these profess probably a thousand different systems of religion. That ours is but one of that thousand. That if there be but one right, and ours that one, we should wish to see the nine hundred and ninety-nine wandering sects gathered into the fold of truth. But against such a majority we cannot effect this by force. Reason and persuasion are the only practicable instruments. To make way for these, free inquiry must be indulged; and how can we wish others to indulge it while we refuse it ourselves?

Pursuing his case, Jefferson noted that two of Virginia's sister states, Pennsylvania and New York, had long prospered with no religious establishment. These commonwealths did not hang more malefactors than Virginia, he noted, and yet they enjoyed unparalleled harmony among their many sects. This happy state he ascribed to "nothing but their unbounded tolerance." The conclusion should be clear "that the way to silence religious disputes is to take no notice of them." He urged, "Let us too give this experiment fair play, and get rid, while we may, of those tyrannical laws."

Many agitated for religious freedom from no deep conviction of the rightness of such a principle but only to relieve their particular creed of legal disqualification or handicap. But not Jefferson. To his mind, forced submission to a church or theology was wrong, even it were his own. Diversity is a law of nature to be honored as the plan of nature's God. *The Act Establishing Religious Freedom in Virginia*, written by Jefferson and prized as an accomplishment for which he wished to be remembered by posterity, cited the weighty matters of divine and human justice that argued for such a step:

> Well aware that God hath created the mind free; that all attempts to influence it by temporal punishments or burdens, or by civil incapacitations, tend only to beget habits of hypocrisy and meanness, and are a departure from the plan of the Holy Author of our religion . . . ;
>
> that the impious presumption of legislators and rulers, civil as well as ecclesiastical, who, being themselves but fallible and uninspired men, have assumed dominion over the faith of others . . . ;
>
> that to compel a man to furnish contributions of money for the propagation of opinions which he disbelieves, is sinful and tyrannical; . . .
>
> that it tends also to corrupt the principles of that very religion it is meant to encourage, by bribing . . . those who will externally profess and conform to it; . . .
>
> and finally, that truth is great and will prevail if left to herself, that she is the proper and sufficient antagonist to error. . . .
>
> *Be it therefore enacted by the General Assembly,*
>
> That no man shall be compelled to frequent or support any religious worship, place or ministry whatsoever, nor shall be enforced, restrained, molested, or burthened in his body or

> goods, nor shall otherwise suffer on account of his religious opinion or belief; but that all men shall be free to profess, and by argument to maintain, their opinions in matters of religion, and that the same shall in nowise diminish, enlarge, or affect their civil capacities.

Against this Jeffersonian counsel, it has recently been popular in right-wing religious circles to argue that the constitutional founders intended only *freedom for* religion, and did not contemplate or condone *freedom from* religion. Those who assert this, insofar as they are honest, have not read Jefferson, Madison, or even Washington. The prohibition on governmental interference prescribed in Jefferson's Virginia Act is absolute in its language, and as every well educated schoolchild knows, or ought to learn, Virginia's statute served as model and inspiration for the religious-freedom clause of the First Amendment of the US Constitution and for many subsequent state constitutions.

Jefferson held it to be a matter of justice, which he believed could be divined in the beneficent scheme of the Great Architect, that the opinion of the atheist had an equal right to that of the "orthodox" to exist and be expressed. Doubts and disbeliefs were part of the moral economy of human reason, necessary for testing and cleansing the channels of thought.

> The varieties in structure and action of the human mind as in those of the body, are the work of our Creator, against which it cannot be a religious duty to erect the standard of uniformity. The practice of morality being necessary for the well-being of society, he has taken care to impress its precepts so indelibly on our hearts that they shall not be effaced by the subtleties of our brain.

The righteous deed in man, Jefferson thought, was impelled by the ingrained moral sense of the heart, regardless of creed or lack of creed. This was no reckless, intellectually indifferent notion on Jefferson's part. His moral theory was the outcome of more than a century of philosophizing in England and Scotland, the product of a school that held moral truth to be independent of scripture, theology, or ecclesiastical council. Jefferson eagerly embraced this school, known as the "moral sense philosophy," since it placed conscience within the same natural order as the physical sciences. If the moral sense were part of our native endowment as social beings, then we could free ourselves from the spiritual tyranny of two thousand years of Platonized Christianity and we could return to the demystifying ethical message of the Sermon on the Mount. That message is written in our hearts as social beings, and we would be able to follow its precepts even if Jesus of Nazareth had never lived.

Jefferson despised the official Christianity of the churches, which he sharply distinguished from what he regarded as the simple moral teachings of Jesus. Although his views on Christianity are usually regarded by intellectual historians as more moderate and friendly to the Christian faith than those of the militant deist, Thomas Paine, a careful reading of Jefferson's *private* views as expressed in letters to trusted friends disclose a mind that vigorously rejected the theological formulation of Christian orthodoxy. Jefferson confided his conviction that the Christian plan of salvation, based on the scheme of a God-man who had become flesh and redeemed mankind through the shedding of his blood, was a fraud perpetuated by priests who "knowing the importance of names . . . have assumed that of Christians, while they are mere Platonists." Writing in this vein to a correspondent in 1820, Jefferson declared, "The priests have so disfigured the simple religion of Jesus that no one who reads the sophistications they have engrafted on it, from the jargon of Plato, of Aristotle, and other mystics, would conceive these could have been fathered on the sublime preacher of the Sermon on the Mount."

Did Jesus himself give any credence to, or even foresee, this account of his teaching "as mangled by our Pseudo-Christians"? No, it was not his doctrine in the least, said Jefferson. In 1810, he spelled out his thoughts in a letter on the real origin of Christian doctrine:

> But a short time elapsed after the death of the great reformer of the Jewish religion, before his principles were departed from by those who professed to be his special servants, and perverted

> into an engine for enslaving mankind. . . . The purest system ever before preached to man has been adulterated and sophisticated by artificial constructions, into a mere contrivance to filch wealth and power. . . . They raise the hue and cry of infidelity, while themselves are the greatest obstacles to the advancement of the real doctrines of Jesus, and do, in fact, constitute the real Anti-Christ.

Was there any basis in fact or in Jesus' concept of himself for the orthodox doctrine that Jesus was God, the second person of a triune godhead? Jefferson believed these were corruptions derived from the Greek metaphysics of Paul. Writing to his old Revolutionary War comrade and erstwhile political rival, John Adams (with whom he had become reconciled after both had retired from office), Jefferson remarked that it was "too late in the day for men of sincerity to pretend to believe in the Platonic mysticisms that three are one, and one three; and yet that the one is not three, and the three are not one." As a Unitarian, Adams had no problem in agreeing with Jefferson.

But this "mystification" that displaced the pure religion of Jesus, "constitutes the craft, the power and the profit of the priests," Jefferson wrote. "Sweep away their gossamer fabrics of factitious religion, and they would catch no more flies." If we did so, he continued, "we should all then, like the Quakers, live without an order of priests . . . follow the oracle of conscience, and say nothing about what no man can understand, nor therefore believe." To another correspondent, Jefferson had written in 1809:

> Reading, reflection and time have convinced me that the interests of society require the observation of those moral precepts only in which all religions agree (for all forbid us to murder, steal, plunder, or bear false witness) and that we should not intermeddle with the particular dogmas in which all religions differ, and which are totally unconnected with morality. In all of them we see good men, and as many in one as another.

The failure to observe this restraint and instead plunge into dispute over obscure and even incomprehensible metaphysical subtleties had only added to human delusion and misery. This he argued in a letter of 1816, declaring he would refrain from participation in that gladiatorial spectacle:

> On the dogmas of religion, as distinguished from moral principles, all mankind, from the beginning of the world to this day, have been quarreling, fighting, burning and torturing one another, for abstractions unintelligible to themselves and to all others, and absolutely beyond the comprehension of the human mind. Were I to enter that arena, I should only add an unit to the number of the Bedlamites.

Could there be any profit to the soul, either here or hereafter, by adhering to doctrines that distinguish each sect from all others and are often held to be necessary to escape perdition? None whatever. Not if the deity were the beneficent and rational Architect of the universe in whom Jefferson placed his confidence. To buttress his belief in a Creator of rationality and benevolence, he recalled approvingly in a letter to William Canby the example of a Quaker preacher who "is said to have exclaimed aloud that he did not believe there was a Quaker, Presbyterian, Methodist or Baptist in heaven." The preacher had reasoned, Jefferson continued, that "in heaven God knew no distinctions, but considered all good men as his children, and brethren of the same family." For himself, Jefferson added: "I believe, with the Quaker preacher, that he who steadily observes those moral precepts in which all religions can concur will never be questioned at the gates of heaven as to the dogmas in which they all differ."

Despite foreswearing theological disputation in public, Jefferson indulged privately in the lusty sport of polemics with an abandon that even Tom Paine would have relished: "Ridicule is the only weapon which can be used against unintelligible propositions," he wrote in 1816. "Ideas must be distinct before reason can act upon them; and no man ever had a distinct idea of the trinity. It is a mere Abracadabra of the mountebanks who call themselves the priests of Jesus." Their security, like that of the cuttlefish, he mused, "is in their faculty of shedding darkness . . . and making it impenetrable. . . . There they will skulk."

His deepest anger and condemnation was reserved for Calvin's doctrine that original sin had totally corrupted man's moral sense and was the antithesis of Jeffersonian rationalism. Calvin had taught that only a portion of the human race, arbitrarily chosen for redemption, would escape everlasting damnation. This doctrine was still fearfully believed by a substantial proportion of the population in Jefferson's day. In a letter to Adams in 1823, Jefferson expostulated:

> I can never join Calvin in addressing *his God*. He was indeed an atheist, which I can never be; or rather his religion was daemonism. If ever a man worshipped a false God, he did. The being . . . is not the God whom you and I acknowledge and adore, the creator and benevolent governor of the world, but a daemon of malignant spirit. It would be more pardonable to believe in no God at all, than to blaspheme him by the atrocious attributes of Calvin.

Jefferson's indignation extended to the body of Christian clergy most closely identified with Calvin's theology:

> The Presbyterian clergy are loudest; the most intolerant of all sects, the most tyrannical and ambitious; ready at the word of the lawgiver, if such a word could now be obtained, to put the torch to the pile, and to rekindle in this virgin hemisphere, the flames in which their oracle Calvin consumed the poor Servetus. . . . They pant to reestablish, *by law*, that holy inquisition, which they can now only infuse into *public opinion*. We have most unwisely committed to the hierophants of our particular superstition, the direction of public opinion. . . . We have given them stated and privileged days to collect and catechise us, opportunities of delivering their oracles to the people in mass, and of molding their minds as wax in the hollow of their hands.

Drawing the contrast between his concept of a human (and humane) Jesus and the theological Christ of the creeds, Jefferson was confident that in the former he had the key to a restored and purified Christianity, the sure foundation for an ethical system far removed from the superstitions and dogmas of history. "I am a *real* Christian," he wrote, "very different from the Platonists who call *me* infidel and *themselves* Christian and preachers of the gospel, while they draw all their characteristic dogmas from what its author never said nor saw."

A careful student of the literature of the Englightenment who drew freely from its leading ideas, Jefferson was especially indebted to his older contemporary and friend, Joseph Priestley, one of the boldest and most knowledgeable moral and religious writers of his age. Priestley was the only theologian with whom Jefferson felt comfortable. Differences in their thinking were not so great as to render the ideas of the other alien or repugnant. Jefferson's religious opinions and their philosophical and historical sources became clearer when we examine the theology of his revered friend, to whom he acknowledged a heavy debt.

Priestley, remembered in the history of science for the discovery of oxygen, one of the major accomplishments of his century, was internationally celebrated long before he and Jefferson met in Philadelphia. At the beginning of England's troubles with the American colonies Priestley, always the revolutionary sympathizer, had written a pamphlet supporting the American cause–to the elation of Dr. Franklin and other Americans who maintained an active correspondence with him on both scientific and political matters. Franklin, while representing the colonies in England, had induced Priestley to write *The History and Present State of Electricity*, which included Franklin's contributions to electrical theory, most notably the celebrated experiment with the kite during a lightning storm.

At the outbreak of the French Revolution, Priestley again took up the pen in defense of republicanism and for the abolition of the ancient privileges of altar and crown. With national feeling rising in Britain against Revolutionary France, on Bastille Day 1791 a mob set fire to Priestley's library, destroying his books, scientific apparatus, and personal effects. Barely escaping with his life, Priestley fled to the now independent United States, disembarking in Philadelphia in 1794.

Long in correspondence with Franklin's American Philosophical Society in Philadelphia, Priestley had been voted into its membership in 1785. He therefore arrived in America to be met by confirmed friends and admirers. Franklin's successor as president of the Society, David Rittenhouse, a mechanical wizard who had designed and built a celebrated planetarium, warmly received Priestley and introduced him to the scientific and intellectual community of Philadelphia. On Rittenhouse's death in 1796, Jefferson succeeded to the presidency of the Society and remained deeply immersed in its affairs for the twenty years of his tenure. In addition to Rittenhouse and Franklin (who had died in 1790) this circle of philosophically-minded Americans included such notables in American scientific and political history as the physician and chemist, Dr. Benjamin Rush; the botanist of North American flora, Benjamin Smith Barton (nephew of Rittenhouse); the Revolutionary War portraitist and museum curator, Charles Willson Peale; and Thomas Paine, a captive abroad in a French prison when Priestley arrived. Into this gifted company the refugee Priestley made his way at the age of sixty. (For a brilliant recounting of the story of this circle and their influence on Jefferson's maturing philosophy, Daniel J. Boorstin's *The Lost World of Thomas Jefferson* is recommended.)

Priestley remained in America until his death in 1804, spending his final years in Northumberland, Pennsylvania, to the distress of Jefferson who had sought him as a neighbor in Monticello. But in the years prior to the removal of the U.S. capital to Washington, Jefferson remained in close association with Priestley, opening himself to a deepening influence that had begun much earlier through the study of Priestley's theological works. While science was Priestley's avocation, as it was that of many of England's other scientific putterers–including some of the most celebrated–he was by vocation a clergyman and profound student of religious history.

A nonconformist minister of advanced Unitarian views, Priestley had published in England his widely read masterpiece, *A History of the Corruptions of Christianity*. Many of the themes already encountered in Jefferson's letters reflect Priestley's biblical analysis and historical scholarship. The orthodox doctrines of the deity of Christ, original sin, the atonement, and the immortality of an immaterial soul were rejected as corruptions of Christianity, imported from the speculative metaphysics of pre-Christian Greece. In none of his concepts could Jefferson's maturing religious philosophy be attributed solely or even originally to Priestley; what Priestley taught and Jefferson adopted was in the air of the Enlightenment philosophy and representative of the thought of many of the ablest thinkers of the age. But Priestley succeeded in synthesizing and systematizing the Enlightenment mentality as it came to be expressed in the English-speaking nations–a formulation always more reserved and cautious than its counterpart among the tumultuous and iconoclastic French.

Yet there was nothing timid or halting in either Priestley or Jefferson as they weighed the truth and falsehood in Christianity. Jefferson combined a veritable religous passion for truth with a radical impulse for reform. In the figure of Jesus he saw a preeminent exemplar of these impulses, if that figure were stripped of the mendacious accretions of theological mystification. Yet, as a fallible human being, Jesus had perhaps viewed himself as a channel for divine revelation:

> That Jesus did not mean to impose himself on mankind as the son of God, physically speaking, I have been convinced by the writings of men more learned than myself in that lore. But that he might conscientiously believe himself inspired from above, is very possible. . . . Elevated by the enthusiasm of a warm and pure heart, conscious of the high strains of an eloquence which had not been taught him, he might readily mistake the coruscations of his own fine genius for inspirations of an higher order. This belief carried, therefore, no more personal imputation, than the belief of Socrates, that himself was under the care and admonitions of a guardian Daemon.

Thus, with fine discrimination Jefferson answered those who insisted that Jesus had to be accepted as "very God of very God," deity incarnate, or else be convicted of insanity or fraud. The purity of his motives and the exalted quality of his ethics did not make Jesus all-wise or beyond error. Writing in 1820 on the limitations and fallacies which he believed were mingled in the philosophy of Jesus, Jefferson stated:

> It is not to be understood that I am with him in all his doctrines. I am a Materialist; he takes the side of Spiritualism; he preaches the efficacy of repentance towards forgiveness of sin; I require a counterpoise of good works to redeem it. . . . It is the innocence of his character, the purity and sublimity of his moral precepts, the eloquences of his inculcations, the beauty of the apologues in which he conveys them, that I so much admire; sometimes, indeed, needing indulgence in eastern hyperbolism. . . . I find many passages of fine imagination, correct morality, and of the most lovely benevolence; and others, again, of so much ignorance, so much absurdity, so much untruth, charlatanism and imposture, as to pronounce it impossible that such contradictions should have proceeded from the same being. I separate, therefore, the gold from the dross; restore to him the former, and leave the latter to the stupidity of some, and roguery of others of his disciples.

Jefferson expanded on this contrast between the simple purity of the principles of Jesus and the "stupidity . . . and roguery" of his successors–among whom he accounted Paul "the great Coryphaeus," and first corruptor–in explaining to a correspondent his undertaking to extract the authentic sayings of the Nazarene from the "dross" of the gospels. He produced a "little book" which he professed would be of use in preaching the unalloyed teachings of Jesus to the American Indians. His method was literally to employ scissors and paste, to snip out the words of Jesus as they appear in the four Gospels and to assemble them in the order that he thought correctly restored the original message. As an accomplished polyglot, he prepared his gospel in four parallel columns–in English, French, Latin and Greek–to compare the various translations. In explaining to Adams his method in producing *The Life and Morals of Jesus of Nazareth*–commonly known as "The Jefferson Bible"–he wrote:

> In extracting the pure principles which he taught, we should have to strip off the artificial vestments in which they have been muffled by priests, who have travestied them into various forms, as instruments of riches and power to themselves. . . . We must reduce our volume to the simple evangelists, select, even from them, the very words only of Jesus, . . . There will be found remaining the most sublime and benevolent code of morals which has ever been offered to man. I have performed this operation for my own use, by cutting verse by verse out of the printed

> book, and arranging the matter which is evidently his, and *which is as easily distinguishable as diamonds in a dunghill.* [Emphasis added.] The result is an octavo of forty-six pages, of pure and unsophisticated doctrines, such as were professed and acted on by the *unlettered* Apostles, the Apostolic Fathers, and the Christians of the first century.

Jefferson's high esteem for the sayings of Jesus as well as his disapproval of the "Platonized" metaphysics and myths in which they were set is evidenced by the painstaking toil he gave to producing *The Morals of Jesus.* He undertook this operation twice, the first and less elaborate version while still in the White House. (It is this version which is described above in the 1813 letter to Adams.) The second version, reflecting the conscientious application of his retirement years in Monticello, is the form that has since been reproduced in facsimile and other editions.

Readers of Jefferson's private correspondence (it was not available to the public during his lifetime) will discern a Voltairean fury in his invective against "the infamy" of "priestcraft"–which in Jefferson's usage applied to Protestant divines (Calvinists especially) and equally to their Greek and Roman predecessors. That the strength of conviction behind this indignation was a major influence in shaping his defense of intellectual freedom and the strict separation of church and state is evident throughout his writings. "In every country," he declared, "the priest has been hostile to liberty. He is always in alliance with the despot, abetting his abuses in return for protection for his own."

Once in the White House, Jefferson strove to put his principles into effect. To Attorney General Levi Lincoln he forwarded a Baptist appeal for church-state separation with a comment of his own:

> Averse to receive addresses, yet unable to prevent them, I have generally endeavored to turn them to some account, by making them the occasion, by way of answer, of sowing useful truths and principles among the people, which might germinate and become rooted among their political tenets. The Baptist address, now enclosed, admits of a condemnation of the alliance between Church and State, under the authority of the constitu-

> tion. It furnishes an occasion, too, which I have long wished to find, of saying why I do not proclaim fasting and thanksgiving, as my predecessors did.

Then, noting the predictable effect of his action on the quarter that had subjected him to exceptional calumny, Jefferson added: "I know that it will give offense to the New England clergy; but the advocate of religious freedom is to expect neither peace nor forgiveness from them."

In their private thinking Jefferson and his circle liberated the secular democratic state from religion, and religion and ethics from theology. Historian Daniel J. Boorstin has summarized their creed: "The essence of religion was not theology but morality; not what men thought but how they acted."

How men acted, as we have seen, was in their view less a matter of logical deduction than of responsiveness to the inborn moral sense of the human heart, a faculty that was strengthened by exercise–by the habitual giving of kindness and the receiving of it derived not from thinking but from feeling. Jefferson's friend Dr. Rush observed how often an atheist equals or exceeds a believer in the excellence of his character. To his nephew, Peter Carr, Jefferson wrote advice that morality is not to be learned by attending lectures or accepting correct doctrines but by exercising the natural faculty of sociable living. We are born with the moral sense, Jefferson argued; it is "as much a part of a man as his leg or arm," present in stronger or weaker degree in all: "This sense is submitted, indeed, in some degree, to the guidance of reason; but it is a small stock which is required for this. . . . *State a moral case to a plowman and a professor. The former will decide it as well, and often better than the latter.*" [Emphasis added.]

Jefferson's materialism, in which he remained firm even against the teaching of his venerated Jesus was a doctrine championed by Priestley, who like many other enlightened clergymen of his time accepted the fundamentals of the philosophy of eighteenth-century Enlightenment. The concept of an immaterial soul, Priestley had written, was not based on biblical authority but was an intrusion of Greek speculation. The Platonists not only asserted the immortality of the soul but also insisted on its preexistence. The Hebrew account, on the contrary, taught that human beings were entirely compounded from earth material. Deity had "breathed" the breath of life into Adam and Eve. Life was literally a process of breathing and the combustion of matter.

The doctrine of an immaterial "spirit" introduced baneful mystification and mischief into an otherwise rational universe. To those who persisted in the absurdity of attributing "mind" to matter Priestley answered that since the phenomena of electrical attraction and magnetism were known to be actions of matter, there could be no objection to the hypothesis of consciousness and thinking arising from actions of material organisms. Jefferson seized upon this explanation to make his moral and material universe of one piece: human beings, like all living and inanimate forms, were expressions, however attenuated and refined, of the Creator's primordial act of establishing nature and nature's laws. Nothing else did or could exist. The deity himself was assumed to be of an infinitely finer but nevertheless real substance. With the vagaries of spiritualism and metaphysical idealism swept away, the great boon to "priestcraft" had been removed. Thus mankind might learn to practice self-government in matters of morality as well as in affairs of state.

The philosophy of Enlightenment, as it permeated Jefferson's thought, was no incidental or extraneous feature. It was the philosophical core of his moral humanism and the foundation of his faith in popular government. He summarized that faith in many epigrams, of which the following can stand as a capstone: "Every man, and every body of men on earth, possess the right of self-government. They receive it with their being from the hand of nature. Individuals exercise it by their single will; collections of men by that of their majority."

10

Imperative Thinker:

Immanuel Kant

(1724–1804)

Although born earlier than either Paine or Jefferson, Kant established a philosophy of religion and ethics that belongs to the era succeeding theirs. Human skepticism and Enlightenment rationalism received a major shock from this East Prussian grandson of a Scottish emigrant named Cant. Liberal in both religion and politics, Kant nevertheless belongs to an age-long succession of exacting schoolmasters who find it necessary to rap their desks for order when their freethinking charges become too exuberant.

Human beings with a normal regard for other people acknowledge a consciousness of moral obligation, a duty to treat others justly–"to do what's right." But *what* is right, *why* is it right, and *how* do we know? This puzzle has bewildered philosophers and plagued ordinary people since the human race first began to make moral decisions.

In traditional societies the question, "What is right, why is it right, and how do we know?" has usually been answered in terms of custom or of prevailing religious authority. For most people in the Western world, God has served as the ultimate sanction. An action is said to be right or wrong because God commands or prohibits its performance; God's will makes an action right or wrong, and the divine will is revealed through a prophet, a sacred tradition, or (in the case of philosophical rationalism) through the deductive powers of the mind, reasoning from God-given, self-evident truths. In all of these cases, belief in God, supported by a claim to know God's will, is accepted as the necessary foundation of right behavior.

But while this view has been dominant through the ages, it has had its challengers. Among these challengers have been avowed atheists or skeptics. But many others, while assuming the existence of a Supreme Being, have held that morality does not require belief in a divine intelligence or the knowledge of what such a Being would demand of us. According to these thinkers morality rests directly on some trait or disposition of human nature, such as social feeling, inborn sympathy, or intuitive knowledge of what is right.

Into this welter of conflicting opinions stepped a slightly built man of delicate health, a professor of philosophy already legendary among his townspeople for his regular habits and simple, self-disciplined life. He examined the problem of how we know the right–or how we know anything–and proposed a radical solution. The answer he offered two hundred years ago caused a revolution in philosophy. The man's name was Immanuel Kant, whom many consider to be the greatest philosopher since Plato and Aristotle. Some have hailed him as the greatest of all time. Even those who, like Bertrand Russell, do not share this opinion, have nevertheless recognized the magnitude of Kant's revolution even though they try to prove him mistaken.

Although a modest man, Kant did not hesitate to describe his work as a Copernican revolution–daring to compare his achievement in philosophy with that of the Polish astronomer Copernicus, whose theory that the Earth revolves around the sun forever altered our ideas about the cosmos. What was this solar revolution in philosophy that Kant believed he had brought about? We begin with this question because to understand his ethics, a general conception of his philosophy is necessary.

In much previous Western thought ethics or moral philosophy was regarded as the satellite of religion; it was like a planet circling the central sun of theology. Kant's daring act was to reverse this relationship. The sense of moral obligation, he argued, is primary. Moral experience is the sun of our understanding. Belief in God, said Kant, is derived from moral experience and depends on our moral sense for its justification. In the terminology that Kant introduced and which has become familiar in philosophical discussion, ethics is autonomous–that is to say, the experience of moral obligation is not determined by anything else, not theology, not belief in the existence of a God, and not on knowledge of the external world. Ethics cannot be grounded in anything other than moral intuition itself. Moral consciousness is irreducible, basic, independent, and autonomous. The heart of Kant's fundamental idea is the conviction that the moral will must be free from the law of cause and effect that governs the world we know through the senses. Its freedom to act transcends the phenomenal world of cause and effect.

Yet it is essential to understand that in subordinating theology to moral consciousness Kant did not question belief in the existence of God, the immortality of the soul, or the freedom of the will. On the contrary, he asserted that the existence of God, immortality, and free will are secure beliefs, finding their justification in our moral experience. Thus, he reversed the classical theological argument, making the existence of God, immortality, and free will dependent upon the reliability of our moral intuition and our consciousness of moral obligation rather than the other way around. In simple language, he argued that since we *know* we experience a sense of moral obligation, requiring that justice be done, we have, as a matter of practical reason, grounds to assume that the real world must include the means to fulfill the moral purpose we experience. Therefore, on grounds of practical reason, we act as if God, immortality, and free will are assured to achieve the moral ends that we find basic to our natures. It is especially this part of Kant's philosophy that subsequent thinkers have found the hardest to accept. But to pursue their objections here would get us ahead of our story.

Kant was at the height of his intellectual powers during the period of the American Revolution. *The Critique of Pure Reason*, his first great work that made his fame secure as a major philosopher, was published in 1781, the very year that Lord Cornwallis surrendered at Yorktown, and the equally important sequel, *The Critique of Practical Reason*, appeared seven years later. Kant of course was far removed from the momentous events then stirring America, living his quiet and steady life as a professor of philosophy at the university in Königsberg, East Prussia, his native city.

Even in Kant's day, East Prussia was a Germanic island surrounded by a Slavic sea, the extreme northeasterly borderland of the German-speaking peoples, From the middle ages, Königsberg had been a vital military bastion of the Teutonic Knights. Books containing old prints of the house where Kant lived show the massive fortress of Königsberg towering in the background. Military prowess and discipline were part of the Prussian soul, especially in the region of this Germanic Gibraltar where the kings of Prussia were traditionally crowned.

In an important respect Kant fitted his environment. Few figures in history have been more committed to the disciplined life than this frail but physically fit professor, who even in old age never neglected his vigorous walks regardless of weather. In his iron fortitude, he seemed pure Prussian, although in fact he was of Scottish ancestry. But the discipline of Kant was internal to the man–an inward, moral imperative. Beyond that inner disposition, his Prussian character ceased. He was no admirer of military virtues or of the authoritarian state. In political philosophy, he was a steadfast champion of liberty and at heart a citizen of the world who in his old age turned to the problem of perpetual peace, which he believed could be achieved through controlling the war-making power by plebiscite and development of an international system of law. When less than a decade after the close of the American Revolution a serious rebellion began in France to assure the people "liberty, equality, fraternity," the usually stoical philosopher of Königsberg is said to have wept tears of joy and to have exclaimed, quoting the New Testament: "I can say with Simeon–Lord, let Thy servant depart in peace, for mine eyes have seen Thy salvation."

In religion as in social philosophy Kant was a rebel, a fact that brought him into collision with the Prussian government, finally forcing him into public silence on religious topics. Reared in a severe pietistic sect calling itself the Soldiers of God, he developed a firm personal code that remained unchanged throughout his life. When as an adult he came to reject the traditional dogmas of Christianity, this inner conviction of moral duty became for him virtually the whole of religion. Forced as a child to attend the devotional exercises of the sectarian school in which he was educated, he acquired such a strong aversion to formal worship that he declined to attend religious services when he grew up. His first academic interests had been science and natural philosophy and when, as he approached the age of sixty he began to publish his major philosophical works, the influence of his early scientific training could be seen clearly.

Most of his scientific studies have been forgotten, but one work remains a milestone of cosmological theory. In that early work Kant developed a hypothesis to explain the origin of the solar system in terms of Newtonian physics, thereby anticipating the work of the French astronomer and thinker Laplace. It is also interesting to note that he put forward the possibility that primates could evolve into human beings, but carefully disguised this evolutionary theory as speculation about future development of a race of intelligent beings descended from the apes, a prudent disguise in view of Prussia's religious authoritarianism. But as his interests matured, what attracted him most about science was the meaning and validity of the scientific method itself. What are the logical foundations of knowledge? What, for example, constitutes proof in science? How does proof in experimental science differ from proof in logic? What is the relation of mathematical proof to logic on the one hand and to experimental science on the other? Does mathematics combine the nature of both logic and experimental science? Kant concluded that it does, and on that rather abstract foundation initiated a revival of an idealist philosophy that had dominated the world for more than a century. Many recent philosophers have concluded that Kant was in error on this point; pure, formal mathematics is simply an extension of logic, containing no trace of knowledge about the world we experience through our senses or discover through observation.

Kant's philosophy is a critical analysis of the empirical philosophy of John Locke and David Hume. The mind, said John Locke, is a tabula rasa, a blank slate on which the senses write. The infant enters the world knowing nothing; there are no *innate* ideas. All ideas develop from sensations, built up by habitual association into concepts.

Kant admitted that ideas may have their origin in experience, but, he thought, the mind is no passive blackboard recording the undecipherable graffitti of bare sensation. On the contrary, the mind is a grammarian of meaning, a traffic controller of experience, guiding incoming impressions along certain paths of flight. Experience is organized like the flight of airliners approaching an airport that must descend to a landing along the runways of the intellect, although Kant did of course not put it that way. The mind is a controlling, dynamic, operating system. Like the airport, the mind is so constructed that experience must enter it along the channels it provides, governed by the laws of perception it imposes, or not successfully touch ground at all. So much for John Locke's "blank tablet."

What are these flight controllers that turn mere blips (sensations) on the mind's radar screen into an intelligible pattern of traffic? Kant called them the "categories" of the mind that shape our perception of the world.

He recognized twelve categories, neatly grouped into four sets of three, a happy arrangement that much amused his skeptical successors. The function of the categories is to order into meaningful patterns the welter of chaotic impressions that bombard the mind. Kant was convinced that the empirical philosophy of Locke and Hume had not succeeded, strictly within the limits of their own principles, in bridging the chasm between raw sensations and ideas.

What we experience as the external world is known to us through the senses, but only as interpreted by the forms and categories of the mind. Space and time are the forms without which the mind cannot perceive reality. Among the categories is Hume's elusive concept, causality. Hume was right, said Kant, in recognizing that we never *discover* cause by mere observation. This is so because the concept (category) of cause is built into our minds prior to experience. It is one of the tools of the mind necessary for the ordering and classification of experience.

Thus all we know of the world and the phenomena in it comes to us from sensations organized by the mind into ideas through the forms of the categories. Yet Kant reasoned, there is a transcendental world *behind* the phenomenal world, the world of "things in themselves" which we cannot know directly but which we have ample reason to believe exists. Why this abrupt introduction of "things in themselves" that must always remain hidden behind the knowable world of phenomena? The answer seems to be that Kant had no other way to account for an essential element of his moral theory. Everything depends upon the sovereign authority of the "ought," the sense of moral obligation which, as we have seen, is the nucleus of his theory of ethics and religion. But the ought is not sovereign unless the will is free. It is not enough for us to feel subjectively that we are free to make choices as we will. Freedom of the will must be genuine and unconditional. But as we have seen, according to Kant the external world that we experience through the senses is a world of cause and effect, a determined world. This has to be so because the cause-effect relationship is one of the categories by which the mind perceives the world. Therefore, said Kant, the principle of cause and effect, as a category of the mind, does not apply to things-in-themselves, that hidden real world *behind* the world of experience. Thus, the moral agency of the will, as a thing-in-itself transcending the phenomenal world, is not under the law of causation. It is free, it is self-governing, it is autonomous. The theory of a realm transcending the senses in which causes do not determine events is Kant's way of expressing the idea of free will.

The freedom of the will, the existence of God, and immortality are called postulates of practical reason, that is, they are simply assumptions, not subject to proof by means of "pure reason," or *theoretical* reason. This distinction between pure reason and practical reason runs throughout Kant's philosophy and an understanding of it is essential to grasping his thought. He used the term "practical" in the original Greek meaning of *praktikós*, that is, active, fit or suitable for doing, standing in contrast to "pure" (speculative) reason, derived from the Latin root *speculari*, to see, to spy out. These root meanings help us to grasp Kant's special semantic usage. Pure or speculative reason is the function of the mind as a seeing eye attempting (in vain, it turns out) to penetrate the higher realities of metaphysics. In contrast, practical reason is an active function of the moral sense that succeeds where pure reason fails.

This distinction between pure and practical reason not only exalts moral intuition into a foundation for belief in free will, God, and immortality, but sharply limits speculative reason as a source of knowledge. Classical philosophy had sought to prove the existence of God by pure reason; but Kant showed that a crucial argument of the theoretical proof was based on a fallacy. The elaborate metaphysical castles of medieval theology collapsed into rubble; that is, the little that remained standing after several centuries of modern thought prior to Kant's final assault collapsed.

But since Kant affirmed on grounds of practical reason what he had denied was possible to know by pure reason, the effect of his work on later philosophy was to supplant rationalistic theology with religious philosophies based on faith, although this was hardly his intent. Kant himself took only a short step in this direction with his postulates of practical reason. Theologians and philosophers in the century to follow would take much longer leaps of faith without the support of Kant's practical reason, and sometimes would embrace faith against reason.

Kant himself recognized that his religion of duty, treating God as a postulate of moral experience, could not serve to support the particular supernatural claims of historic Christianity; with rigorous consistency (and perhaps with a sense of shedding an unnecessary burden) he gave up belief in orthodox Christianity, becoming simply a deist, or a believer in religion based on reason. In contrast, those who accepted the negative conclusion of his analysis of speculative theology but who were unwilling to give up the metaphysical dogmas of the church had no way open to them except to forsake reason for faith. But even the more perceptive of these, such as the widely influential Schleiermacher, recognized that the medieval edifice was beyond repair–in content as well as in architecture, and set about constructing a more liberal interpretation of Christianity, emphasizing the ethical teachings of Jesus as an expression of radical dependence on the divine will. Schleiermacher's was neither Kant's solution nor Spinoza's but it reflected the influence of both.

In America, the Kantian upheaval in religion reached its fullest expression in Emerson's Transcendentalism and later in Felix Adler's development of Ethical Culture. But Emerson discarded Kant's doctrine of personal immortality, maintaining solely a belief in free will as the expression of the autonomous Self and the idea of God (revised in Emersonian pantheism as the Oversoul). Going still further in modifying Kant, Felix Adler abandoned the idea of God as well as immortality, staking all on the concept of moral autonomy and the postulate of the unconditional worth of the person which it implies.

When Kant turned from the task of refuting Hume's skepticism, an undertaking that had led him into some highly dubious arguments about mathematics and logic, he took up the task of describing what is distinctive and essential to ethical judgment, articulating insights and principles that have remained of value throughout many subsequent changes in moral philosophy.

What does the moral law require of us, stripped of all accidental or purely situational aspects? In answer to this question, Kant sought a general law that might provide the kind of unfailing guidance we would expect from a proposition of logic. Such a moral law would have two features: (1) It would be universal, that is, it would apply equally to all people everywhere and at all times; and (2) it would have the feature of necessity–that is, it would always follow from its assumptions and not be subject to failure. Its imperative would not be hypothetical but unconditional. In Kant's terminology, it would be a categorical imperative.

And what is the rule that Kant formulated to meet these rigorous requirements? His categorical imperative states: "Act only on that rule whereby you can at the same time will that it should become a universal law." As commentators on Kant's thought have pointed out, his rule is an abstract reformulation of the Golden Rule and beset with the same problems as more familiar statements of that rule found in a number of the world's scriptures and moral philosophies.

Kant himself drew some rather harsh and sometimes cruel conclusions from his famous moral principle–a fact that no doubt reflects his puritanical training and the influence of a culture steeped in military devotion to order. On Kantian principles, we should never lie, since we cannot wish to make lying a universal practice; obviously that would make human society impossible. This argument lets Kant also insist that we should not resort to falsehood even to save the life of an innocent person from a murderous pursuer. The argument is curious. For Kant's rule should also tell us with equal force that because we cannot will the betrayal of an innocent victim we are morally constrained from betraying the victim. In such a conflict situation, where different moral principles clash, rational beings must avoid committing the greater evil. This would seem to follow from Kant's own logic, although his devotion to the ideal of a perfect moral order led him to many a conflicted result.

But how within the limits of Kant's principles shall we decide the greater evil? In his discussion of the meaning of moral obligation Kant noted that it means recognition of the duty to respect each human being as an absolute end in himself or herself. A human being must never be reduced to the status of merely a means to an end or, more strictly, a human being must never be used in a manner that degrades or violates the person as an end in himself. In simpler words, each of us is obligated to treat others, and to be treated by others in return, as of supreme value; human beings are not to be degraded or sacrificed only to advance one's own purpose or power. This is expressed in the statement that each person is a being of worth beyond all price, with worth understood to mean absolute intrinsic value.

While Kant's ethical philosophy does not provide us with a handbook of moral rules for particular situations or a detailed road map to make our way through all the avenues of human conflict it does provide us with a reliable compass for determining the moral direction of our actions. It has the advantage over conventional morality in not linking moral rules or definitions of justice to the fortunes of a particular creed, ideology, or party. It affirms our common identity as rational human beings; it asserts our worth as rational beings with irreplaceable lives of our own; and it confirms the moral basis of the community of free wills and free minds that is ideally the human family. We learn the nature of right conduct, the necessity for right conduct, and the value of right conduct through our inner consciousness as morally responsible beings in a community of morally responsible beings. In recognizing that foundation as the rational basis for the ethical and spiritual life, Immanuel Kant gave to humanity a moral philosophy capable of correcting all incomplete and fallible systems of thought, including his own.

11

Patriot of Humanity:

Friedrich Schiller

(1759–1805)

Kant had saved philosophy–and ethics in particular–from Hume's seminal and highly influential but also excessive skepticism. Even Bertrand Russell, his most enthusiastic revivalist, showed that by carrying Hume's principle of doubt in everything not experienced by the senses to its logical extreme Hume had made even such doubt unsupportable.

When Schiller settled in Jena in 1787, it was the center of Kantian philosophy. The general enthusiasm for Kant at that time is almost incomprehensible in view of the difficulty of his subject matter and his involved style. Schiller, too, was powerfully attracted by Kant's philosophy based on the premise that the world of reason is more real than the sensual world and superior to it. But what made Schiller a disciple of Kant was above all else "the great idea of self-determination" based on freedom. In a letter to his friend Christian Gottfried Körner he wrote: "No greater words were ever spoken by mortal man than these of Kant which represent at once the essence of his entire philosophy: 'Determine yourself from within.' " In greater detail he developed this idea in his essay, "On the Sublime": "All other things must; man is the being that wills. It is precisely for this reason that nothing is so unworthy of man as the toleration of force; for force negates him. Whoever inflicts it upon us denies us nothing less than our humanity." When man obeys laws without being able to consent to them, this deproves his action of any moral value.

It was the apostle of freedom in Schiller that was attracted by the principle that the human spirit is free and independent. But although Kant's moral philosophy, treated in more detail in the previous chapter, made a deep impression on Schiller, one aspect of it was antithetical to his view of human nature. In a letter to Wilhelm von Humboldt he wrote: "Speculative philosophy, if ever I went for it, repelled me by its empty forms; I found in its barren fields no quick water and no sustenance." But he saw as eternal treasures the principles of the independence and the autonomy of the spirit of man. Schiller's main departure from Kant's moral philosophy was his call for union of the sensual and moral impulses, the marriage of "sensual happiness and peace of soul (*Sinnenglück* and *Seelenfrieden*)." "Man," he says, "has been given two natures, a sensual and a moral, and it cannot possibly be his duty to use one to repress the other." He also disagreed with the idea that if a moral action is in accord with the inclination of an individual rather than against it, it loses its moral value. Such a demand leads to a hostile attitude toward life.

The years Schiller had spent wrestling with the philosophy of Kant were not wasted. In the end he arrived at a new position that was peculiarly his own. It was this that made his friendship with Goethe possible. For Goethe, too, found abstract philosophy confusing and unprofitable. It was not his way of grasping the essential nature of the world. Truth, he held, was more closely approached through the emotions and the senses. Only the fusion of the sensual and the spiritual forces was equal to encompassing the world of phenomena.

As Hitler's armored forces plunged ever deeper into the heartland of European Russia and the Ukraine, reports filtered to the West that secretly trained "elite" forces of Himmler's Gestapo, the *Einsatzgruppen*, were systematically slaughtering the Jewish population of the occupied territories; whole communities were transported by motor truck to isolated woodlands where gigantic pits had been prepared. Old men, women, young children, and infants in their mothers' arms, driven by blows from truncheon and rifle butt, were herded into these excavations, where they were machine-gunned to death. The victims were hastily covered with earth even while the moans of the dying remained audible.

Gestapo chiefs complained to their superiors that the unremitting bloodshed was imposing an unbearable emotional strain on the executioners of this carnage. Even the hardened supermen of the Nazi corps found it difficult to make a vocation of mass murder. An improved, more elegant method had to be devised, not out of consideration for the victims but for the convenience of their killers. The outcome, as all the world knows, was that monstrous factory of death, the gas chamber that was to be a major industry of the failing Third Reich.

When reports of this atrocity first circulated in the West, in most quarters they were totally disbelieved. Atrocity stories were quite common in wartime. They must be fabrications of Stalin's propaganda, concocted to raise the fever of belligerence and to pressure the Allies into opening a second front. At the war's end, when photographs of the deathcamps and their mountains of corpses left no longer any room for doubt, people demanded to know how this could have happened. After all, the Germans were a civilized people. Despite the racist ideology of the Nazis, it was nearly impossible to believe that a highly developed culture could relapse into such degradation.

Was not Germany the land of such peaks of moral philosophy as Kant, Goethe, and Schiller? Few other nations had produced their equal.

At the time when Franklin, Jefferson, and their associates appointed to draft the Declaration of Independence were presenting their work to the Continental Congress in Philadelphia, the dream of freedom was firing the imaginations of German idealists, although they found little evidence of liberty in their fragmented, autocratically governed land. Germany was an unrealized hope, existing only in the shared identity and aspiration of its people. Its many lilliputian duchies and principalities were governed by a motley of princes who were hardly different from the petty lords of feudal times. Vienna and Berlin–Austria and Prussia–coveting this patchwork of fiefdoms and principalities, fought for control in a contest that remained unresolved until Bismarck, the "iron chancellor" of Prussia, succeeded almost a century later in making Germany a nation.

In 1776, when the Liberty Bell sounded over the waters of the Delaware, freedom's intellectual triumvirate in Germany–Kant, Goethe, and Schiller–were in full vigor, pursuing the labors that would earn them places in the pantheon of humanity's greatest benefactors. Kant at fifty-two the eldest, was at work on the *Critique of Pure Reason*. Goethe, already famous as a poet and author of *Werther* and as an intellect of exceptional promise, had embarked on a career as counselor and government administrator to the Duke of Weimar. Already at work on *Faust*, his masterpiece, he would live to see himself acclaimed as the prince of German letters.

The youngest of our trio, not yet seventeen, was perhaps learning the most valuable lesson of all: the supreme value of personal dignity, taught through suffering the outrage and humiliation inflicted upon him by his ruler, Duke Earl Eugen of Württemberg. Young Schiller had aspired to enter theological studies at Tubingen. But the Duke had other plans for this adolescent son of one of his army surgeons. By the duke's command, Schiller was enrolled in a military academy recently founded by the duke to prepare young men for a life of duty to the state; there would be no nonsense about a theological career–or anything else not authorized by the autocratic ruler.

Thus, beginning at the age of fourteen, Friedrich underwent a seven-year regimen that inoculated him forever against autocratic government and militarism. Thereafter, freedom, not mere political freedom, but one's moral autonomy would be his passionate goal. He learned to hate the martial traits and narrow loyalties that make men killers, and serfs of their military masters. He wrote later:

> We of the modern world are endowed with a realm of interest unknown to Greek and Roman alike. With it the patriotic interest simply cannot compete. This latter is really significant only for immature people. . . . The philosophical mind can take an interest in one nation or national occurrence only insofar as it appears significant as a condition for the betterment of the entire human race.

Imploring fellow Germans to have a higher ambition than the pursuit of national power, which became an obsession of Germany for generations, Schiller wrote in rebuke, "Vainly you Germans attempt to set yourself up as a nation. Strive to grow freer instead, freer as man and succeed."

To his sister-in-law he confided, "I do believe that every individual human soul that develops its powers is more than the largest accumulation of people taken together." States exist only to facilitate the development of their individual citizens who should always strive toward achieving a *universal* humanity. Confiding this ideal to the Christian thinker Friedrich Heinrich Jacobi, he wrote:

> Let us remain citizens of our age *in the flesh*, for there is no other way. But *in the spirit* it is the privilege and the duty of philosopher and poet to belong to no nation and no age but to be in the full sense of the term a contemporary of all ages.

Schiller fled from his forced service to the Duke of Württemberg and for years afterward lived with the fear of extradition and punishment. Embarking on a career as playwright, stage director, historian, and poet, he moved restlessly and insecurely about the German states–to Mannheim, Leipzig, Dresden, Weimar, Jena, and back to Weimar. Goethe was helpful, providing for him a professorship of history at the University of Jena in 1787, a post that illness forced him to relinquish two years later. Goethe had invited him to come and stay for a prolonged visit, so that they might be able to clarify their thoughts in discussion, thoughts they had entertained before in a fascinating and rightly celebrated exchange of letters. Goethe readily acknowledged his large debt to his younger friend, especially in writing for the stage, in which Schiller was unexcelled; the younger poet in turn owed to Goethe a balancing influence in shaping his philosophy of ethics and art.

Prior to this final phase of his short life, which was to end in 1805 after years of struggle with tuberculosis, Schiller had established himself as one of the masters of historical writing in the German language. As we might expect from his character, his historical works revolve around the theme of freedom–the forty-year struggle of the Dutch Republic to throw off the despotism of Phillip II of Spain, and the sufferings and outrages of human rights of the Thirty Years War. His mature tragedies center on the same thought, especially in *Don Carlos*, where in the midst of the terror of the Holy Inquisition an unquenchable yearning for liberty is put into the mouth of Marquis Posa, the protagonist of the drama, and in *Wilhelm Tell*, archetype of the unconquerable will of the human spirit in the face of oppression.

If ever a visionary spoke as a prophet to his nation and the world it was Schiller. As the prophets of Israel forewarned of impending disaster and divine judgment, so Schiller delivered to humanity–and especially to Germany–a warning of the scourge awaiting every people that succumbs to the false glories of nationalism and the intoxication of war.

He expressed this prophetic vision in an essay, "The Legislation of Lycurgus and Solon." Even if he had written nothing else, this work alone would establish him as a master analyst of collective psychohistory. The fateful path of every nation infected with the totalitarian spirit is warned against, with Sparta as a deterring example. We need not wonder that during the days of the Third Reich, Hans and Sophie Scholl, brother and sister, student leaders in Munich, were executed for resisting the Nazi ideology; their crime included the distribution of Schiller's "Lycurgus and Solon."

Schiller saw two paths open in history, the way of Athens, represented in the lawgiver, Solon, and the way of Sparta, seen in Lycurgus. These two contrasting figures became types for all subsequent history: Athens for personal liberty, limitation on government, free inquiry, and respect for the individual; Sparta for absolute state control over every facet of life, the effacement of individuality, subordination of family to the state and suppression of everything that might interfere with the will of the all-controlling state. The engine of Sparta is the cult of war, for which the young are prepared from infancy. The young girl is indoctrinated to harden herself to be a fit mother of future warriors.

Youths were given sparse rations and by their hunger encouraged to steal, but they were punished if they were so clumsy or lacking in wile as to be caught. The helots, a class of slaves captured in war, were fair game to be murdered, if chanced upon at night by marauding squads of youth honing their military skills. Sparta, it would appear, had every accoutrement of the modern totalitarian society. Indeed, it was a more painstakingly crafted fascistic system than was ever achieved by Hitler's Germany. It required no führer and allowed for none: control of the totalitation establishment was held by a rigid collective leadership that no individual could modify or even hope to challenge. In this respect Sparta closely approximated the Leninist model of the highly disciplined, centralized, and self-perpetuating political elite.

Schiller does not specifically foretell that Germany may become a future Sparta. As a universal man he addresses himself to all nations, warning all of the same path. The impulse to violence and tyranny is strong, and without moral preparedness of the human spirit, without a true transformation of the collective character of a people there is no escape from the curse of oppression. Revolutions will go full circle and replace old absolutisms with new ones. As he expressed this thought in another of his writings, new *secular* tyrannies will replace the old theocratic despotism:

> The old principles will remain, but they will be clothed in the garb of the century, and philosophy will lend its name to an oppression which was formerly authorized by the Church. Terrified of the freedom, which in their first attempts always appears to them as an enemy, men will in one case throw themselves into the arms of a comfortable slavery and in another, driven to despair by a pedantic tutelage, they will escape into the libertinism of the natural state. Usurpation will plead the weakness of human nature, insurrection its dignity, until at length the great sovereign of all human affairs, blind force, steps in to decide the sham conflict of principles like a common fist fight.

The two contrasting lawgivers, Lycurgus and Solon, provide Schiller with the opportunity to apply the materials of legend and history to his humanistic purpose. Yet he never misuses his materials; he informs as a philosopher and poet, not as a propagandist in the facile or deceiving sense. The purpose of art–and here history becomes art in Schiller's hands–is to penetrate beneath the surface of events, to fathom causes and connections to illuminate the consequences, and thus the meaning and moral significance of human behavior. The conclusion is not imposed like the moral of a fable, but resurrected from the past as living flesh. The opposite approach reduces the artist to a falsifier or at least to a simplistic and dreamy moralist who repels rather than elicits the inner life of moral experience.

Schiller's method deftly awakens the moral imagination and draws us into *living* the history he portrays. It enables us to breathe and expand in the freedom of Athens and be crushed in Sparta.

> The Athenian was generous in prosperity, steadfast in adversity. . . . He treated his slaves humanely; an ill-treated slave was permitted to bring suit against his master. Even animals were generously treated by this people. After the completion of the temple Hekatompedon, it was decreed that all animals that had assisted in the work should be relieved of any further labor and should be allowed for the rest of their lives to pasture in the richest meadows. Afterward one of these animals returned to work of its own accord, running mechanically in front of the

> others that were pulling loads. This spectacle so touched the people that the order was given that the animal should in future be given special care at the public expense.

Better to be a beast of burden in Athens than a king in Sparta! From habit, an animal might take its place beside its fellows at toil, but the warm-hearted Athenian read this as an act of spontaneous solidarity and sympathy which even the beast expresses. But the only solidarity allowed to Spartans was participation in robbing fellow beings of their freedom and happiness, while extinguishing all gentle and generous feelings in themselves. And the consequence? Sparta was a desert. "Where in Sparta was there a Socrates, a Thucydides, a Sophocles, a Plato? Sparta could produce only rulers and warriors."

With the case studies of Sparta and Athens before him, Schiller concluded: "The character of an entire people is the most faithful expression of its laws and the most reliable criterion of its worth or worthlessness." By their fruits ye shall know them. Lycurgus succeeded in establishing a social order that thrived and proved its effectiveness over centuries. By his standards and intentions, Lycurgus was an honorable man. He carefully articulated every feature of the social and political order to promote its desired end: Gold and silver were outlawed, replaced by bulky coins of iron, which were specially processed to render the metal unfit for working into useful objects. Private land was divided into plots of exactly equal value, and the produce had to be turned over to the state for consumption in public dining halls where all citizens had to take their meals. Materials for housing were carefully prescribed, as were the few tools that could be used to construct them in order to prohibit luxury in style, decoration, or furnishing. Children at the age of seven were turned over to the state for training in the martial arts and to be molded to a precise social conformity. Slaves were steadily supplied by Sparta's perpetual aggressions and were, as we have seen, treated as chattel to be abused or killed at will. Most forms of labor were not considered befitting citizens and fell on these captive workers.

War provided not only the vocation of the state but served

as the only sanctioned emotional outlet. Where even sex and procreation had a national and martial purpose, war and games preparing for war offered diversion and excitement:

> It was undoubtedly a fine trick on the part of the lawgiver to associate festivity and mirth with dangerous ordeals and thus to eliminate the element of dread. He went still further. In time of war, he somewhat relaxed the severe discipline. . . . Hence war became a sort of recreation for the Spartans and they anticipated it with delight like an occasion for merry-making. At the approach of the enemy, Lycurgus ordered the Castorean hymn to be sung and, accompanied by the music of flutes, the soldiers marched out . . . joyous and unafraid.

As Schiller reconstructed Sparta's legislation and history, it anticipates twentieth-century totalitarianism so fully in overall impact as in innumerable particulars, that we find the effect overwhelming. Was Schiller only describing a remote past or was he warning our own age? In his youth he had hoped that casting off tyranny would suffice; the spirit of liberty, once unfettered, would prevail. But as he observed the debasement of revolutionary France and pondered the irrational forces that had brought down democracy in Solon's glorious Athens, he began to foresee a steeper, more difficult ascent for freedom.

This chastened understanding coincided with his moving from professional historian back again to dramatist and poet, but to a vision of poetry and drama more sharply focused by a maturing knowledge of human character. Here Schiller's immersion in Kant, critically revised by Goethe's world view, ripened in him to produce a profounder realization of the artist's mission. Human beings could not create a free society without attaining the virtues and controls of freedom within themselves, and this required the harmonizing of flesh and spirit. In his *Letters on the Aesthetic Education of Man* he wrote that we must "look for some support to ensure the continuation of society," which is "not to be found in the natural character of man which, being selfish and violent, is far more calculated to destroy society than to preserve it." Where is the support for social rejuvenation to be found?

> Should we, perhaps, expect this action to come from the state?

> This is not possible, for the state, as it is now constituted, is responsible for the evil, and the state, as reason conceives it in idea, instead of being able to establish this better humanity, must itself be founded upon it. . . . The present age, far from exhibiting the form of humanity that we have recognized to be the necessary condition for the moral reform of the state, shows us rather the precise opposite.

Without a secure psychological and moral grounding in its individual members, the collective force of the state will overpower and destroy the very qualities of life necessary for individuality to flourish. "The law of conformity becomes a tyranny against the individual," he writes, "when it is combined with an already pervasive weakness and physical limitation, and so extinguishes the last glimmering sparks of spontaneity and individuality."

But this vicious and apparently unbreakable circle must be broken if mankind is to progress toward liberty. "All improvement in the political sphere," Schiller observes, "is to proceed from the ennoblement of character of the individual–but how, under the influence of a barbarous constitution, can character be ennobled?" We must, he answers, secure "an instrument not provided by the state . . . that will remain pure and clear despite all political corruption." He thinks he has found it, and here Schiller assumes an optimism that, at first glance, his study of ancient totalitarianism would not seem to support–and which, ruefully, a history of nearly two hundred years since his time has made even bleaker. This "instrument," he tells us, is the creative, restorative spirit of art, which he proceeds to compare with that other pillar of spiritual autonomy, science, as the spirit of free inquiry.

But before we write off Schiller's solution as disproved by modern history, we should hear his case. Perhaps, despite the horrors of recent decades and centuries, the final verdict is not yet in. Lycurgus expelled art and high culture from Sparta, and Sparta prevailed militarily over Athens. But Athens is alive in the prophetic visions of civilization while Sparta remains only as an object lesson in tyranny.

> Art, like science, is free of everything that is . . . established by human conventions, and both rejoice in an absolute immun-

> ity from human arbitrariness. The political legislator can close off its domain, but he cannot govern it. He can ostracize the friend of truth, but truth endures. He can humiliate the artist, but art he cannot debase. . . . Where character is devitalized and loose, science will strive to please and art to enrich. For entire centuries philosophers and artists have been seen to engage in plunging truth and beauty into the depths . . . , but truth and beauty fight their way victoriously back to the surface with their own indestructible vitality."

Translated into twentieth-century ideological struggle, Schiller foresees that hack artists and intellectual sycophants will have their hour, but they write in water. Despite the worst that political and moral despotism can inflict–and enduring more than would seem to be humanly possible–the Thomas Manns, Pasternaks, and Solzhenitsyns inscribe their truths in their unconquerable spirit. Why then do injustice and oppression prevail, when everywhere the knowledge needed for moral deliverance is at hand? In the anguish of a year when revolutionary France was plunged into terror, and all of Europe trembled, Schiller asked, in an echo of St. Paul, why we cannot live the truth if we know it:

> The age is enlightened, that is to say such knowledge has been obtained and disseminated which would suffice to rectify at least our practical principles. The spirit of free inquiry has dispelled the erroneous conceptions that for a long time barred the approach to truth and undermined the foundations on which fanaticism and fraud erected their throne. Reason has been purged of the illusions of the senses and of deceptive sophistry; and philosophy herself, which first caused us to forsake nature, calls us loudly and urgently to return to her bosom–why is it that we are still barbarians?

He responds to his own question by answering, "Energy of spirit is needed to overcome the obstacles that both indolence of nature and cowardice of heart have set in the path of our enlightment. . . . The greater part of humanity is too weary and exhausted from the struggle with want to brace itself for a fresh and sterner struggle with error." In their weakness of natural power and in their poverty of spirit, the majority of mankind are only too glad to "escape the hard labors of thought and gladly leave to others the guardianship of their thinking." If they feel higher impulses, most will "embrace with eager faith the formulas that state and priesthood hold in readiness for this to happen."

To energize the free spirit in its liberation from this peonage, the artist becomes a catalyst, facilitating the union of the soul's strong emotional powers with the guiding ideals that give direction but which, in themselves, are powerless to bring about the necessary transformation. Art, we remember, accomplishes this best not by preaching or imploring but by touching the sources of motivation. "That art alone is genuine which provides the highest enjoyment," he writes in the introduction to "The Bride of Messina." "And the highest enjoyment is freedom of the spirit in the vivacious play of all its powers."

The creative element of art prepares and actualizes the free play of the self's humanizing elements. "Genuine art . . . does not have as its object a merely transitory game. Its serious purpose is not merely to transform the human being into a momentary dream of freedom, but actually to make him free."

Art accomplishes this not by imposing an ideology, or even truth itself, from without. It rather elicits it by "awakening a power within. . . . Precisely because genuine art aims at something real and objective, it cannot be satisfied with the mere appearance of truth. Upon truth itself, on the solid bedrock of nature, it rears its ideal structure."

Contrary to Kant, Schiller and Goethe insisted that human liberty is found in the radical unification of the sensuousness of the natural human being with his spiritual identity. Reason and understanding, flesh and spirit, the natural and the ideal must be one. Also in an older, religious terminology, the problem of human life is to find salvation; but salvation is not redemption in another world but a healing to be accomplished in this world. It is illuminating that an early translation of the Bible into English rendered the word salvation as "healing." The purpose of faith is the *healing* of the world. The bifurcation into body and spirit is overcome, the severed self is made whole again and so healed in the unifying experience of true art.

Art, therefore, is not just a decoration of life but an expression of its creativity and moral power. This recogniton has driven tyrants in all ages to the need to control and manipulate the creative mind.

Lycurgus set a model for all later tyranny when he attempted to extirpate the powerful impact of the aesthetic sense. Such suppression of the human spirit was an integral feature of his totalitarian rule. After Sparta prevailed over Athens, the authoritarian infection penetrated the city of Solon, as we see it in Plato's model constitution where the muses are either expelled or turned to purposes of ideological control. That Plato's *Republic* was no utopian fancy can be seen starkly in the reality of an absolutist church. Catholic Christianity had adopted Plato's ideals and Platonized its theory and practice. When Augustus of Hippo turned at last to embrace his mother's Christian faith, he retained a mind-set of despotism that traced its sources back to Plato, this authoritarian-minded Athenian who out of hatred for the democratic traditions of Athens found his model constitution in the garrison state of Lycurgus. There is little of the Sermon on the Mount in Augustinian absolutism; the *City of God* rises less from the vision of the New Jerusalem than from Plato's old *Republic*.

Schiller understood with a clarity seldom equaled in the history of ideas that the reality of freedom cannot be erected by elevating coercion to an ideal. As Marxist-Leninists have confirmed in practice, the "temporary" dictatorship of the proletariat becomes permanent dictatorship *over* the proletariat. To end tyranny, we must purge our minds of all traces of despotism.

"It must be admitted," Schiller wrote of the Spartan system, "that nothing could be more carefully conceived or be more adequate to its purpose than this constitution, . . . and, if rigidly enforced, would necessarily maintain itself indefinitely." Effective for its dire purpose, Schiller saw the very perfection of the totalitarian state as monstrous, and he rejected it as humanity's constant peril.

Schiller lived for only a year after he completed *Wilhelm Tell*. It was a year of painful physical suffering. All his last dramas were written in the intervals between attacks of tuberculosis that followed one another ever more closely. When he died on May 9, 1805, Wilhelm von Humboldt wrote in his essay, "On Schiller and the Progress of His Thought": "His goal was so exalted that he could never have reached the end. He lived surrounded only by the highest ideas and most brilliant imagery."

For Goethe, the survivor, the image of his departed friend became transfigured into one of pure piety. His admiration for Schiller's spiritual and moral greatness inspired him to write the immortal verses in his "Epilogue to Schiller's Song of the Bell." "There was in him," Goethe wrote to Zelter on November 30, 1830, "an innate Christ-like tendency. He never touched anything common without ennobling it. This lofty and elevating quality is the result of the forceful determination with which he stipulates that human life has an absolute meaning: even in the prison of the circumstances man can preserve his inner freedom and 'as the great task of his life can realize the idealistic human being' that everyone bears within him."

No intellectual history of Europe can pass over Schiller's influence. To trace the path (progress) of his spirit and take possession anew of the great legacy he left to all those coming after him is an intellectual and ethical experience of unique power. In the words of Hugo von Hufmannsthal, "The light of Schiller greets us like a lodestar of the ages."

12

The Inner Eye at Large:

Ralph Waldo Emerson

(1803–1882)

The original church of the pilgrims—the First Parish of Plymouth—became unitarian and liberal during the first years of the nineteenth century. It forced the orthodox Calvinist minority to withdraw and this minority established its own "Church of the Pilgrims" in order to reestablish doctrinal discipline. The Harvard Divinity School fell to the liberals at about the same time. These early exponents of "liberal Christianity" believed they could maintain both a rationalized Christianity and a Christianized rationalism. This synthesis failed as criticism came from two sources: the spiritual or transcendentalist party that, following Kant's British apostle Coleridge, believed that the old rationalism was blind to the higher truths of the spirit; and on the opposite side, from a more aggressive rationalist and scientific party that refused to compromise with a metaphysics considered untenable. Emerson belonged to the transcendentalist trend of thought; his English friend and admirer, Harriet Martineau, veered into the antimetaphysical and materialist camp. Both exponents should be met without prejudice. They can be good companions to the two sides of human nature, the mystical and the rational.

Ralph Waldo Emerson was the most celebrated and also most frequently quoted American writer of his generation. In Europe, where his fame was unparalleled for an American thinker and poet he was hailed as evidence of America's coming of age as a distinctive culture. His influence in liberalizing religion was itself a major accomplishment. He had left the active ministry of Boston's historic Second Church (the Old North Church)–which was Unitarian–after only three and a half years, in part because he was not temperamentally suited to pastoral duties but mainly because he objected to conducting the formal prayers and communion service of even this most liberal of Christian denominations. Within his lifetime he saw his influence carry many of the younger Unitarian clergy beyond the boundaries of historic Christianity to formulate a universal religion based purely on ethics and to organize the Free Religious Association to serve this end.

Emerson was the principal prophet for several generations of men and women who were more likely to find inspiration in a walk through the woods or by gazing upon the starry heaven than in regular attendance at church. There is much in the American free spirit that one cannot understand unless one knows Emerson. His transcendentalist philosophy was a religion of the spiritually emancipated mind and heart, unbounded by church or party.

In his 1842 lecture, *The Transcendentalist*, Emerson attempted to explain in a few sentences what this new, and allegedly incomprehensible development of idealist philosophy, was about:

> It is well known to most of my audience that the Idealism of the present day acquired the name of Transcendental from the use of that term by Immanuel Kant of Koenigsberg, who replied to the skeptical philosophy of Locke, which insisted that there was nothing in the intellect which was not previously in the experience of the sense, by showing that there was a very important

> class of ideas or imperative forms, which did not come by experience, but through which experience was acquired; that these were intuitions of the mind itself; and he denominated them *Transcendental* forms. The extraordinary profoundness and precision of that man's thinking have given vogue to his nomenclature in Europe and America, to that extent that whatever belongs to the class of intuitive thought is popularly called at the present day *Transcendental*.

This school of thought, given fresh and forceful expression by our American poet-philosopher, enabled several generations of Americans to heal the supposed breach between ideas and action.

Americans were doers before they were thinkers–or so it had always seemed to the old established cultures of Europe and to many Americans who, with the inferiority complex of an upstart people, accepted prevailing opinion about their alleged poverty of thought. But history does not confirm this lack of ideas and vision in the American character. Quite the contrary: America was founded on dreams and ideal blueprints for the making of an idealized commonwealth. From the Puritan city on a hill to James Oglethorpe's attempt to plant a model society of independent farmers and artisans on the Savannah, America from its inception was a richly patterned quilting of Utopia, New Jerusalem, and El Dorado. In that respect, Emerson–the social critic and visionary, the angry prophet of a new Israel, castigating his people for their low-minded interest in commerce and their philistinism was only the carrier of the torch of reform that had been burning brightly since America's creation. New England pilgrim and Puritan, Rhode Island Baptist and Jew, New Jersey and Pennsylvanian Quaker and Mennonite, Carolina Moravian and Huguenot, and Georgia Salzburger–the entire seaboard of English North America was generously inlaid with the jewels of fresh revelations and original, if sometimes eccentric, social experiments. These in turn were followed by French-inspired utopian communities and other experimental colonies so familiar to Emerson–Brook Farm, Hopedale, and the Fruitlands community of his friend and mentor Bronson Alcott.

To recognize that Emerson stood in a long tradition of

American visionaries and oracles does not deprive him of his unique greatness. On the contrary, without Abraham and Moses, there would have been no Micah or Isaiah. The Puritan and perfectionist traditions clashed and blended for two hundred years–for eight or more generations–before transformation in the creative mind of America's most representative sage.

Does Emerson deserve to be counted among our nation's great philosophers? Is he to be regarded as a philosopher at all, or as a poet or spiritual teacher without an organized church? John Dewey, who spoke with some authority on what constitutes philosophy, observed: "Perhaps those are nearer right . . . who deny that Emerson is a philosopher, because he is more than a philosopher. . . . His own preference was to be ranked with the seers rather than the reasoners of the race."

Dewey recalled lines from Emerson in which he says, "I think that philosophy is still rude and elementary; it will one day be taught by poets. The poet is in the right attitude; he is believing; the philosopher, after some struggle, [has] only reasons for believing."

Dewey rejected the deprecation of those who dismissed Emerson as something less than a philosopher:

> I would not make hard and fast lines between philosopher and poet, yet there is some distinction of accent in thought and or rhythm in speech. The desire for an articulate, not for silent, logic is intrinsic with philosophy. The unfolding of the perception must be stated, not merely followed and understood.

With the poet or spiritual visionary it is otherwise. The seer or poet speaks from immediate experience, inward revelation or insight, as one having authority. This oracular style in Emerson repels many people. There is a suggestion of "Thus saith the Lord," in many of his pronouncements. The style of composition, particularly in his later works, is disorganized and abrupt, somewhat reminiscent of St. Paul who breaks off one thought to take up another. Aphorisms follow one another so closely that one feels cannonaded with verbal grapeshot. To contemporary ears many of these Emersonian maxims sound stentorian and pedantic.

These defects of style were noted by critics in Emerson's lifetime, including Matthew Arnold in Britain and James Russell Lowell in America, who did not place him among writers of the first rank. But these are blemishes on the countenance of a titan. Taken in its entirety, considered as a vision of the whole of things, the Emersonian accomplishment seems constructed on a larger than human scale. Yet there is nothing forbidding or intimidating in Emerson–not in a single line. He is always approachable and completely human. He is a lawgiver, equal in our age to Moses or Mohammed; yet he urges us to accept no law from God or man for which we do not find warrant in our own consciousness. He believed in absolute being but he rejected institutional absolutism absolutely. Trust yourself, he said. Prove every moral truth within your own being.

When in 1837 he delivered his oration before the Phi Beta Kappa Society, entitled *The American Scholar*, he urged his hearers to throw off America's two-hundred-year-long dependence on European thought. It is time for us to come into our own as a civilization, to think our own thoughts, to create our own philosophy, our own poetry and vision of life. We have been pupils of Old-World schoolmasters too long already: "Our day of dependence, our long apprenticeship to the learning of other lands draws to a close. The millions that around us are rushing into life cannot always be fed on the sere remains of foreign harvests."

This seemingly impractical New England recluse proved himself the representative American by proclaiming the close connection between doing and thinking that has always been characteristic of the American character, and which is the genius of pragmatic philosophy, however idealistic in its grounding:

> The mind now thinks, now acts, and each . . . reproduces the other. When the artist has exhausted his materials, when the fancy no longer paints, when thoughts are no longer apprehended and books are a weariness,–he has always the resource *to live*. Character is higher than intellect. Thinking is the function. Living is the functionary. . . . A great soul will always be strong to live, as well as strong to think. . . . This is a total act. Thinking is a partial act.

Here in a nutshell is the essence of the American philosophy and an undeclared prophecy of the form that philosophy has taken for the century and a half since Emerson. It is no accident that William James and John Dewey, for all their metaphysical differences with Emerson, admired his thought and found in his insight themes that continued to be reflected in their own pragmatic definitions of truth and value and of the relation of doing to thinking.

Despite the mystical strain in Emerson's philosophy, or perhaps because of it, he recognized that the action gives birth to the thought, providing the American mind with its unmistakable signature: "The preamble of thought, the transition through which it passes from the unconscious to the conscious, is action. Only so much do I know, as I have lived."

Returning to the theme of originality and action, the thirty-four-year-old Emerson concluded his remarkable address by again urging American uniqueness:

> We will walk on our own feet; we will work with our own hands; we will speak our own minds. The study of letters shall be no longer a name for pity, for doubt, and for sensual indulgence. . . . A nation of men will for the first time exist, because each believes himself inspired by the Divine Soul which also inspires all men.

In these closing sentences of his oration, *The American Scholar*, Emerson returned to an argument made earlier in his presentation that human beings have lost their entirety or wholeness as persons. We have become, he said, not men but merely fragments of men. This is one of the liveliest and most prescient passages in the Emersonian canon. Its perceptiveness is striking when one considers the preoccupation with alienation that has characterized philosophy and psychology throughout subsequent history. Emerson described the human situation in terms still recognized.:

> It is one of those fables which out of an unknown antiquity convey an unlooked-for wisdom, that the gods, in the beginning, divided Man into men, that he might be more helpful to himself; just as the hand was divided into fingers, the better to answer its end.

* * *

> The old fable covers a doctrine ever new and sublime; that there is One Man,–present to all particular men only partially, or through one faculty; and you must take the whole society to find the whole man. Man is not a farmer, or a professor, or an engineer, but he is all. Man is priest, and scholar, and statesman, and producer and soldier. In the *divided* or social state these functions are parcelled out to individuals, each of whom aims to do his stint of the joint work, while each other performs his. The fable implies that the individual, to possess himself, must sometimes return from his own labor to embrace all other laborers. But, unfortunately, this original unit, this fountain of power, has been so distributed to multitudes, has been so minutely subdivided and peddled out, that it is spilled into drops and cannot be gathered. The state of society is one in which the members have suffered amputation from the trunk, and strut about so many walking monsters,–a good finger, a neck, a stomach, an elbow, but never a man. Man is thus metamorphosed into a thing, into many things. The planter, who is Man sent out into the field to gather food, is seldom cheered by any idea of the true dignity of his ministry. He sees his bushel and cart, and nothing beyond. . . . The tradesman scarcely even gives an ideal worth to his work, but is ridden by the routine of his craft, and the soul is subject to dollars. The priest becomes a form; the attorney a statute-book; the mechanic a machine; the sailor a rope of the ship.
>
> In this distribution of functions the scholar is the delegated thinker. . . . In the degenerate state, when the victim of society, he tends to become a mere thinker, or still worse, the parrot of other men's thinking.

When Emerson composed these bitter words on the alienation of labor and social function as determining consciousness, Karl Marx, whose name would be linked to these leading ideas, was still a youth of nineteen.

The ethical problem of democracy, Emerson asserted throughout his long career, is to restore human beings to themselves as whole beings, not to condemn men and women to live impoverished existence as economic fragments. Without grasping this essential motivation, this aim of a restorative humanism that might enable human beings to transcend their physical limitations, Emerson will remain only partially understood. The fable of primordial man, the human original before he had been divided into a society of fragmented people, was Emerson's symbol of human wholeness and freedom, the divine human, expressing the creative spontaneity of living, immortal nature.

Emerson's religion is pantheistic, or more accurately, it is a metaphysical idealism in which, as in Hindu speculative philosophy, the material universe is only the garment, or appearance, of an underlying divine unity expressed in multitudinous individuals. While metaphysical idealism is often considered a conservative philosophy, allied to the status quo, in Emerson it attains an antiauthoritarian, evolutionary outlook. It affirms a spiritual conception of democracy in which each person writes within his own heart the living scripture of personal worth and self-reliance.

Emerson's transcendentalist philosophy was a humanism grounded in an idealist metaphysics, celebrating the aboriginal nature of the person as an expression of Nature's inexhaustible creativeness. It was profoundly an *evolutionary* humanism, based on the pre-Darwinian theory of the French naturalist, Lamarck. Emerson's son Edward, in preparing the centennial edition of Emerson's works, repeatedly emphasized the importance of evolution in Emerson's world view. Lamarck's hypothesis, it will be remembered, assumed the transmission of acquired characteristics to an individual's descendents–a theory overturned by Darwin's theory of natural selection but in its day a potent carrier of the idea of evolutionary ascent.

Lamarck's evolutionary concept agreed with Emerson's gospel of progress through striving; purpose and will become the essential motivations of endless biological and spiritual progress. Thus Emerson's view was vitalist as well as idealist, a thought later resurrected in Henri Bergson's concept of the élan vital. Emerson expressed this spiritualized interpretation of the ascent of the species through eons of time in a poem set as the introductory motto of the second edition (1849) of his book *Nature* (published a decade before the appearance of Darwin's *Origin of the Species*). By the forces of purpose and will moving in history, the lowliest biological forms ascend into intelligent life:

A subtle chain of countless rings
   The next unto the farthest brings;
The eye reads omens where it goes,
   And speaks all languages the rose;
And, striving to be man, the worm
   Mounts through all the spires of form.

Orthodox Christianity's cosmology of a world created four thousand years before Christ held no charm for Emerson; he was convinced by the recent findings of geology of a much older earth, a truth foreshadowed in the Hindu philosophy's vision of a universe of countless eons, bringing forth and extinguishing innumerable forms in the breathing out and breathing in of Brahma, the eternal ground and soul of a cosmos of ever changing appearances. All living and material forms are but the shadows of this eternal, universal self, the underlying identity of all that exists and thinks of itself as divisible:

If the red slayer thinks he slays,
   Or if the slain thinks he is slain,
They know not well the subtle ways
   I keep, and pass, and turn again.

Far and forgot to me is near;
   Shadow and sunlight are the same;
The vanished gods to me appear;
   And one to me are shame and fame.

They reckon ill who leave me out;
   When me they fly, I am the wings;
I am the doubter and the doubt,
   And I the hymn the Brahmin sings.

The strong gods pine for my abode,
   And pine in vain the sacred Seven;
But then, meek lover of the good!
   Find me, and turn thy back on heaven.

–[Brahma]

Emerson, the chief celebrant of individuality and self-reliance, is thus the foremost teacher of the eternal unity and of the essential identity of the individual self with the over-soul, the universal self. This dual aspect poses no problem or contradiction for Transcendentalism, which sees a complementarity, a harmony, of the individual and the universal.

The effect of Emerson's early address, *The American Scholar*, was electric. Dr. Oliver Wendell Holmes called it "our intellectual Declaration of Independence." And writing from Scotland, Emerson's youthful inspirer and lifelong friend, Thomas Carlyle, was characteristically effusive:

> My friend! you know not what you have done for me there. . . . Lo, out of the West comes a clear utterance, clearly recognizable as a *man's* voice, and I *have* a kinsman and a brother: God be thanked for it. I could have wept to have read that speech; the highly melody of it went tingling through my heart. . . . But for you, my dear friend, I say and pray heartily: May God grant you strength; for you have a *fearful* work to do! Fearful I call it; and yet is great, and the greatest.

Carlyle's description of Emerson's work as fearful was realized the following year when Emerson delivered yet another "Declaration of Independence," this a declaration of spiritual emancipation from all Christian dogma, including rejection of the special revelation of the Bible, the miracles of Christ or any notion that Jesus was any more or less than any other human soul. He chose as his stage for this deliverance the senior class lecture of the Harvard Divinity School in July 1838. When he had finished, many of the graduating seniors were enthralled, becoming Emersonian free religionists for life; but the faculty was so scandalized that Emerson was barred from further invitations for the next thirty years.

Emerson was deeply spiritual and profoundly mystical in his own way; he was never iconoclastic in the style of Thomas Paine or Robert Ingersoll, or even given to the bluntness of his younger colleague in the Unitarian ministry, the celebrated abolitionist Theodore Parker. Nevertheless, by the time he had completed his address and sat down, it was clear that this former parish minister, scion of many generations of Puritan divines, had broken from even the advanced liberal Christianity of Unitarian Harvard. The Christian scripture had no inherent authority, Emerson said, except as a record of the struggle of good people in an earlier age to know deity. But there revelations had no sovereignty over us. The Christ is not confined to a Galilean teacher who lived two thousand years ago, however great the man of Nazareth may have been. God is incarnated in every human face that shines with the inward light of creation. The doctrine of special revelation and miracle beggars the perpetual miracle of nature itself.

These themes, which were to effect a spiritual revolution in nineteenth-century America, had been foreshadowed in the oration of the previous summer, *The American Scholar*. In that address Emerson had decried the idea that there can be one holy book, authoritative for all time. "Each age," he declared, "must write its own books. . . . The books of an older period will not fit this." He saw a "great mischief" in venerating ancient books:

> The sacredness which attaches to the act of creation, the act of thought is transferred to the record. The poet chanting was felt to be a divine man: henceforth the chant is divine also. The writer was a just and wise spirit: henceforth it is settled the book is perfect; as love of the hero corrupts into worship of his statue. . . . The sluggish and perverted mind of the multitude, . . . having once received this book, stands upon it, and makes an outcry if it is disparaged. . . . Meek young men grow up in libraries, believing it their duty to accept the views which Cicero, which Locke, which Bacon, have given; forgetful that Cicero, Locke, and Bacon were only young men in libraries when they wrote these books.

These early addresses have none of the random luxuriance of the later Emerson, the renowned lecturer who had to live up to popular expectation to startle audiences with a hundred breathtaking oracles every evening. The style of the early Emerson is clear and orderly, and yet it exhibits the freedom and grace of the poet and original thinker.

But to call Emerson original, to see him as the John Hancock of American cultural independence, is not to question his intellectual heritage. He was deeply immersed in European literature and philosophy and in the scriptures and philosophies of India and the Far East. He was free to invent the future because he had traveled so masterfully through the artifacts of the past without being shackled to that history. American Transcendentalism was a native free-form expression of the Transcendentalist philosophy then ascendent in Germany and Britain. As Emerson had said, its roots were in Kant, but Americans had borrowed their seed of this variable species as it had flowered in Wordsworth and Coleridge. Coleridge's romantic and Platonized mutation of Kant's idealism in particular became the variation cultivated in New England. When Coleridge's popular *Aids of Reflection* was dubbed the "Old Testament" of Transcendentalism, it was only a matter of time before Emerson's first-published work, a little book entitled *Nature* (1836), would be celebrated as the "New Testament" of the emerging philosophy that many referred to simply as "the Newness."

In his 1842 lecture, *The Transcendentalist*, Emerson attempted to draw the boundary between the two great schools of thought that he believed had divided human thought between them:

> What is popularly called Transcendentalism among us, is Idealism; Idealism as it appears in 1842. As thinkers, mankind has ever been divided into two sects, Materialists and Idealists; the first class founded on experience, the second on consciousness; the first class beginning to think from the data of the senses, the second class perceive that the senses are not final, and say, the senses give us representations of things, but what are the things themselves, they cannot tell. The materialist insists on the fact, on history, on the force of circumstances and the animal wants of man; the idealist on the power of Thought and Will. . . . These two modes of thinking are both natural, but the idealist contends that his way of thinking is in the higher nature. He concedes all that the other affirms, admits the impression of sense, admits their coherency, their use and beauty, and then asks the materialist for his grounds of assurance that things are as his senses represent them.

In developing his case Emerson demonstrates considerable powers of logic and rational argument–abilities he is often accused of having only in small measure. He pursues his thesis cogently, with the skill of an accomplished debater:

> The idealist . . . does not deny the sensuous fact: by no means; but he will not see that alone. He does not deny the presence of this table, this chair, and the walls of this room, but he looks at these things as the reverse side of the tapestry, as the *other end*, each being a sequel or completion of a spiritual fact which nearly concerns him. This manner of looking at things transfers every object in nature from an independent and anomalous position without there, into the consciousness. Even the materialist Condillac, perhaps the most logical expounder of materialism, was constrained to say, Though we should soar into the heavens, though we should sink into the abyss, we never go out of ourselves; it is always our own thought that we perceive! What more could an idealist say?

In taking up "the Newness," Emerson and the other young philosophers of his circle, prompted by the slightly senior Alcott, were abandoning the empirical and realist tradition that had dominated British and American thought from the precursors of Locke through the times of Voltaire and Jefferson. The empirical philosophy and its Realist and Common Sense schools of ethics had been a progressive and liberating force in religion, government, and science. But in Transcendentalism its most advanced disciples were arrayed against it. Yet this was no conservative reaction. The young rebels saw themselves as completing a revolution that their fathers had left unfinished. Boston Unitarianism, the most liberal and free-thinking of religious sects, was a halfway house of compromise. The American system of government remained an uneasy mixture of democracy and privilege, of individual rights and legally enforced slavery. Transcendentalism could not rest easily while involuntary servitude existed. Women were not free, as Margaret Fuller and Elizabeth Peabody were sure to remind their Transcendentalist colleagues—although Bronson Alcott and his radical pedagogues were already in the right on the issue of the emancipation and education of women. The new idealism represented itself as a more consistent and coherent gospel of spiritual democracy and free religion than the older rationalism and Jeffersonian deism.

Emerson could credit Kant with the "profoundness" and

"precision" of his system; but as Trancendentalism developed as a living philosophy in America, it assumed the free form of a rambling rose clamoring over the trellises of New England cottages and mansions. Emerson himself was the source of much of the poetry, mysticism, and moral fervor of the New England variant. There was much more of Emerson than of Kant in this new growth. What was a logical deduction in Kant becomes a burning bush of divine fire in Emerson. Revelation is ordinary, or more adequately expressed, the ordinary is elevated to the level of divinity. What you and I are at our human best–in Emerson's terminology as *men*–is nothing less than the actuality of God. The supernatural is naturalized in Emerson and takes its abode in the commonplace. As Whitman, an early disciple of Emerson, would express it:

> Why, who makes much of a miracle?
> As to me I know of nothing else but miracles, . . .
> To me every hour of the light and the dark is a miracle,
> Every cubic inch of space is a miracle.
> Every square yard of the surface of the earth
> is spread with the same,
> Every foot of the interior swarms with the same.

Emerson understood clearly enough that familiarity deprives us of this sense of the *holiness* and mystery of the immediate and the commonplace. He recognized that the far away, the long ago, the inaccessible and the unknown are invested with qualities of sanctity and divinity. He saw the destructiveness of such a view as it deprecates the human and the knowable.

Emerson is our national sage–a New World oracle of Delphi, New England Lao Tze and American Carlyle combined. That such a claim may at first appear excessive does not deprive it of validity. Its reasonableness, indeed its inevitable recognition, becomes obvious when we measure the expanse of Emerson's influence upon our spiritual and intellectual development as a people.

On the first page of his first small volume, *Nature*, he sounded the keynote that was to remain the motif of his thought. In that justly celebrated passage he wrote: "If the stars should appear one night in a thousand years, how men would believe and adore; and preserve for many generations the remembrance of the city of God which had been shown! But every night come out these envoys of beauty, and light the universe with their admonishing smile."

His unequaled influence over American culture, still far from spent, can only be explained by the scope and force of his unmeasured originality. He was a star of the first magnitude; and when a thousand years have passed, our descendants will still wonder at this prodigy that at America's creation illumined the dawn as if at noonday.

13

Ear Trumpet and Ram's Horn:

Harriet Martineau

(1802–1876)

Students of American intellectual history sometimes remember her as an English journalist who wrote an unflattering description of life in the United States during the 1830s. Nevertheless, Harriet Martineau paid American democracy the high compliment of taking its values seriously. An avowed atheist in her mature years, she was an audacious seeker and skeptic who upheld the ideal of the free mind in a century of scientific discovery and religious doubt.

One of the most celebrated but controversial figures of her century, she was sought after by cabinet ministers for her views on political economy, lionized by high society as a prolific and popular writer, gaped at by crowds as a radical abolitionist, and vilified everywhere as an atheist. Standing today as a prime symbol of the struggle for the equality of women, Harriet Martineau would nevertheless be remembered as a force for human freedom and dignity, even if she had never penned a sentence on women's rights. Her career remains a monument to woman as citizen, social critic, and moral reformer–and to men and women alike as persevering freethinker and apostle of liberty.

Her accomplishments were achieved in spite of handicaps graver than those normally imposed on one of her sex. Her physical disabilities and illnesses alone would have blocked the development of a less stalwart will. Born without a sense of smell and very little of taste, she developed progressive deafness that became debilitating by the age of twelve. Suffering chronic dyspepsia in childhood, she was forced to drink milk–to which she was clearly allergic–since medical opinion then supported the popular wisdom that milk was good for children.

When in 1834 this Englishwoman stepped ashore for a two-year American tour, she was already famous. Ear trumpet in hand, she embarked on an arduous expedition that took her throughout the settled regions of the United States, through the East, New England, the Old Northwest, the deep South, and Mississippi valley, crossing and recrossing large regions of frontier America. She bumped along buffalo and Indian roads so rugged that the stage seemed certain to overturn, over hills so steep that male passengers were required to alight from the coach to walk, and across streams so deep that women passengers as well as men had to abandon the conveyance and walk on log footpaths. Making such a night crossing on the southern frontier, Harriet mistook a shadow for the footpath and marched headlong into water up to her waist. Returned to the coach on the far side of the stream, she sat in wet garments smiling at what a ridiculous figure she must have made by her midnight attempt to walk on water.

Her American visit gave the thirty-two-year-old foreign observer ample opportunity to reflect on issues that were to occupy her intellect and conscience until the end of her life: democracy and ethical progress, science and economics, the abolition of slavery, women's rights, and the troublesome question of religion in relation to superstition, intellectual freedom and social justice. To her mind, these never were divisible issues; they all were parts of the same struggle.

In midlife she recollected that during childhood she had

been far more religious than her parents had realized, or perhaps would have desired. But by the time of her American tour, she was already very much a seeker of truth and a freethinker, although still identifying her belief as Christianity purged of its historic superstitions. But in fact there remained nothing distinctively Christian about her religious philosophy, and within a decade she would discard even the vestiges of her earlier creed. By slow but steady steps she evolved from the pious child who communed unselfconsciously with God into the mature woman who fulfilled her spiritual nature through a passionate commitment to science and progress as she understood them, and particularly as they were interpreted by the Positive Philosophy of Auguste Comte.

But at the time of her American visit, her discovery of Comte and his Religion of Humanity was still far in the future. As a young woman, she had revised the Unitarian Christianity of her upbringing into an advanced form of deism, free from belief in miracle or special revelation, a belief that would have commended itself to Voltaire or Jefferson. Indeed, her intellectual development roughly duplicated what Jefferson and other deists had undergone during the previous century. The same thinkers who had influenced Jefferson's mature views on religion–David Hartley and Joseph Priestley in particular–were decisive in shaping Harriet's free thought. But she never stopped where her teachers left off; there was always an unknown (and usually forbidden) region to enter and explore.

Everything she observed and questioned in the course of her sojourn in the United States was viewed in the light of a liberating moral vision; yet she was still as intensely "religious" as the child she once was. Only the content and form of her spiritual passion had changed.

It is clear from *Society in America*, her three-volume study of life in the United States, written in 1837 the year following her return to England, that in her thinking religion had become a metaphor of the moral life. Moral development stimulates the evolution of religious thought, she wrote, not–

as is usually assumed–morality simply following religion. This view anticipated Robert Ingersoll's axiom, stated more than a generation later, "A just God is the noblest work of man." She would also have approved Ingersoll's adage, "Hands that help are holier by far than lips that pray."

Long before her American visit, she had given up praying, together with belief in "free will" and miracles. Like many other rationalists from Democritus to Mark Twain, she became convinced that nothing happens by chance–not even an act of will. To be free, as Spinoza argued, is simply to be unbound by external restraint and thus to act in response to the inner working of the mind, "according to nature." We cannot be other than what we are.

Those who reject this line of reasoning regard determinists as illogical or self-contradictory when they profess to be devoted to ideas of human freedom and dignity. Not so, the determinist philosopher replies. There is no contradiction. The laws of necessity remove behavior from the realm of caprice and chaos, placing it on the firm ground of an orderly nature. Thus Spinoza and other determinists put great emphasis on education–on instilling in the child a love of justice and right. To act according to reason is true freedom; it is to know and act upon the deepest wisdom to be derived from our natures as thinking and social beings. An early expression of behaviorist psychology is recognizable in this philosophy. We punish criminals–or better yet, we strive to rehabilitate them through reeducation in order that they may internalize the desire to act in socially desirable ways.

One of Martineau's biographers, displaying an unprofessional disdain for the "strange sect" of her upbringing–together with an appalling ignorance of Unitarianism's intellectual history–declared: "It was not, of course, to be expected that the somewhat vague tenets of Unitarianism could continue to satisfy so intellectual a person as Harriet. She replaced it by 'necessitarianism'–a doctrine 'the truth of which is so irresistible that, when once understood, it is adopted as a matter of course,' she tells us."

But the biographer was mistaken in supposing that her

"necessitarian" philosophy represented a break from her inherited faith, which in fact she continued to profess for some years afterward. As we saw in our study of Jefferson, the greatest of English Unitarian theologians and scientists had been Joseph Priestley, a forceful exponent of both necessitarianism and materialism, positions he was able to reconcile with his formulation of Unitarian theology–much to the dismay of American Unitarians who, reflecting a different intellectual history, were generally committed to the doctrine of free will.

Lant Carpenter, Unitarian minister and headmaster of Harriet's school, had placed in the hands of his young student the works of Priestley and Hartley, and from these masters she had taken the essentials of her moral and metaphysical philosophy. To understand her intellectual situation, we must recognize that the more radical Unitarians of the early nineteenth century, together with the deists who were not always distinguishable from them, represented the most "advanced" party of religious rationalists, except for the avowed atheists who in English-speaking countries were quite few and usually intimidated into silence. Under these circumstances, we should not be surprised to find freethinkers and skeptics assuming the protective coloration of deism, and of Unitarian Christianity–much to the chagrin and embarrassment of more conservative and socially respectable members of the faith. That the charge of skepticism was more than the slander of their orthodox detractors can be seen in the subsequent histories of many members of this circle and in the steady evolution of Unitarian institutions toward agnosticism and humanism.

William Johnstone Fox, M.P., who in Moncure Conway's appraisal, "for forty years made the South Place pulpit famous," was conspicuous among this number–and Fox was crucial to Harriet Martineau's development as her mentor, supportive critic, and sole publisher during the first discouraging years of her writing career. Upon becoming the minister of London's South Place Chapel (now the South Place Ethical Society) in 1816, Fox insisted that the bond of union be altered to make dedication to "virtue" rather than theological belief the prerequisite of membership. This bold break with customary church discipline was made a generation before Emerson's call for "a church of moral science" and sixty years prior to the accomplishment of that dream in the founding of Felix Adler's Society for Ethical Culture in New York. Throughout his long ministry at South Place, Fox championed a bold philosophy of intellectual freedom that set no limit to the free exercise of reason. Becoming editor of the Unitarian publication, the *Monthly Repository*, he opened its pages to expression of social and theological liberalism, and it was in this periodical that Harriet Martineau saw her first articles and stories in print.

It is hardly surprising that Harriet, still in her twenties, evolved rapidly into a dauntless questioner and critic. She soon dared to doubt that human understanding had fathomed the existence or attributes of God. Most of those who have written about her life have accepted the prevailing opinion that she remained a Christian believer until a physical and spiritual crisis in the early 1840s prompted her to begin a slide into doubt that resulted in her becoming an atheist by the end of the decade.

But actually her spiritual development towards free thought came earlier despite the fact that she adapted the word "christian" (often written lower case) to her purposes.

By the time of her American visit, 1834–36, she was judging issues and religious doctrines from a rationalist standpoint. While she still believed in the immortality of the soul–although not in physical resurrection–she based this conviction on the argument that belief in personal immortality is virtually universal. By this reasoning, she echoed earlier Unitarian and deistic opinion, which would have gratified Franklin or Paine. But by the age of forty she had given up this last remnant of traditional belief and accepted the thought that this life is the totality of human existence, quite sufficient in and for itself.

Our evidence for dating back to the mid-1830s the dawning of her skepticism is to be found in *Society in America*. Devoting almost one hundred pages of the third and final volume to religion in the United States, mixed with her reflections on religion generally, she speaks of God as "the unknown" and the "assumed First Cause." Here she presses her argument that religion springs from morality–echoing W. J. Fox and anticipating Matthew Arnold. Opening her reflections with her own definition of religion:

> In its widest sense, "the tendency of human nature to the Infinite:" and its principle is manifested in the pursuit of perfection in any direction whatever . . . It is in this widest sense that some speculative atheists have been religious men; religious in their efforts after self-perfection; though unable to personify their conception of the Infinite.

Was she already beginning to speculate along these lines or only defending others who might be inclined to doubt or deny the personality of God? She does not spell out her opinion, and perhaps did not recognize how far she had moved toward the "atheistic" materialism that fourteen years later she would avow at the cost of losing many friendships and even family bonds.

Whether or not she foresaw clearly how far her advancing views would take her, the direction of her future course is discernible in every passage of *Society in America* dealing with religion. Having defined religion "in the widest sense," she proceeded to offer a definition in "a somewhat narrower sense": it is "the relation which the highest human sentiments bear toward an infinitely perfect Being." And adding for emphasis:

> There can be no further narrowing than this. Any account of religion which restricts it within the boundaries of any system, which connects it with any mode of belief, which implicates it with hope of reward or fear of punishment, is low and injurious, and debases religion into superstition.

She continued to go to church, usually seeking out the Unitarian church wherever it existed in American cities she visited, depicting herself as a Unitarian and Christian. At this stage of her intellectual development, she retained Christianity by stripping it of its historic errors without always being specific in identifying what she considered those errors to be. As a Unitarian, she would, of course, have regarded the doctrine of the Trinity, the deity of Christ, the orthodox conception of redemption, and the existence of an everlasting hell as superstitious. But she goes beyond this, stripping historic Christianity of every doctrine that supports belief in a divinely favored mission or destiny. After having been shorn of its "corruptions," Christianity is reconceived in her thinking as the Revolutionary-Enlightenment doctrine of human rights, grounded in natural law:

> The Christian religion is specified as being the highest fact in the rights of man from its embodying (with all the rest) the principle of natural religion–that religion is at once an individual, an universal, and an equal concern. In it may be found a sanction of all just claims of political and social equality; for it proclaims, now in music and now in thunder–it blazons, now in sunshine and now in lightning,–the fact of the natural equality of men. In giving forth this as its grand doctrine, it is indeed "the root of all democracy," the root of the maxim (among others) that among the inalienable rights of all men are life, liberty, and the pursuit of happiness. The democracy of America is planted deep down into the christian religion; into its principles, which it has in common with natural religion, and which it vivifies and illumines, but does not alter.

Thus "the christian religion" is defined in terms identical with Jeffersonian liberal democracy–and with the radical British republicanism and free thought of her age. *Society in America* is a platform for the reformist agenda in Britain, even as it ostensibly serves as a commentary on life and politics in the United States. Although containing much fascinating description of landscape and people and offering many astute political judgments (along with some that are less distinguished), *Society in America* is a flawed book, as its author makes it a complex hybrid: part journal, part political tract, part economics textbook, part travelogue, part philosophical treatise–and throughout, a three-volume nonstop sermon. As a literary achievement, the whole is considerably less than the sum of its parts. Nevertheless it is a document of the times providing an inexhaustible mine of artifacts of its period. Among its most acute and fascinating portions are the ninety-eight pages of the section "Religion in America."

Viewing popular religion in America as a mass of superstition masking social indifference and injustice, with rare exceptions, she found ministers of every denomination, including her own, deficient in moral commitment. Watching them walk with their eyes closed to the enormity of slavery, she recorded:

> It appears to me that the one thing in which the clergy of every kind are fatally deficient is faith; that faith which would lead them, first, to appropriate all truth, fearlessly and unconditionally; and then to give it as freely as they have received it. They are fond of apostolic authority. What would Paul's ministry have been if he had preached on everything but idolatry at Ephesus, and licentiousness at Corinth? . . . If he had stopped short from the expediencey of not dividing a household against itself, in case such should be the consequence of giving true principles to the air; if, dreading to break up the false peace of successful lucre and overbearing profligacy, he had confined himself to speculations like those with which he won the ear of the Athenians, carefully avoiding any allusions to Diana at Ephesus and temperance and judgment to come at Corinth, what kind of an apostle would he have been? Very like the American clergy of the nineteenth century.

One group in America was preaching "judgment to come," a judgment to be rendered not at Corinth, but at places with such names as Antietam, Gettysburg, Richmond, Vicksburg, Atlanta, and Appomattox. It is to Martineau's everlasting credit that she openly acknowledged her sympathy and support for the much abused, vilified, and endangered Abolitionists. Her antislavery views preceded her arrival in America thanks to the militance of her writings. Fearing for her safety, the captain of her ship declared he would not have permitted her to disembark had he known her views. Friends paled on hearing her plan to tour the South. She was not content to stop in comparatively cultured Virginia but determined to proceed to Charleston, and on through Georgia, a state then threatening war to expunge Creeks and Cherokees from their territory–and to send to damnation with ball and powder their Yankee schoolteachers and protectors. This was clearly no country for a meddlesome Englishwoman.

She proceeded through Georgia despite all warning. West of Augusta she found a pioneer land of ubiquitous violence and intolerance. On the road crossing central Georgia to the frontier town of Columbus, founded only a decade earlier on Georgia's Chattahoochee River boundary with Alabama, she heard tales of grudge killings and other acts of precipitous violence. The "West" then included everything beyond the Atlantic seaboard, and the "West" already meant a region where gunpowder was the law.

Despite the rudeness of the country, she was charmed by its luxuriant beauty and bounty. The breakfast table of the crudest, most ill-kept inn burdened under an almost unimaginable abundance of meats, breads, jams, and preserves; and dinner produced an even more glorious array, including "salads"–probably cooked greens, according to the usage of the time–and assorted vegetables and fruits, the hallmarks of the rural southern kitchen, with many basically similar courses and garnishes never considered redundant by the rural folks. Other aspects of southern frontier living were less agreeable. Rooms at wayside taverns were often unclean and ill furnished. Travelers were expected to share accommodations and even beds with strangers. And everywhere was the smoldering violence of an economy fueled by the steady dispossession of the native American and expansion of the forced labor of the African. The trail which would lead Harriet through Alabama crossed the territory of the Creek Nation, soon to be forcibly removed–at great cost in suffering and life–to Indian territory, now Oklahoma.

On her arrival at Columbus, she noted the look of the native Americans, especially the women:

> During the evening, I could do nothing but watch the Indians from my window. The place swarmed with them; a few Choctaws, and the rest Creeks. A sad havoc has taken place among them since; . . . Groups of Indians were crouching about the entries of the stores, or looking in at windows. The squaws went by, walking one behind another, with their hair growing low on the forehead, loose, or tied at the back of the head, forming a fine

> contrast with the young lady who had presided at our breakfast table at five that morning, with her long hair braided and adorned with brilliant combs, while her fingers shone in pearl and gold rings. These squaws carried large Indian baskets on their backs, and shuffled along, barefooted, while their lords paced before them, well mounted; or, if walking, gay with blue and red clothing and embroidered leggings, with tufts of hair at the knees, while pouches and white fringes dangled about them. . . . By eight o'clock they had all disappeared; but the streets were full of them again the next morning.

Leaving behind the pine forests and farmlands of Georgia as she journeyed beyond Columbus, her trail passed through woodlands where fellow stage passengers were always "on the lookout for Indians" actually peaceable and civilized by the time of her visit. They bumped along poor roads to Montgomery and down to the Gulf Coast of Mobile.

If Martineau recognized the injury to the Indian, her conscience burned on confronting the plight of the slave. Southern Indians, or at least their wealthy upper class, owned African slaves–understood at the time as a sign of the native American's advancement to "civilization." Black slaves hoped to be purchased by Indians, Martineau learned, because the Indians were regarded as considerate masters who treated their slaves in the manner of tenant farmers, interfering little in their domestic life and respecting their leisure.

But it was not so with the grasping newly rich of the white plantation houses. She heard of burgeoning fortunes on every hand, all resting on the toil and blood of the miserable troops of black slaves whom she saw herded westward to the slave markets and bottomlands of the lower Mississippi valley. While the polite plantation masters of Charleston and Augusta had sought to impress her by displays of fondness for their liveried and crisply aproned house servants, she had been forewarned not to regard such masters and servants as typical of the vast agricultural factories of the South. Recalling the "common sight of companies of slaves traveling westward," she wrote:

> Sometimes these poor creatures were encamped, under the

> care of some slave-owner, on the banks of a clear stream, to spend a day in washing their clothes. Sometimes they were loitering along the road; the old folks and infants mounted on the top of a wagon-load of luggage; the able-bodied, on foot, perhaps silent, perhaps laughing; the prettier of the girls, perhaps with a flower in the hair and a lover's arm around her shoulder. There were wide differences in the air and gait of these people. It is usual to call the most depressed of them brutish in appearance. In some cases they are so; but I never saw in any brute an expression of countenance so low, so lost, as in the most degraded class of negroes.

Yet she knew blacks free of slavery to be a radiant, life-loving people; slavery was a shocking evil that she felt compelled to drive into the consciousness of every American and European white.

Philosophical apologists of the slave system, including statesmen and clergy, called it euphemistically "negro subordination," representing the system to be mutually beneficial to both races, as one rescuing blacks from a life of savagery and pagan darkness. Theologians found sanction for slavery in their scriptures and condemned those who sought to end the system as rebels against God's plan for the African's salvation.

Martineau had heard these arguments before. She and her English compatriots had participated in the successful campaign to end slavery in the West Indies colonies, a goal accomplished by peaceful means in 1832, just two years before her arrival in America.

On returning to New England following the southern expedition, she accepted an invitation to attend a meeting of Abolitionists. Harriet had once accepted the popular criticism that the Abolitionist movement had acted recklessly to the detriment of emancipation. She believed that no longer. Making the acquaintance of Maria Weston Chapman, Harriet recognized her as a talented, tireless champion of the cause–and a beautiful and resourceful woman as well. William Lloyd Garrison, unlike the fanatic of popular imagination, was a prophet of liberation and a saint of social justice.

The Abolitionists met behind bolted doors in a house before

which threatening hecklers loitered. Garrison had earlier been mobbed, escaping probable lynching only because of the intervention of friends. Members of the mob were discovered to be no rabble, but "gentlemen of standing" in the community. This she noted was a distinction between mob violence in America, whether north or south, and the riots of Europe. In America, it was the "best" elements of the community that knotted the rope and lit the faggots.

The status of women was another anomaly in the practice of the democratic creed. "One of the fundamental principles announced in the Declaration of Independence," she noted, "is, that governments derive their just powers from the consent of the governed." How, she asked, could this be reconciled with the political position of women in America?

> Governments in the United States have power to tax women who hold property; to divorce them from their husbands; to fine, imprison, and execute them for certain offenses. Whence do these governments derive their powers? They are not "just," as they are not derived from the consent of the women thus governed.

"The democratic principle condemns all this as wrong," she observed, but women are said to be subject to the law by long-accepted submission, by "acquiescence."

> I, for one, do not acquiesce. I declare that whatever obedience I yield to the laws of the society in which I live is a matter between, not the community and myself, but my judgment and my will. Any punishment inflicted on me for the breach of the laws, I should regard as so much gratuitous injury; for to those laws I never have, actually or virtually, assented. I know there are women in England who agree with me in this–I know that there are women in America who agree with me in this. The plea of acquiescence is invalidated by us.

Martineau demonstrated the viciousness and folly of the customary excuses used to cheat women of legal equality. She exploded the claims of the "inconvenience" and the detrimental moral and social effects of women's participation in government. In all this she showed her considerable powers of irony in blasting the flimflam of the antifeminist case:

> That woman has power to represent her own interests, no one can deny till she has been tried. . . . The fearful and absurd images which are perpetually called up to perplex the question . . . have nothing to do with the matter. . . . The kings of Europe would have laughed mightily, two centuries ago, at the idea of a commoner without robes, crown, sceptre, stepping into the throne of a strong nation. Yet who dared laugh when Washington's super-royal voice greeted the New World from the presidential chair, and the old world stood still to catch the echo.
>
> The principle of the equal rights of both halves of the human race is all we have to do with here. It is the democratic principle which can never be seriously contraverted, and for only a short time evaded.

She understood the principle of American democracy and of democracy universally more clearly than did most of the Americans who ridiculed this frequently caricatured moralist, as she strained forward with her ear trumpet to catch the murmurings of the future. She made many good friends in America and won the respect of the nation's greatest. Former president James Madison received her. At home on his Virginia hilltop plantation near where Jefferson lay recently buried, the eighty-three-year-old Madison expatiated impressively on American government and society. Also Emerson made her aquaintance. Their admiration was mutual and lasting.

A decade after her American adventure, she made an equally arduous expedition to Egypt and the Holy Land, retracing the steps of the patriarchs and apostles, writing what is generally conceded to be a much better book than *Society in America*. Both friends and detractors acknowledge *Eastern Life, Past and Present*, published in 1848 in three volumes, as one of her most impressive accomplishments, a classic of world travel.

The tendency toward agnostic free thought subtly acknowledged in *Society in America* becomes explicit in *Eastern Life*. The publisher who had commissioned the work was disturbed by her dismissal of Judaism and Christianity as only stages in the evolution of religious thought from animism and polytheism on the long road to contemporary rationalism. Martineau had shown the chronology of the Bible to be in error, a disclosing shocking to the publisher although hardly a novel finding of biblical scholarship. Like other scholars she regarded the Pentateuch as dependent on Egyptian sources for the account of creation. Christianity also had incorporated pagan beliefs in its conception of Christ's divine nature. The giving of the Law on Sinai and the forty years wilderness wanderings were likewise recognized as legend and symbol. She indignantly refused to delete the offending passages and found a publisher less intimidated by orthodox opinion. Surprisingly little attention was later paid to this aspect by critics and readers who accepted the work as essentially a book of travel.

But three years later appeared a volume that changed the public perception of Harriet Martineau, costing her many of her most cherished friendships and causing an irreparable breach between her and her favorite brother, James. Thereafter the name of Harriet Martineau would be synonomous with "atheism." Soon she would turn to the positivist philosophy of the French thinker, Auguste Comte, and find in Positivism confirmation of her ideas on religion and the implausibility of all theologies.

The book that brought public awareness of her apostasy from Christianity (albeit a tenuous "Christianity") was written in collaboration with a prominent mesmerist of the period, H. G. Atkinson, a figure of disputed reputation in his own time, and since dismissed as a nonentity.

In *Letters on the Laws*, Atkinson argues the case for a wholly materialistic view of reality. He took an uncompromisingly atheistic position and ruled out any thought of life after death as wishful thinking, with Harriet enthusiastically seconding his opinion. She had finally jettisoned the last remaining article of her childhood faith. Not only was there no hell, as she had learned from her Unitarian teachers; she now believed there was no heaven either. Her brother James was dismayed–and outraged.

Of the eight Martineau siblings, Harriet and James had

been the closest. Three years her junior, James had shared with Harriet a keenness of intelligence and religious inquisitiveness that distinguished the careers of both. Neither was bound by traditional views, and when James was named professor of religion at Manchester College, the most prestigious position in English Unitarianism, Harriet remarked honestly that the appointment was a mistake; James was not entirely conventional, even by liberal Unitarian standards. From childhood he had read his Bible with a critical mind, "skipping the nonsense" with an unruffled ease that Harriet could not muster.

But if James was more placid in his Bible reading than his sister, he was also a subtler and more profound thinker. Living a very long life which spanned all but the first five years of the nineteenth century, and outliving Harriet by a quarter century, James established himself as a leading religious philosopher and ethicist of his time. Among British Unitarians the number of important thinkers was disproportionate to their small numbers. James Martineau ranked philosophically with the great Joseph Priestley. Henry Sidgwick, noted historian of the philosophy of ethics, wrote his intellectual biography, helping to assure James a permanent place in the history of ideas.

For such a man, despite his love for his sister, Harriet's collaboration with a figure of Atkinson's repute was intolerable. James took an uncharacteristically harsh view of the matter. Harriet, in a wholly characteristic reaction, never forgave him.

When Henry Atkinson appeared on the scene, all the building blocks of Harriet's conversion to pure rationalism lay at hand, ready to be assembled. The office of confidant and catalyst, previously served by her brilliant younger brother—who had always in some sense held her in awe—fell to the still younger Henry Atkinson.

With James in spiritual banishment, Harriet could come entirely into her own, with no lingering censor to veneer her rationalism. James could dress up in Christian clothes if he liked. Harried had passed the point of deferring to hereditary opinion. Even Henry became less necessary as she found her own voice as an emancipated freethinker.

In one respect she owed Henry Atikinson and his fellow mesmerists a lasting debt, and she freely acknowledged it. Much of the scorn felt for Atkinson by James and others can be traced to Harriet's cure by mesmerism. Although Atkinson had not treated her case personally, he had been consulted and had recommended the practitioner who effected Harriet's return to health. After having been bedridden for nearly five years, suffering from an affliction that had been diagnosed by her physician as prolapse of the uterus, she had learned of the cures said to have been produced by mesmerism. Desperate for help, she arranged treatment and responded almost immediately. Soon the invalid was so restored to health that she was walking several miles a day and could maintain a rigorous schedule of work. Her cure was long-lasting and made possible the strenuous, two-year expedition to Egypt and Palestine.

Two years after publication of the Martineau-Atkinson book, Harriet undertook the work that gave her a permanent niche in the temple of intellectual history. Upon reading Auguste Comte in the original French she became convinced that his systematic philosophy offered the foundation for a new age of science and progress. Comte's argument that human thought had advanced through three historic stages–the theological; the metaphysical; and finally the positivist or empirical, the highest stage–confirmed her own view that religion progresses from primitive magic and miracle to scientific rationalism.

Embarking on the colossal task of translating into English Comte's basic six-volume work, *The Positive Philosophy of Auguste Comte*, Harriet was persuaded by a publisher to condense it to not more than two volumes. Despite her recognition that a skillful condensation would be more difficult than a full translation, she agreed to accept the assignment and acquitted herself with such success that Comte preferred the result to his original as an introduction for the general reader. It was even seriously considered to translate her version back into French.

Martineau lived another twenty years after having thus established herself in the world of ideas. Never a completely orthodox Comtist–his worship of the ideal of womanhood offended her egalitarian humanism–she became the veritable embodiment of the Victorian radical democrat and freethinker. Growing older, she also maintained a keen interest in public affairs on both sides of the Atlantic, following the struggles of the American abolitionists through the violent climax of the Civil War.

She aged gracefully and was the pride of the freethinkers and atheists of Britain, who still suffered severe legal discrimination and social prejudice. Despite ostracism and personal insults, she adamantly rejected all religious conventions. The old dream of personal immortality vanished altogether from her consciousness, so that she found perfect peace in the conviction that life, although limited in time, was fully satisfying. When she died in 1876 the entire thinking world sensed that it had lost a great human being. In her own way, Harriet Martineau had saved her soul.

14

Pilot of a Brooding Heart:

Mark Twain

(1835–1910)

The literary father of *Huckleberry Finn* could not have been blind to human nature. The working together of mind and heart was his great gift that made him see all, understand all, and forgive all–all except the cruelty that Twain saw as ingrained in the structure of the world, the fiendish creation of an uncaring deity that was indistinguishable from Satan. He could never forgive that. This dark vision made him use bitter satire; pessimism and despair were real enough. He believed that human beings were condemned to act out an unremitting, merciless fate. Yet he celebrated the dignity and recorded the pain of ordinary people, as well he might–since without dignity there can be no ground for genuine tragedy.

In "Captain Stormfield's Visit to Heaven" Mark Twain relates the tale of an old sea captain who dies and goes to his reward.

"When I found myself perched on a cloud, with a million other people, I never felt so good in my life. Say I, 'Now this is according to the promises; I've been having my doubts, but now I *am* in heaven, sure enough.' I gave my palm branch a wave or two, for luck, and then I tautened up my harpstrings and struck in."

But soon Stormfield's enthusiasm begins to lag and he wonders if this business of playing harps on a cloud bank is all it is cracked up to be. He casts aside his harp and wanders away. And so ends Captain Stormfield's career as a harp-playing angel in the heavenly choir.

One of the time-honored ways to deal with fanaticism and exalted ignorance is to expose it by a blast of satire. Mark Twain believed that irony was the best weapon to dispel doubts and foolish superstitions.

In *The Mysterious Stranger* his use of satire assumed an angry tone. Of the human race he declared:

"You have a mongrel perception of humor. Nothing more. A multitude of you possess that. This multitude sees the comic side of a thousand low-grade and trivial things–broad incongruities, mainly: grotesqueries, absurdities, evokers of the horse-laugh. The ten thousand high-grade comicalities which exist in the world are sealed from their dull vision. . . . Against the assault of laughter nothing can stand. You are always fussing and fighting with your other weapons. Do you ever use that one? No; you leave it lying rusting. As a race, do you ever use it at all? No; you lack sense and the courage."

The "mysterious stranger" of the title is an angel who, according to the romance, reveals himself to three young boys in Austria in 1590. He promises to bring happiness to an old man who has suffered a great deal. The boys learn to their horror that the angel accomplishes this purpose by making the old man insane. When the boys next encounter the angel, they reproach him. He had promised to make the old man happy, but had only made him insane. The angel protests:

"Ah, you mistake; it was the truth. I said he would be happy the rest of his days, and he will, for he will always think he is the Emperor, and his pride in it and his joy in it will endure to the end. He is now, and will remain, the one utterly happy person in this empire."

The angel explains, "No sane man can be happy. . . . Only

the mad can be happy, and not many of those. The few that imagine themselves kings or gods are happy, the rest are no happier than the sane."

Delusion would thus seem the only basis of human well-being. Human behavior may be saintly or abominable, but since there is no genuine free will, there is no cause for pride or blame. Twain presented this portion of his gospel in the form of a dialogue between an old man and a young man, published under the title "What Is Man?"

Mark Twain's answer is uncompromising–man is a machine and nothing more than a machine. This judgment, which the young man considers degrading to the race, is defended by the old man who insists that he is not to be blamed for recognizing a fact. He is merely reporting what God created. The fact that man is a machine is his salvation, because the machine cannot be faulted for the way it operates–it operates according to its make. It cannot operate any other way.

The old man says: "There are gold men, and tin men, and copper men, and leaden men, and steel men, and so on–and each has the limitations of his nature, his heredities, his training, and his environment. You can build engines out of each of these metals, and they will all perform, but you must not require the weak ones to do equal work with the strong ones."

The old man continues, "Whatsoever a man is, is due to his *make*, and to the *influences* brought to bear upon it by his heredities, his habitat, his associations. He is moved, directed, *commanded*, by *exterior* influences–*solely*. He *originates* nothing, not even a thought.

"*Personally* you did not create even the smallest microscopic fragment of the materials out of which your opinion is made; and personally you cannot claim even the slender merit of *putting the borrowed materials together*. That was done automatically–by your mental machinery, in strict accordance with the law of that machinery's construction. And you not only did not make that machinery yourself, but you have *not even any command over it*."

The old man drives home to his point. Not even Shakespeare could claim personal credit for his achievement. "Shakespeare created nothing. . . . He exactly portrayed people whom *God* had created; but he created none himself. . . . Shakespeare could not create. *He was a machine, and machines do not create.*"

The young man breaks in protesting, "Where *was* his excellence, then?"

The old man answers: "He was not a sewing-machine, like you and me; he was a Gobelin loom. The threads and colors came into him *from the outside*; outside influences, suggestions, *experiences* framed the patterns in his mind and started up its complex and admirable machinery, and *it automatically* turned out that pictured and gorgeous fabric which still compels the astonishment of the world. . . . You and I are but sewing-machines. We must turn out what we can; we must do our endeavor and care nothing at all when the unthinking reproach us for not turning out Gobelins."

The young man inquires, "I suppose, then, there is no more merit in being brave than in being a coward?"

"*Personal* merit?" the old man asks. "No. A brave man does not *create* his bravery. He is entitled to no personal credit for possessing it. It is born to him."

The young man counters: "Sometimes a timid man sets himself the task of conquering his cowardice and becoming brave–and succeeds. What do you say to that?"

The old man replies: "That it shows the value of *training in right directions over training in wrong ones*. Inestimably valuable is training, influence, education, in right directions–*training one's self-approbation to elevate its ideals.*"

The dialogue proceeds in this vein as the old man and young man debate the age-old question whether man really possesses free will and is responsible for his actions, or whether his actions are directed by unconscious, immutable forces and influences over which he has no command.

Mark Twain defends his position as not being lawless or amoral; on the contrary, he argues that it is the foundation for a morality by which people can live without the absurdities and contradictions to which he believed the philosophy of free will is subject. Why do we do the things we do? To achieve personal satisfaction. Even the things we do out of idealism, out of love, we do because we are so made that idealism and love are necessary ingredients to our happiness.

To oneself the act must do good first. Otherwise we will not do it. We may think we are doing it solely for the other person's sake, but it is not so, Mark Twain insists.

He framed this into what he called the one law, the one source that determines all human behavior. "This is the law," he says. "Keep it in your mind. From his cradle to his grave a man never does a single thing which has any first and foremost object but one–to secure peace of mind–spiritual comfort for himself."

Mark Twain stressed the importance of what he called "good education," which he understood in strictly deterministic terms as behavioristic conditioning. The good consists simply of such actions and attitudes as produce happiness for others at the same time that we pursue our primary and involuntary interest of finding emotional balance and satisfaction for ourselves. He framed this into a moral imperative: "Intelligently train your ideals upward and still upward toward a summit, where you will find your chiefest pleasure in conduct which, while contenting you, will be sure to confer benefits upon your neighbors and the community."

"Every man is a result," he said, "of two forces. Training and another thing. That other thing is temperament. That is the disposition you were born with. You can't eradicate your disposition nor any rag of it."

Twain hated religious fanaticism, regarding the single-minded orthodoxy of Christian evangelicals as slightly ridiculous, and saying so humorously, in many of his books. In the so-called "dark writings" of his final years, which he decreed should not be published until long after his death, he abandons lighthearted satire and invokes withering scorn of a religion that he regards as both absurd and morally debasing.

The closing passage from *The Mysterious Stranger* reduces Mark Twain's pessimism–his view of divine perversity and human impotence–to its starkest outline. The mysterious stranger–the angel who is now revealed as Satan–takes his final farewell, explaining to the boys that life is a dream; they have deluded themselves into thinking that a reality so monstrous as this world can be real:

> "Strange! . . . Strange, indeed, that you should not have suspected that your universe and its contents were only dreams, visions, fiction! Strange, because they are so frankly and hysterically insane–like all dreams; a God who could make good children as easily as bad, yet preferred to make bad ones; who could have made every one of them happy, yet never made a single one happy; who made them prize their bitter life, yet stingily cut it short; . . . who mouths justice and invented hell–mouths Golden Rules and forgiveness multiplied by seventy times seven, and invented hell; who mouths morals to other people, and has none Himself; who frowns upon crimes, yet commits them all; who created man without invitation, then tries to shuffle the responsibility for man's acts upon him, instead of honorably placing it where it belongs, upon Himself; and finally with altogether divine obtuseness invites this poor abused slave to worship Him. . . .
>
> "You perceive now that these things are all impossible, except in a dream. You perceive that they are pure and puerile insanities, the silly creations of an imagination that is not conscious of its freaks. . . . The dream marks are all present . . . there is no God, no universe, no human race, no earthly life, no heaven no hell. It is all a dream–a grotesque and foolish dream.

The cruelty of the Biblical God was especially abhorrent to Twain; he scorned the special pleading of Christians of his time who contrasted the stern, vengeful god of the Old Testament with the merciful and loving Heavenly Father portrayed by Jesus in the New. Jesus himself was not exempt from condemnation, because Jesus had introduced the idea of an everlasting hell with which orthodox Christianity threatened all who were not redeemed in the Church of Christ. This doctrine drew Twain's fiercest condemnation in *Letters from the Earth*, a work that was not published until more than fifty years after his death. With his doctrine of hell, Jesus had given the world a God "a thousand times crueller than ever he was in the Old Testament." As God incarnated in human form, Jesus epitomized for Twain the moral duplicity–and insanity–of the Biblical deity. Christ, the "earthly half" of the deity, Twain wrote in his "Reflections," teaches mercy "and sets us an example by inventing a lake of fire and brimstone in which all of us who fail to recognize and worship Him as God are to be burned through all eternity. . . . Nothing in all history . . . remotely approaches in atrocity the invention of Hell."

Critics of Twain have faulted him for forcing interpretations on the Bible that are not to be found in the text of scripture itself, but such criticism fails to recognize that his target was Christian dogma as it was understood and preached in the fundamentalist and Calvinistic churches of the American frontier. He understood better than literary critics of another century and a more freethinking culture the moral and psychological deformity wrought by fundamentalist Christianity on the minds of millions under its spell. He suffered that deformity in his own tormented psyche. Twain never threw off the terrors of Christian supernaturalism. Many years after he had repudiated it intellectually, its dark angels continued to invade his dreams and agitate his reveries.

In his earlier years, as we have seen in "Captain Stormfield's Visit to Heaven," Twain was capable of treating the topic of God and an afterlife in a lighter vein; in that period, he made an earnest attempt to reconcile himself to the Christian faith, although even then the crude supernaturalism of fundamentalism drew his ridicule.

Captain Stormfield asks his philosophical friend in heaven if people ever get disappointed, and Sandy replies, "Oh, there are a lot of such things that people expect and don't get. For instance, there's a Brooklyn preacher by the name of Talmage, who is laying up a considerable disappointment for himself. He says, every now and then in his sermons, that the first thing he does when he gets to heaven, will be to fling his arms around Abraham, Isaac and Jacob, and kiss them and weep on them. There's millions of people down there on earth that are promising themselves the same thing. As many as sixty thousand people arrive here every single day, that want to run straight to Abraham, Isaac and Jacob, and hug them and weep on them. Now mind you, sixty thousand a day is a pretty heavy contract for those old people. If they were a mind to allow it, they wouldn't ever have anything to do, year in and year out, but stand up and be hugged and wept on thirty-two hours in the twenty-four. They would be tired out and as wet as muskrats all the time. . . . Those are kind and gentle old Jews, but they ain't any fonder of kissing the emotional highlights of Brooklyn than you be."

"Do you think Talmage will really come here?" asks Stormfield.

"Why certainly, he will; but don't you be alarmed; he will run with his own kind, and there's plenty of them. That is the main charm of heaven–there's all kinds here–which wouldn't be the case if you let the preachers tell it. When the Deity builds a heaven, it is built right, and on a liberal plan."

Mark Twain stands as a towering peak in the high Sierras of American literature, ranking easily among our greatest writers. In the literature of the world he is without peer as a humorist and one of the supreme masters in the genre of local color and idiom. Yet literary criticism has had exceptional difficulty in assessing his rank. Beginning with Matthew Arnold, who saw him only as the vulgar celebrant of a stubbornly crass popular culture, many of his critics were too hobbled by their own aesthetic parochialism to recognize his stature.

During most of the years since Twain's death, critics have taken sides in a battle largely fought among lines laid down by Van Wyck Brooks, his primary assailant, and Bernard DeVoto, the chief defender of his aesthetic integrity and literary worth. With considerable justification Brooks entitled his critical study *The Ordeal of Mark Twain*. Brooks recognized the tragic figure behind the face of laughter. The famous humorist was possessed by a melancholy demon; even beyond the pessimism of most tragic authors. But where Brooks went wrong in his criticism was in concluding that Twain's psychological crisis came from betraying his gifts for the sake of popular applause–and to keep peace with a proper, puritanical wife and his overweening literary mentor, William Dean Howells. Surrendering to these influences, Twain fell far below his capacity as an artist, Brooks argued, and this self-betrayal drove him to despair. But failure to achieve artistic greatness is a hard thesis to sustain against the genius who produced *Huckleberry Finn*. To be sure, Twain wrote a vast library of uneven, rambling fragments that he could not bring himself to finish. But would Brooks consider Shakespeare a failure because many of the bard's acknowledged thirty-seven plays are deeply flawed? Like Shakespeare's less successful plays, Twain's most mediocre manuscripts nevertheless show flashes of summer lightning.

The tragedy of Mark Twain lay not in his self-betrayal as an artist but in a much deeper wound as a human being. Too ruthlessly honest to believe what he considered a lie and too compassionate to be reconciled to an unfeeling universe, he suffered an inner torment that was terminated only by his death. His very power as an artist was propelled by a Promethean effort to wrest nobility and beauty out of a universe that seem programmed for unending cruelty, misery and ruin. He made millions laugh, and he learned early to laugh at himself. But the only lasting nobility and beauty he found hovered in the region between the innocence of the very young and the honesty of the mentally uncorrupted. He was an atheist who, like Job and Ecclesiastes, retained God as a symbol of cosmic caprice and indifference. He professed humanity as his religion, yet his humanism expressed a contempt for human cruelty and cunning that was as profound as his compassion was boundless. The contradiction between these two feelings impaled him. Like many self-educated people of his generation, he worshiped reason, yet could argue that man was a machine who by conscious effort could not modify his views in the least. Twain's mechanistic philosophy of science, in which he anchored his pessimism and moral nihilism, was outdated even when he wrote–and was never the primal cause of his despair. For that we must look to the myth of the vindictive God, a demon more horrid than Satan, whose punishments are always outrageously excessive and inflicted without regard to innocence or guilt.

Of all the interpreters and critics of Mark Twain's psyche, Edgar Lee Masters was the most perceptive in recognizing Twain's religious trauma as controlling and overpowering. Especially after his financial ruin following a bad business venture, the sudden death of a favorite daughter, and his wife's extended illness and death, Twain regressed to the Calvinistic fatalism that had always boiled just under the surface of his consciousness. His most angry diatribes against Christianity, as Masters pointed out, reflected a free thought that never quite succeeded in throwing off his adolescent terrors. It was a bitter joke of self-recognition when late in life he described himself, despite his atheism, as a Presbyterian–predestination and all.

Other freethinkers have managed to combine a determinist, or even a mechanistic, philosophy, with the optimism and good cheer that have been characteristic of humanism. But there is a vast gulf between determinism as a doctrine of morally neutral necessity and a supernaturally ordained predestination that necessarily involves hidden moral purposes and unfathomable cruelties. Mark Twain's pessimism yielded to no logical compromises or accommodations. He was chained to a fate from which he could not free himself–and he insisted on staring into the face of his tormentor. He was a great humanist in the same sense that the deeply pessimistic Sigmund Freud was. Those who sentimentalize about "human goodness" are not the true champions of human greatness. Those who confront evil in its fullest monstrosity and yet remain loyal to humane values are our noblest teachers.

If the life of Mark Twain requires a justification–some compensation for the pain that beset him to the end–it is to be found in the very accomplishment that has taken nearly a century of criticism to confirm: He was a literary colossus who, like other supreme artists whose voices turn misfortune into tragic art, won greatness through suffering, giving to other men and women a heroic vision that he often failed to see in himself and the world he made. For who can read

Huckleberry Finn, Tom Sawyer, Innocents Abroad, Roughing It–or even the "dark writings" of his final years–without feeling a certain rugged but gentle loyalty to the flawed but struggling creatures who constitute Mark Twain's "damned human race"? It does him no discredit to recognize that Mark Twain's greatness was thrown up in the contest to wrest sanity from madness, to call into being a kingdom of the imagination where the sun shines and laughter prevails over the hurt of the wounded heart.

15

First Citizen of the Cosmos:

Albert Einstein

(1879–1955)

It is given to very few human beings to reshape our notions of time and space, to remold beyond man's power of imagination those of the cosmos's structure. Perhaps only Euclid, Aristarchus, Ptolemy, Copernicus, Newton, and Einstein belong to this magic circle. And only one, a contemporary, joined this circle and continues to dazzle and perplex our minds. Yet for all the wonder of his intellect, the world remembers Einstein affectionately as a gentle, simple man who placed human dignity and goodness above all else.

When the first atomic bomb burst over Hiroshima in August 1945 Albert Einstein–soon to be hailed (and condemned) as "father of the A-bomb," as well as creator of the dawning nuclear era–learned of the event on radio while vacationing at Saranac Lake in New York State's Adirondack Mountains. For reasons that will soon be apparent, Einstein had not been briefed on progress toward development of the bomb. He had deduced what he knew from his general knowledge of the progress of nuclear research and from the strict secrecy of the work of colleagues, whose very location was carefully veiled, in addition to such clues as were dropped from time to time by nuclear physicists seeking his advice.

Official unwillingness to bring Einstein into the secret is at first surprising in view of the project's history; for it was Einstein's letters to President Franklin D. Roosevelt, stressing the extreme peril of permitting Germany to be first to possess this weapon, that had made necessary the herculean undertaking resulting in the Hiroshima bomb. Part of the explanation lies in Einstein's own ambivalence about such a weapon, although he had informed the president through intermediaries of his willingness to contribute in any way he could to winning the nuclear race and the war against the Nazis. But the principal reason for holding at arm's length the world's most celebrated theoretical physicist can be found in the government's suspicion of any individual, however gifted or valuable, who, noted for his unorthodoxy and frankness, is considered impossible to control. In making this judgment, administrators and their security officers had a correct understanding of Einstein's independent character and personal values. Honest, earnest, and passionate as he was in his hatred of Nazi Germany–and convinced as he was that it must be destroyed–Einstein's sense of himself as a world citizen and of his self-governing conscience did not allow him to work within the rules of a secret bureaucracy. Even scientists who were much more pliable, including the Manhattan Project's scientific director, J. Robert Oppenheimer, would soon enough find themselves cast into official disfavor because of their untoward reflexes of moral judgment.

Almost immediately and for the remainder of his life, Einstein minimized his involvement in the development of the fission bomb that had erased two Japanese cities and would in any future conflict by his estimate, published soon after the war's end, kill two-thirds of the world's population. That his contribution to the bomb's development had been limited to a single letter to the president, he stated many times for the remainder of his life.

Actually, he had written the president more than once, and

indirectly had communicated with him through colleagues on other occasions. He had also produced technical studies whose application to the bomb's development, while not (at least officially) disclosed to him, left little doubt about its purpose. In addition, there were his numerous public and confidential utterances urging the greatest effort by all possible means to destroy the Nazi regime.

In any case, Einstein insisted that he remained a determined pacifist. In the two wars of his lifetime that involved his native Germany he had passionately desired Germany's defeat, and long before World War II he was an early and indefatigable warner of the peril of Nazi barbarism, pleading that the democracies arm themselves against Hitler. Einstein believed in pacifism as a goal and an ultimate principle, but given the circumstances of Prussian militarism in World War I and of Hitler's Reich after 1933, he set aside nonviolence as inapplicable. Thus, in practice he exhibited a realistic determination to resort to force which, like other humanitarians, he rejected in theory.

He reached this decision at the very beginning of the Nazi ascendancy. It could hardly have been otherwise, considering his personal experience with "Aryan" anti-Semitism from his pre–World War I days in Prague and Berlin and his front-seat view of the unfolding of Prussian militarism and German racial fanaticism as World War I progressed. From the capital of Kaiser Wilhelm's empire, Einstein had watched the Junker generals march out their spike-helmeted hordes, and with a daring that in retrospect seems reckless he made little attempt to conceal his passionate hope that Germany would be defeated. For the welfare of humanity and the sake of civilized progress, it had to be so.

In the years 1914–1918 his scientist friends at the Kaiser Wilhelm Institute for Physics joined overwhelmingly the masses of other "good" Germans–from Socialists to ultra-Rightists–in a national crusade to prove German racial and cultural superiority, to humble the "servile" Slav and put the proud Gaul and Anglo-Saxon in their places.

It is still commonplace to assign to Einstein the role of a

saintly bumbler of wishful thinking, an incorrigible believer in human goodness who could see no evil, hear no evil, and think no evil of anyone. The record does not substantiate this false image of the "innocent." Few of Einstein's contemporaries saw so early and so steadily the future course of extreme nationalism joined to a sinister pseudoscience of racial arrogance, and even fewer gave themselves so tirelessly to warning against and combatting this epidemic of twentieth-century race idolatry. In Marxism-Leninism ideological uniformity and "class solidarity" replace racial purity, but the submission of the individual to the claims of the state and the control of a totalitarian party have similar devastating consequences. Einstein saw this and warned against the dangers from both extremes. Yet many portrayed him as a devoted admirer, if not secret adherent, of Bolshevik power. Yet he warned that totalitarian communism would become a greater threat to peace than unrestrained capitalism because of its greater concentration of power. He opposed giving the Soviet Union, or even the presently weak United Nations, the secret of the atomic bomb. He also urged the United States to continue to stockpile the bomb to forestall possible future use of the weapon by the USSR, either to attack or to blackmail the West. He foresaw that Russia would try to frustrate all efforts to create effective world government or other international authority capable of controlling nuclear weapons and enforcing the peace. And he continued doggedly to pursue these objectives despite protests against his views made by Soviet scientists acting under Stalin's orders. So much for the Communist "dupe" or Stalinist "agent" at Princeton! That he also battled against a rising tide of anticommunist hysteria and McCarthyite slander, warning against the danger of an increasingly militarized and nationalistic America, does not compromise Einstein's antitotalitarian philosophy. It rather underscores his clarity and consistency in battling extremism of both Right and Left.

Who was this man, so widely and extravagantly venerated by some, yet so widely misrepresented and denigrated by others? Why were his religious and ethical values so distrusted and deprecated that a fashionable Catholic preacher, Fulton J. Sheen, could publicly ridicule him, scoffing at his conception of "cosmic religion"? Einstein should spell cosmic without an "s," Sheen chortled.

For those born too late to remember him in life, it is difficult to convey the impact Einstein had on his times. From the morning in 1919 when he awoke to find his name exploding over the world press, and retain its lustre until he died in 1955, he occupied a place in the popular imagination that has probably never been approached by any other thinker in history. Only wonder-workers and avatars of the gods seem to have been endowed with comparable gifts. Tens of thousands of people in English-speaking countries–and in Japan–overflowed lecture halls to see the greatest living intellect, and to listen attentively to his voice speaking in a language they could not understand about a subject they were incapable of comprehending. The incomprehensibility of Einstein's mind only enhanced popular interest in him. People tried to envisage "the fourth dimension" and curved space, titillating themselves (and being titillated by charlatan popularizers) with thoughts of looking out into space with eyes sharp enough to see the backs of their own heads, and of such impossible time-machine wonders as traveling faster than the speed of light, thereby being able to return from their cosmic excursions before they had left!

To be "an Einstein" was to shine as a peerless prodigy. From religion and politics to the secrets of the universe, people expected the good doctor to know everything. His legendary omniscience alternated with its opposite. Actually, he was said to be exceedingly gullible and ignorant about all matters beyond his specialization. His religion was "comic" (according to the Catholic cleric) as well as perilous; his politics pernicious and darkly treacherous; his life-style eccentric and his path through the world blundering and odd to those superior beings who congratulated themselves on having been born with a normal quotient of brains.

Reporters followed him everywhere, making every casual utterance a matter of holy writ–and of permanent record.

When Einstein guessed wrong about expected events, when he proved to be mistaken in his opinions, the evidence was taken as proof of incorrigible naiveté or perversity. In the period following the First World War, he threw himself into the movement of a permanently demilitarized world–urging the world's people to swear off military training and service, and to accept prison if need be rather than to march in file or shoulder a rifle, articulating the view of millions that the Great War had demonstrated convincingly the futility and untenability of all future war. Millions had been slaughtered in the trenches and skies of Europe. Weapons had become too terrible, war too costly in both material and human terms. At long last, people had awakened to citizenship in a shared world. Now was the time to end war–now, while the memory of Verdun and Flanders was sharp!

From the beginning of the war, Einstein in Germany, like Bertrand Russell in Britain, had recognized the criminal futility of the conflict between Europe's most advanced nations; Russell had been imprisoned for his outspoken opposition, and Einstein, while not prosecuted, had suffered considerable rebuke. Had the authorities read his wartime correspondence, sent during visits to neutral Switzerland to such figures as Romain Rolland, the French internationalist and peace advocate, Eintein well might have been incarcerated. There is no question that his pacifism was genuine, total, and virtually congenital. His statements in support of his principles were bold, intense, and unyielding. But he recognized the special deadliness of the Nazi ideology when it first appeared and its rule over Europe seemed almost inescapable. Einstein never wavered. He complicated public perception of his stand by continuing to call himself a pacifist, but to the chagrin of his pacifist friends he tirelessly called for Europe to stop Hitler by force, to arm quickly for the inevitable conflict. Thus, whether one agrees with the "total" pacifist of the pre-Hitler era or the Einstein who cast aside nonviolence to argue the necessity and justification of armed might to vanquish Nazism, one must recognize that he drastically altered his position as night over Europe threatened. He changed his position long before it was popular to advocate such extreme measures against Hitler, while many were still willing to accept the Nazis as a bulwark against Russia's Tartar hordes. Let the date be noted: Einstein foresaw the conflagration in January 1933. Indeed, in the fall of 1932, when he and his wife, Elsa, closed their house near Berlin for a temporary teaching visit in the United States, he voiced the foreboding that they would never again see their beloved home. Even after the defeat of the Third Reich, Einstein declined to set foot on German soil. His expressions concerning German national guilt, for the war and the Holocaust, were unequivocal and unforgiving. He did not conform to the image of the unearthly "saint" of popular imagination who would refuse to judge where judgment was required.

Even the infancy and childhood of Einstein were tailored to fit the journalistic impression of eccentric genius. What dullard in school was not told that the boy Einstein had been as stupid as any? He could not master elementary arithmetic, it is alleged. But, in fact, as a young student devouring advanced problems that a gifted relative prepared for his delight, he had been brilliant in mathematics. The very small molecule of truth in stories of childhood dullness seem to have come from accounts of his withdrawn nature and his lateness in beginning to talk. More to the point was his rebelliousness as a Munich schoolboy in the face of dehumanizing discipline–a distaste for regimentation that he developed early and never lost. This memory may have provoked his hostility to German "order" and determined his youthful decision while still a foreign student at the Swiss Federal Polytechnical High School in Zurich, to become a resident and citizen of Switzerland. While he returned to Germany, he never renounced his Swiss citizenship, even though under German law he became once more a German national.

To Switzerland he owed his higher education in physics, his first breath of democratic air, and his first job. It was in Berne, while working as an examiner in the Swiss Patent Office, that the twenty-six-year-old Einstein wrote in 1905 the Special Theory of Relativity, the paper that reconceived the nature of the physical universe. Almost simultaneously he produced a paper on the photoelectric effect that alone would have established him as a major figure in science. When in 1921 he belatedly received the Nobel Prize in Physics, the already legendary sorcerer of relativity received his award not for his epochal theory of relativity but for the discovery of the laws of the photoelectrical effect.

The peculiar judgment of the Nobel Committee is perhaps understandable because of the hard-to-grasp implications of Einstein's two papers on relativity, the Special Theory of 1905 and the equally epochal General Theory, published in 1915 after years of intellectual toil, frustration and final triumph. Although both papers won immediate champions among the world's physicists, others, including some of the greatest names in science and philosophy, remained unconvinced.

Explaining relativity to "the millions" tested the interpretive powers of the most ingenious. Some were as brilliant, but only as moderately successful at the task as Bertrand Russell, Alfred North Whitehead, and Arthur Eddington. Others, less competent at exposition, failed to communicate at all what they understood, while still others amazed multitudes with marvelous disclosures having little relationship to Einstein's conception. Even among the best commentators, probably none was as clear and to the point as Einstein himself. He had a child's facility for vivid imagery–as if carrying about in his head a visual simulator capable (after hard cogitation) of displaying on a mental screen "thought experiments" elucidating otherwise arcane propositions. He came later to believe that he and other mathematical physicists had overestimated their ability to communicate the principle of relativity to nonmathematical minds. But fortunately he reached this discouraging and, no doubt, accurate assessment of the limits of popular comprehension only after he had enriched our understanding with explanations that bring the lay reader about as close to a knowledge of the theory as most of us are likely to get.

Einstein recognized, as certain nineteenth-century mathematicians had suggested, that the familiar view of space set forth in the classical geometry of Euclid is not absolute and under all but limited conditions is an inaccurate rendering of physical reality. Time is not absolute any more than space, and in fact both merge into a single continuum. Gravity, that mysterious force of Newtonian mechanics, resolves into a physical field affecting space. One radical outcome of the relativity theory, Einstein explains to his lay readers, is that "the physical properties of space are affected by ponderable matter."

He never tired of reminding us that there is nothing esoteric in his methods or conclusions. He had simply applied his powers of deduction to account satisfactorily for phenomena that had been observed in the laboratory, but which were not accounted for in terms of classical Newtonian physics.

Those who were bewildered by this new view were naturally inclined to give it a mysterious quality. When people suggested to Einstein's second wife, Elsa, that her husband was a mystic, in amusement she dismissed this idea as absurd. He was very much the opposite. Einstein himself attributed a religious motive to his quest for knowledge, but he explained time and time again that his conception of religion was the very opposite of belief in a quixotic personal deity who engaged in producing "mysteries" to befuddle. "God is subtle, but He is not malicious," became one of Einstein's most quoted maxims. In fact, Einstein's God is not a "He" or a "She" but an "It." The ultimate source of the world in his conception is wholly impersonal; it is an unworthy egotism, a sign of pettiness rather than spirituality, that leads human beings to imagine a god who is concerned with our personal destinies or even with the human race.

When in 1929 his religious views were under heavy attack, especially in the Catholic press, Rabbi Herbert Goldstein of New York City telegraphed Einstein asking him to verify his belief. He responded in words that have become famous. He said that he believed in "Spinoza's God," revealed "in the harmony of all that exists, not in a God who concerns himself with the fate and actions of men."

Our ethical values, Einstein repeatedly explained, are

responsive to human feelings and needs. The Universe, or God, does not provide or guarantee our values; morally we are responsible for ourselves. This does not invalidate our ethics or make questions of human behavior any less significant. The paradise or hell we create on earth is of our own making. Einstein further revealed his thoughts on the relation between religion and ethics in a message sent from Princeton to the New York Society for Ethical Culture in 1951 on the seventy-fifth anniversary of the Society, and of the Ethical Culture movement which grew from it. To the Society, dedicated to ethics as the essence of the religious life, independent of all ritual and theology, Einstein expressed his emphatic agreement. After noting the disturbing setback of humane values of the previous seventy-five years, and stressing that science per se cannot determine our values, he concluded: "Without ethical culture, there is no salvation for humanity."

While agreeing with Ethical Culture on the reconception of religion as humanistic sympathy and moral concern, Einstein expressed special affinity for another religious body. "If I were not a Jew," he once declared, "I would be a Quaker," a tribute to the untiring humanitarian and peace-making labors of the Society of Friends.

Einstein's Jewish consciousness was something, he admitted, that he did not experience until mid-life. After the close of World War I he soon became sensitive to the increase of anti-Semitism, which resulted in many attacks on Jews, including the assassination of Walther Rathenau, a Jewish cabinet member of the Weimar Republic. Einstein had reason to fear that he might be next on the assassination list, a possibility widely discussed in view of his outspoken pacifism, his strong democratic socialist beliefs, and his visible connection with the Zionist movement.

His response to these fears was not to become silent but to join again and again with other liberals and humanists in protesting acts of discrimination or violence directed against Jews and their friends. As a result, Einstein began to identify with the Zionist cause, which he had earlier deplored as a throwback to regrettable attitudes of nationalism and ethnocentricity. But in the developing European environment he saw Zionism as a necessary expression of the Jewish community's will to survive biologically and as a culture. To help establish a base for Jewish culture in Palestine, he gave his services in repeated lecture tours, both in Europe and America, to raise funds to support the creation of a strong Jewish University in Jerusalem. In a world in which Jews were persecuted and despised, he argued, a national center in the Holy Land could provide the basis for self-respect and recognition that Jews hitherto had lacked.

But such a Jewish Center, he argued until after World War II, did not mean establishment of a Jewish state with the deplorable trappings of military power and national ambition. Above all, the Jews and the Arabs must be brought together to create a pluralistic cooperative community that could serve as a model for the world. This dream was beyond fulfillment, given the urgencies and antagonisms that surrounded a desperate refugee population flooding into Palestine following the Holocaust. Nevertheless, Einstein never wavered in his conviction that reconciliation between Jew and Arab in a secular democratic state had to be the goal of the Zionist cause.

He remained consistent in his view that being Jewish transcended the question of religion. He did not regard himself as religiously a Jew; but that fact, he insisted, in no way invalidated his Jewishness. Nevertheless, once circumstances and political forces dictated the creation of Israel as a Jewish state, Einstein gave it his support, although he rejected the figurehead presidency when it was offered him on Weizmann's death, and also declined to move to Israel, saying he was too old and ill to begin life again in a new land.

From his arrival in the United States just weeks before Hitler's rise to power in January, 1933–for what had been planned as a brief visiting lectureship–until his death in 1955, Einstein made his home in Princeton, New Jersey. When he retired in 1945, he had been continuously an academic member of the Institute for Advanced Study. Even after retirement, he kept his study at the Institute and pursued, unsuccessfully, the elusive search for a solution to support a unified field theory, combining the laws of gravity and electromagnetism into a single, comprehensive formula.

He became something of a dissenter in the field of quantum physics, in which his own early work had played such a crucial part. Physical theory seemed to support the views of those who rejected the principle of causality in favor of indeterminacy, a view championed by Heisenberg in Germany, and the Danish physicist Niels Bohr–who dramatically escaped occupied Denmark in a small sailboat to Sweden, whence he was secretly flown by a high-altitude spy plane to England, to join his colleagues in the United States in the race against Hitler for the A-bomb. Einstein and Bohr had already enjoyed many friendly arguments in Europe about causality versus chance and were to continue the debate throughout their lives in America. Indeterminacy is only seemingly so, insisted Einstein, a result of our ignorance of more fundamental principles. Not so, responded Bohr. At the level of quantum mechanics, chance prevails. It signifies the fundamental nature of the universe, not our ignorance. Despite the fact that each advance in knowledge seemed to support Bohr against Einstein, the latter never wavered. God, he said, would not play dice with the universe.

He believed in "Spinoza's God" to the end: order prevails; and the cosmos is comprehensible if we know where, and how, to look. Many physicists viewed this outcome as the fixation of a brilliant imagination finally arrested in the thought of an earlier era; Einstein, it was said, had not kept abreast with the development of a science that he had done so much to advance. But who can say whether Bohr or Einstein will finally be vindicated–if there can be a "final" verdict in science or philosophy? Right or wrong, Einstein lived and died faithful to his principles–his "cosmic" belief, that the reality we inhabit is rational: It *can* be comprehended.

16

A Lord Unsanctified:

Bertrand Russell

(1872–1970)

Bertrand Russell proved that if you are born smart, rich, and healthy, you need not cultivate the "further social disadvantages" of being ponderous and dull. He showed also that a philosopher can change his mind, although some members of the philosophical fraternity never forgave him for doing so. With dismaying frequency, he was outrageously right; and when he was not, he was outrageously wrong.

Raised to the peerage on the death of his older brother as the third Earl Russell, the philosopher wore his rank lightly. An ascetic looking man—King George VI thought him most peculiar in appearance—Russell had an indefatigable appetite for life and fun. Behind his smile and witty retort lay a brain that discerned human folly and cruelty and longed "to alleviate the evil, but I cannot, and *I* too suffer." Nevertheless, looking back on nearly a century of his life, he wrote: "I have found it worth living, and would gladly live it again if the chance were offered me."

The twentieth century has been one of increasing mystification in science, obscurantism in religion, and barbarism in ideology. One man above all others threw himself against these specters of his age, providing it with an example of sanity that was as shining as it was rare.

Bertrand Arthur William Russell, the third Earl Russell, was born in 1872 and died in 1970. Even a mind of Russell's vigor and versatility could hardly have produced so formidable a legacy in a lesser span. In his later years he could look back on childhood memories of an aged grandfather who had been the British prime minister during the potato famine in Ireland of the 1840s; yet he lived far enough into the age of space travel to witness the landing of astronauts on the moon. He remembered his terror as a youth of seventeen on being left alone at his Victorian grandmother's table to entertain her formidable dinner guest, the great statesman and former prime minister, William Gladstone; but in later life he overcame such awe for men of power. As a renowned octogenarian, he dispatched the fateful telegrams that provided Soviet Premier Nikita Krushchev with a face-saving way to step back from the Cuban missile crisis of 1962.

He was a passionate champion of human decency and reason; yet he is often remembered only for his negations and disbeliefs. Throughout his long life he conducted a four-front war on the dogmas and insanities that hold contemporary humanity in thraldom: religious and philosophical delusions which rob us of independent thought; puritanical moralities which despise and cripple the capacity for happiness; nationalistic passions which incite us to commit unspeakable cruelties; and ideological fanaticisms which would make the earth a prison. These four horsemen of the twentieth-century apocalypse were the nemeses that Russell fought unrelentingly.

While still a young man, in collaboration with his colleague and former teacher, A. N. Whitehead, he became the most celebrated mathematical logician in the world. Some historians of philosophy have maintained that his name will be among the very few of our century who will be remembered a thousand years hence–perhaps one of a select company of only two or three. Yet, of the millions in his lifetime who admired or hated Bertrand Russell, probably only a mere handful had any understanding of his contribution to the advancement of free thought. They knew him principally or solely as gadfly, critic, skeptic, war-resister, crusader, or iconoclast. He owed his broad reputation to his exceptional gifts as a writer and controversalist. One of the supreme stylists of the English language, whose merits brought him the Nobel Prize for Literature in 1950, he used his abilities primarily to instruct, and only secondarily to entertain.

In the decades that opened the present century, miracle-mongers discovered new opportunity to compound confusion. Baffling uncertainties in physics and psychology provided unexpected chances for discredited dogmatisms to reassert themselves. Irrational doctrines that throughout history have thrived on credulity, returned to virulence. Russell was in hot pursuit of the purveyors of mystification, explaining to all willing to listen the fallacies concealed within the revived obscurantisms.

He refused to see a divine revelation in any new complexity of physics or of logic. On the contrary, many extrapolations that reputed sages made from the new physics were without merit, Russell insisted. Their arguments were logically rigged to produce what they wanted to prove, no matter which way the evidence pointed. Does our knowledge of the way the world works suggest the principle of universal causation? If so, with chance ruled out, we can rest secure in the knowledge that our world is one of order, perhaps of design. But if, on the contrary, we live in a world not based on any certainty, what then? Why, another miracle is installed; we have vindicated "free will," since uncertainty sunders the chain of determinism, making room for choice. Of course, physicists and mathematical logicians aware of the limitations of knowledge drew no such conclusions. But on every hand we see wishful thinking detecting the ramparts of God on every airy pinnacle glimpsed through the speculative mists.

It was Russell's intellectual passion to clear up the muddles and confusions in people's thinking about philosophy and science. His purpose was not to destroy but to illuminate, acting always on the assumption that respect for truth is the supreme value, even if error and illusion are more comforting. To believe something because we find it reassuring was to Russell unworthy of the principled mind. He liked to point out that strict honesty of thought in the intellectual sphere represents the same spirit of truthfulness as the great religions prescribe in the moral. It is not the sincere doubter who is the sinner; it is rather the dogmatic believer who disregards evidence or stifles free inquiry.

Weighing the good against the evil that religious belief has been responsible for in human history, Russell found religion to be on balance more harmful than beneficial. But the worst of contemporary dogmatisms, he said, is Communism, the newest contender in the field of dubious truths. He was one of the first to argue that Communism is properly classified as a religion, despite its professed secular and "scientific" character. On analysis, he reasoned, Marxism-Leninism is a crusading mystical faith, masquerading as a science while violating the very principles of scientific thinking. The church of Marx, authoritatively interpreted by his prophet Lenin and a succession of Soviet popes from Stalin to the present, constitutes the most dangerous fanaticism of the present era, more brutal and insidious than the traditional religions, since new fanaticisms are more virulent than those mellowed by time.

In a widely read essay, "Ideas That Have Harmed Mankind," Russell wrote: "In our day the sword of the Lord has passed to the hand of the Marxists. . . . This doctrine has kinship with the earlier doctrines of the Chosen People and Manifest Destiny. In its character of fatalism it has viewed the struggle of opponents as one against destiny."

Lenin imagined he was an atheist, Russell noted, but Lenin was mistaken, since he attributed to a mythical entity, the dialectic, the role of a divine power directing the course of history. These opinions struck many as odd, coming as they did from Russell, an avowed socialist, and many of his fellow socialists were quick to disavow him. He certainly was no Marxist.

His distinctive variety of democratic socialism derived from the reformist Whig tradition of Britain, not from the doctrines of the Communist Manifesto. As early as 1896, when Russell's first book, *German Social Democracy*, was published, he expressed forebodings about the authoritarian character of Marxist theory, a trait that he rightly predicted would be fatal to the development of a free and open society. Later he was to write that Marx, like Nietzsche, was a philosopher of disruption, and that fortunately, his doctrines had only temporarily triumphed among socialists. The doctrines of class warfare and the dictatorship of the proletariat are particularly pernicious and likely to be sources of great harm.

The problem of power concerned Russell throughout his life; arbitrary and unrestrained, it has always been a curse, and its concentration in a centralized state is an acute threat to human progress. And state socialism provides a cloak of legitimacy for this deadly accumulation of power. Russell's socialism, in contrast to Marxism, was strongly antistatist. Like Norman Thomas of the American Socialist Party in his last years, Russell sought a social model that would distribute power prudently, but Russell came to his position much earlier in his career than did Thomas, and also with greater consistency. For many years Thomas tried to work with Communists; Russell, in contrast, understood from the very beginning that democracy and Marxism-Leninism are absolutely antithetical.

Individualism was always at the basis of Russell's socialism. Capitalism's fault is concentrating power in the hands of a few persons of wealth; to answer the human need for personal self-realization that democratic socialism addresses, the transference of the power of the capitalists to a new oligarchy of commissars and bureaucrats must be avoided. Guild socialism, the distribution of power among workers' associations or "guilds," was Russell's safeguard to this danger. Thus, while Russell, like most members of the intellectual community in which he moved, was avowedly anticapitalist and strongly committed to the British Labor Party, he never idolized Marx but rather sounded the alarm against the growth of totalitarianism, which he saw rising on every hand, especially with the simultaneous advent of Communism and Fascism in Europe.

But even Russell found no satisfactory answer to the problem of how to maintain diversity in the arts and freedom of expression for writers and thinkers in a strictly socialist society. Without an independent press supported by private capital the free dissemination of opinion must languish. Proponents of Guild socialism could suggest nothing better than that authors subsidize their own work!

Russell's anti-Soviet views were not welcome in British intellectual circles during the years immediately following the Communist rise to power. But from 1920, when a visit to the Soviet "experiment" confirmed his worst fears, he refused to mute his opposition to Marxist-Leninist totalitarianism.

One-third of a century later, when the developing nuclear contest of the great powers convinced him that both sides had to set limits to their competition in order to safeguard human survival, he finally moved toward a less vocal anti-Communist stand. Nevertheless, his effort to awaken Western liberals and social democrats to the consequences of Communist theory and practice remains one of his lasting services to human freedom.

As a reward for his painful efforts he was ostracized by many in the British Labor Party and the socialist movement. As a friend confided to Russell, many comrades felt he should not write as he did about the Soviet Union, even if it was the truth, since reactionaries would use his arguments to attack socialism and worsen relations with Russia. Russell, however, saw much more at stake than partisan advantage or diplomatic decorum. He recognized that contemporary totalitarianism represents a recrudescence of the barbarism and mental slavery that had taken centuries of struggle to overcome. He understood that, once installed, the tyranny of the modern pharoahs would not fade away as Marx had so blithely–and wrongly–predicted.

On his 1920 visit to Russia, Russell interviewed Lenin and was deeply shaken by the Bolshevik leader's brutish arrogance, intellectual narrowness, and undisguised glee in contemplating the misery of his defeated opponents. Nearly half a century later, recalling his first impression of Communist rule, Russell recorded:

> For my part, the time I spent in Russia was one of continually increasing nightmare. . . . Cruelty, poverty, suspicion, persecution formed the very air we breathed. Our conversations were continually spied upon. In the middle of the night one would hear shots, and know that idealists were being killed in prison.

He related the bewilderment of a Russian poet whom the government permitted to earn his living by lecturing on rhythmics with the stipulation that this art must be taught from a Marxist perspective. Thirty years later, Stalin compelled Soviet geneticists to explain the operations of the genes in terms of Marxian dialectics, producing a biological science of humbuggery that prevailed until Stalin's death permitted a partial regaining of sanity.

Russell's attitude toward the Soviets was never uncomplicated. He shared with a generation of Western democrats and liberals the problem of dealing with a regressive system that despised and subverted liberal, humanitarian values, yet which became an increasingly vital ally in resisting the aggressions of Fascism. Even Winston Churchill, who had deplored the failure of the Western powers to smother Bolshevism in it cradle, found it expedient to forge an alliance with Stalin, once Hitler, renouncing the notorious Molotov-Ribbentrop Pact, sent tanks across the Soviet border.

But while Russell might favor assistance to Russia to prevent the Nazi conquest of Europe–or after 1954 might advocate accommodation with the Soviets to avoid nuclear annihilation–he never relaxed his opposition to the ideology of Communism or refrained from pointing out its dictatorial and reactionary nature. Communism is a throwback to Sparta, disguised as the new Jerusalem, a regression to primitive tribal absolutism masked in humanitarian costume. Even when in the 1960s he was seen as the leading international symbol of the campaigns to achieve nuclear disarmament and to end the war in Vietnam, he never shared the illusion of many that Communism was "no worse" than Western capitalism, or that the systematic denial of freedom in Marxist-Leninist societies could be likened to the miscarriages of justice of the Western democracies. Communist suppression represents something much more systematically destructive and antagonistic to freedom.

Russell's attitude may be fairly summed up as the conviction that while Communist ideology is one of the major threats to the free mind in our time–and probably will remain so for the foreseeable future–it is not the *only* threat: Even in pursuing the necessary task of combatting its missionary aggressiveness, lovers of freedom must not destroy the basis of liberty in a spasm of irrational, blindly hostile reaction. It is a hard lesson, one that, even properly understood, is exceedingly difficult to put into practice.

But even with the danger of nuclear war not present, the effort to win greater intellectual and spiritual freedom would require a broader vision than mere anti-Communism. The best answer to Communist totalitarianism is not the rabid fanaticism of Fascist reaction or of McCarthyite demagoguery, but the enlightened democratic pluralism of Jefferson, Madison, and Franklin Roosevelt. In Great Britain a democratic social philosophy designed to meet the needs of the British laboring classes was developed by the Fabian socialists (despite the penchant of many Fabian intellectuals to romanticize Russia) and put into practice by the postwar Labor government of Clement Atlee and his chief deputies, Herbert Morrison and Ernest Bevin, practical democrats who harbored no illusions about Communism. Their approach, combining social reconstruction at home with resistance to Communist tyranny, appealed strongly to Russell and drew his support in the critical years following World War II.

Russell's personal and intellectual life can be divided into four major periods, each corresponding to the particular phase of the world crisis in which he lived: (1) The Victorian and early twentieth-century era of European peace; (2) the war resistance and antimilitarist years, beginning in 1914 and continuing throughout most of the two decades between the two World Wars–when Hitler's aggressions finally prompted Russell to renounce pacifism and support armed struggle against the Nazis; (3) the post–World War II decade, 1945–54, in which Russell urged federation of the world's democracies to confront Stalin's expanding empire and use of the West's nuclear arsenal to contain Soviet annexations; and (4) the age of mutual nuclear deterrence, beginning with Russia's development of the H-bomb in 1954 and continuing through the remaining fifteen years of Russell's life.

To a surprising degree, Russell's four marriages fit into these distinct phases of his life. Thus, the years of his marriage to Alyce, the American Quaker who was his first wife, fell within the prewar era, blending easily, at least to the outsider's eye, into the apparently placid career of the young mathematical logician.

The wife of Russell's bohemian, unconventional "second period" was Dora Black, who took precedence over Russell himself in their joint creation of the controversial Beacon Hill School, a celebrated example of the experimental "free school" of the 1920s. More radical than her husband on the subjects of sex and free love, Dora had precipitated a spirited argument with "Bertie" on their first acquaintance, announcing preemptively that when she became a mother she would regard the child as entirely her own; the father should have nothing to say about its rearing. "Then I shan't marry you!" Russell recalled having answered.

But marry her he did and together with Dora developed the theories of childrearing and sex education that scandalized respectable opinion and returned to plague him many years later when he was barred from teaching at the City College of New York.

Patricia ("Peter") Spence, his third wife, married Russell in 1936 and was with him during the wartime years when he taught and wrote in the United States. Arriving in 1938 for a temporary academic appointment, the Russells were stranded by the outbreak of hostilities and the beginning of submarine warfare in the Atlantic.

When, in 1944, the Allies had restored a measure of safety

to ocean travel, the family returned to England. The marriage ended four years later. With "Peter" and Bertie during their American sojourn were all three of Russell's children. Conrad, only a baby when they sailed in 1938, was Russell's son by "Peter". John and Kate, his two older children, by Dora, joined them during the summer of 1939 for a visit with plans to return to England for the opening of the fall term of school. Hitler's invasion of Poland on September 1, 1939, frustrated this intention, requiring Russell to enroll seventeen-year-old John and fifteen-year-old Kate in the University of California at Los Angeles, where he was then teaching.

Russell's fourth and final marriage, to Edith Finch, who like Alyce was American, took place in 1952, when Russell's views on marriage had become more conservative. In subsequent years Russell came to place a higher value on permanence in marriage than he had at any time since his divorce from Alyce more than thirty years earlier. It was with Edith that Russell finally found marital happiness; she was, he acknowledged, the great love of his life and the much-valued confidant and mainstay of his final years.

As important as were Russell's views on sex education and marriage–views that today seem far less shocking than when he espoused them–his most characteristic and enduring contribution to popular enlightenment was in the field of religious criticism. His views follow in general the opinions of earlier rationalists and freethinkers outlined in this volume. Russell, however, spoke with the precision and authority of a logician whose reputation for incisive thought added luster to his opinons. Lesser philosophers might complain that Russell was always changing his views; but they seldom considered that such change was steadily in the direction of jettisoning metaphysical ballast as he dug through layer after layer of logical fallacy and presumption.

Briefly stated, Russell's philosophical work expelled from mathematics and logic all basis for believing that deductive reasoning offers an avenue to a higher truth, or a path to "the Absolute." Russell showed that even a philosopher as great as Kant had been muddled about the logical foundations of mathematics, as mentioned in our chapter on Kant.

Russell's theoretical masterpiece, *Principia Mathematica*, written early in his career in collaboration with Alfred North Whitehead, his former teacher at Cambridge, provided the reasoning to reduce mathematics to pure logic. Much mystification about numbers was thereby eliminated, and bad metaphysics was exposed as fallacious.

Before World War I most of Russell's attention was devoted to theoretical investigations. His life was well regulated, his concentration prodigious, and his demeanor studious. But the collapse of his first marriage, and even more the ghastly slaughter on the battlefields of Europe after August 1914 shook Russell forever out of the academic cloister. The tranquil years of his youth and early middle age, outwardly placid but often desperately lonely and melancholy, were put behind him; the forty-two-year-old Russell devoted most of the remaining fifty-five years of his life as war protester (including time behind bars in His Majesty's prison), social nonconformist, political and educational rebel, heretic, and skeptic. It is the last of these categories–heretic and skeptic–that furnishes the fullest and most personal portrait of his moral passion and intellectual incorruptibility.

His parents, Viscount and Lady Amberley, were freethinkers, but their wish that their sons be reared as agnostics was not honored after their early deaths. Kate Amberley contracted diphtheria while nursing Bertie's older brother and sister. Both mother and daughter died, leaving the six-year-old brother, Frank, and two-year-old Bertie in the care of a chronically ailing father who suffered from a mysterious ailment diagnosed, probably incorrectly, as epilepsy. Eighteen months later Viscount Amberley died at the age of thirty-three.

The impetuous six-year-old Frank and his younger brother came under the care of their paternal grandmother, the widow of the late prime minister, John Russell. The Russells had been aristocrats for many generations and their family seat, Woburn, remains a showplace among British estates. When Bertie was still too young to remember the occasion, Queen Victoria came to call, and a gratified Aunt Agatha was pleased to record that the usually impetuous little boy made "a nice little bow" and had not treated Her Majesty with "the utter disrespect I expected." Apparently Aunt Agatha was always expecting the worst of the Amberley orphans. Years later an outraged Frank protested to Bertie that Aunt Agatha was a malicious old gossip since she had roundly condemned Bertie's domestic living arrangement of the moment, presumably with good reason.

With the boys' parents dead, Lady Russell took charge of their education, which included a generous exposure to Christian piety. Years later Russell would recall with continuing distaste this early exposure to Victoria indoctrination. Yet Grandmother Russell's variety of religious moralism had something to recommend it in strengthening traits that served Russell for a lifetime. Lady Russell was herself a rebel; in advanced years she left the respectability of Christian orthodoxy to espouse Unitarianism. She presented her impressionable grandson with a Bible, on the flyleaf of which she inscribed from Deuteronomy: "Thou shall not follow a multitude to do evil!" This single verse remained holy writ for Russell throughout his life.

Lady Russell's halfway house of Unitarian Christianity offered no attraction to a grandson who found almost nothing in Christian belief to approve. Its only positive doctrine was the counsel to love one another and that, he noted, was a teaching not original with Christianity and one that Christian churchmen and kings had conspicuously ignored throughout history. He did not know what to make of a religion that teaches the eternal damnation of most the human race, that condones the moral callousness enabling sainted church fathers to contemplate with satisfaction the endless torment of their fellow beings. Jesus was morally inferior to Buddha, Russell declared, because he taught the doctrine of hell; no proper teacher of morality should put fear of that sort into the world.

When asked whether he was an atheist or an agnostic, Russell replied that he had never resolved the question. It is clear enough from his many utterances that Russell gave no more credence to the existence of the Judeo-Christian deity than to the reality of Wotan, Neptune, or the tooth fairy. Yet his theory of knowledge set all such entities beyond the possibility of knowing. As improbable as elves, trolls and angels may be (and there is no basis for assuming that any one class of these putative beings is more or less likely than any other) in strict logic we cannot deny the possibility that they (or some of them) may exist; at the same time we can quite properly deny that there is any plausible reason to believe in *any* of them. Strictly speaking, we are standing on the ground of agnosticism; yet outright denial could hardly add emphasis to our strong inclination to disbelieve. (Merriam-Webster's dictionary defines atheism as "denial or disbelief," leaving unresolved the distinction between denial and disbelief.)

Nevertheless, Russell's systematic logical empiricism saved him from the absurdity (and futility) of trying to disprove the incomprehensible. Facing Father F. C. Copleston, S. J., in what must have been one of the most remarkable radio debates in history, Russell took the agnostic position. The program, broadcast on the BBC's Third Programme in 1948, brought together Britain's most celebrated skeptic and a Roman Catholic intellectual highly regarded for his authoritative studies in the history of philosophy. For the student of theology the exchange is instructive as an example of the subtlety but inconclusiveness of metaphysical discussion. The more interesting statements are Russell's. Copleston set out to convince by rational argument alone; and Russell, to prevail, only had to assert his grounds for finding Copleston's logic unconvincing.

Father Copleston argued the Aristotelian-Thomist case for the existence of a "necessary being"–which Russell met with the counterthrust that "necessary" is a useless word, except as applied to analytic propositions, not to things. Analytic propositions are functions of logic, such as the mathematical assertion that one and one are two. Strictly speaking propositions of this class define rather than describe. "Necessary beings" belong solely to the formal realm of definitions and cannot be shown to exist in the real world of nebulae, tricycles, and cucumbers.

Russell's view that classic and popular "proofs" for the existence of God rest on fallacious reasoning was, of course, not original. With the outstanding exception of Roman Catholic scholastic philosophy derived from Aristotle and Thomas Aquinas, most modern philosophy had been profoundly shaken by Hume's skepticism and Kant's celebrated demonstration of the failure of the medieval proof of God's existence. Kant, as we saw, hoped by "practical reason" to undo the effect of Humean skepticism and to restore a basis for believing in freedom of the will, personal immortality, and God, which he had shown could not be established by "pure reason." But since Kant, European theology and religious philosophy have generally turned to intuition or to faith to justify religious belief. There we must let the matter rest; if metaphysical and theological entities are to be accepted in the modern world, faith rather than reason must be their final resort.

While Russell's attitudes and beliefs with respect to popular religion did not differ from that of probably a majority of secular philosophers, his popular writings made him the target of bitter reprisal, occasioning in our country the most celebrated case of the century affecting the academic freedom of an individual.

In February 1940 while Russell was teaching in California, the faculty of the City College of New York nominated him to teach in the Department of Philosophy. The Board of Higher Education accepted the nomination, appointing Russell without a dissenting vote. City College thus hoped to distinguish itself by acquiring the services of one of the world's most accomplished logicians and certainly the most renowned philosopher of the time. Instead it suffered an academic humiliation that inspired adverse comment throughout the civilized world; except for the competition of news of the war in Europe, rapidly moving toward the fall of France and the beginning of the Battle of Britain, the controversy would have achieved even greater notoriety.

The controversy broke when Bishop Manning of the Episcopal Church wrote a letter to the press condemning the appointment of "a recognized propagandist against both religion and morality, and who specifically defends adultery." Calling attention to Russell's published statement that "outside of human desires there is no moral standard," the bishop asked rhetorically: "Can anyone who cares for the welfare of our country be willing to see such teaching disseminated with the countenance of our colleges and universities?"

Defenders of the appointment pointed out that Russell's courses would be in areas of technical philosophy and far removed from the moral issues that critics found so offensive. The celebrated controversialist would teach only three classes and these were described in the school catalogue in terms hardly calculated to arouse prurient interests: "Modern concepts of logic and of its relation to science, mathematics, and philosophy; problems in the foundations of mathematics; relations of pure to applied sciences and the reciprocal influence of metaphysics and scientific theories."

The Tablet, Roman Catholic diocesan newspaper of Brooklyn, called the appointment a "brutal, insulting shock to . . . all real Americans" and dubbed Russell "professor of paganism" and "the philosophical anarchist and moral nihilist of Great Britain." The Hearst publication, *Journal and American* (later the *Journal-American*), represented Russell as favoring the "nationalization" of women, of bearing children out of wedlock, and of rearing children as "pawns of a godless state." Mrs. Jean Kay, a Brooklyn resident, instituted a taxpayer's suit to block the appointment, claiming to be an interested party on behalf of her daughter (who was not eligible to enroll in the all-male college). Her attorney did not hide the religious motive for the complaint, contending that it was "contrary to public policy to appoint as a teacher anyone believing in atheism." The attorney, Joseph Goldstein, who had served as a magistrate under the previous city administration, depicted Russell's works as "lecherous, libidinous, lustful, venerous, erotomaniac, aphrodisic, irreverent, narrow-minded, untruthful, and bereft of moral fiber." Having thus exhausted the thesaurus, the attorney charged that Russell had conducted a nudist colony in England and that his wife, children, and he himself had paraded nude in public.

In statements to the press and to friends, Russell denied that he had ever run a nudist colony or that any member of his family had ever gone naked in public. The case was argued before a Roman Catholic judge whose written opinion is a cornucopia of religious bias, unrestrained by a semblance of respect for academic freedom or the constitutional principle of church-state separation. Writing his autobiography nearly thirty years later, Russell summarized laconically this specimen of American jurisprudence: "The suit came before an Irishman who decided against me at length and with vituperation. I wished for an appeal, but the Municipality of New York refused to appeal."

Oddly enough, the mother in Brooklyn whose daughter ran no risk of encountering Russell at City College was ruled to have standing before the court, while Russell, the individual most affected, had no standing to testify or to appeal, since the case was technically between the complainant and the City of New York. The City, wishing to dispose of the issue, left Russell with no recourse to clear himself or to confront those who had so blatantly defamed his reputation under the cloak of legal immunity. The outraged protest of John Dewey, Morris Raphael Cohen, Horace M. Kallen, Robert M. Hutchens, Frank Graham, A. N. Whitehead, and many other leading professors and college presidents was contemptuously disregarded by the press and governing bodies. Russell had been widely depicted as a pro-Communist and therefore worthy of any and all outrages he suffered.

Not content with this mischief, his pursuers attempted to have him dismissed from a similar teaching stint at Harvard, already scheduled to follow his temporary assignment at City College. The effort failed, but after the Harvard visit ended, Russell found himself an academic pariah in wartime America, with a family to support and no way to return to Britain. Only an opportunity to lecture at the Barnes Foundation near Philadelphia saved him from total financial embarrassment. (Most Americans, including his academic colleagues, assumed that as an English lord he must be fantastically rich, not knowing that he had given away his inheritance earlier in life out of the conviction that every person should earn his own living.) Barnes, a wealthy and eccentric art collector, soon quarreled with Russell and dismissed him without notice, complaining when Russell took him to court for breach of contract that Russell's lectures were of poor quality. For once, a court agreed with Russell, although the law's delay denied the funds when they were most needed. In 1943 the lectures that Barnes found of so little merit were published (with additional chapters) as *The History of Western Philosophy*, a work that surprised both author and publisher by immediately becoming a best seller; the work remained for many years one of the most widely purchased books in print, totally reversing Russell's financial situation.

Two generations have passed since Russell was denied a chance to teach at City College because of alleged moral turpitude. Those who knew him best stressed his personal integrity, kindliness, and devotion to humane values. He hated and fought brutality, intellectual arrogance, and dictatorship. But what of the charge–even now made against nonabsolutist ethics–of moral subjectivism and nihilism? As an author who enjoyed writing lucid, vivid prose, Russell sometimes sacrificed caution for the sake of emphasis, obvious exaggeration providing levity and playfulness in his writing. His temperamental disposition to be as forthright as possible led him to make occasional judgments that lacked the care of his usual logical rigor. Bishop Manning took full advantage of Russell's lack of precision in citing his assertion that "outside of human desires there is no moral standard." Given the spirit and context of Russell's ethical writings, the assertion is defensible. But in the mouth of a monster or a nihilist justifying his crimes, or quoted by a demagogue to illustrate the "amorality" of humanism, Russell's words easily lend themselves to parody and misrepresentation. Those sharing his ethical perspective might wish he had developed a more adequate description of the nature and function of ethics, since he was clearly no advocate of nihilism or moral indifference. His formulation becomes tenable as the foundation of a rational ethical humanism if we replace the excessively private and subjective notion of "human desires" with the more verifiable concept of human needs, recognizing "needs" as empirically demonstrable in terms of human aspiration and development.

In making this restatement, we are not departing from the spirit of Russell's thought that morality rests upon purely human purposes or ends, but we make explicit–as his statement of the case did not–those features of human interdependence and mutuality that make moral judgments both reasonable and necessary.

Such reformulation removes ethics from the domain of a psychology of purely subjective mental states where preference, passions, and desires reign unevaluated and unrestrained; Russell himself recognized the insights of depth psychology and was acutely aware of the deceit of consciousness. But given the powers of critical intelligence, morality becomes a matter of rational inquiry applied to the restraint of cruelty and injustice and the maximizing of human well-being. In such an inquest, rational good will takes the preeminent position it held in Russell's personal and public life.

Thus in humanizing ethics as in reformulating the foundations of logic, Russell offered a fresh point of departure from which others may undertake worthwhile voyages of discovery, unhampered by absolutist traditions which through the ages have tethered the inquiring mind.

17

Prisoner of Conscience:

Andrei Sakharov

(1921–   )

Religious dogmatism and heresy hunts have been recurring features of Western civilization. The twentieth century has also witnessed these cultural obsessions. It has done so in a new guise, the secular totalitarian ideology that systematically suppresses all spiritual rivals and installs itself as a "historically" mandated orthodoxy. Bertrand Russell made the case for unmasking Marxism as a secular religion and correctly forecast the Marxist-Leninist dictatorship as the most virulent persecutory creed of our time. At great personal hardship and risk, the Soviet scientist Andrei Sakharov, and his wife, Elena Bonner, have confronted this earthly messianic power in the name of the ethical values of humanism, liberalism, and true democracy.

On a day early in July 1973 Swedish television correspondent Olle Stenholm interviewed Sakharov, the legendary father of the Soviet thermonuclear bomb and more recently a celebrated "dissident." Three years earlier Sakharov had helped to organize Moscow's much-harassed Human Rights Committee. Stenholm's interview prompted the Soviet government to expel him and to begin a propaganda campaign to discredit the USSR's distinguished physicist and human rights activist. "But in fact," Sakharov reflected on recalling the Stenholm interview, "what I said was almost trivial."

For once Sakharov, passionately devoted to truth, stated less than the full truth–perhaps a reflection of his genuine modesty and a seeming inability to recognize, despite all evidence, that Soviet officialdom regarded his free-ranging intellect as a serious threat to the regime's firm control and influence. The twentieth century has indeed shown scant advance over the ages of ancient tyrants who feared and persecuted freethinker and doubter. In the eyes of oppressors freedom is a contagion that calls for extreme measures to destroy its dreaded virus.

In the Stenholm interview Sakharov forthrightly described how his views on government, socialism, economics, and ideology had changed. It is "the most natural thing" he explained, to believe that the social system of one's nation is the best. That's what he once thought. But that belief was not supported by the facts. On the contrary, he declared, Soviet pseudosocialism offers nothing new: "It is only an extreme form of that capitalist path of development found in the United States and other Western countries but in an extremely monopolized form."

The Soviet Union is therefore plagued with the same social problems and personal alienation as is the West. He expressed these views many times in the decade to follow, pointing to the epidemic of absenteeism and alcoholism in Soviet society as among the few "freedoms" and psychological escapes open to the populace.

Reflecting on Marxist-Leninist claims that the Soviet society represents a higher form of social development he added: "Very characteristically, we are also the most pretentious–that is, although our society is not the best, we pretend that we are much more."

Whether Soviet society is to be considered a classless society, he argued, is a matter of definition: "It is similar to our past arguments as to what kind of society is to be called fascist." In any case, Soviet society is one "of great internal inequality." A few years later he characterized an earlier phase of Soviet tyranny as "the blood horror of Stalin's fascism," sweeping aside the claim of Marxist-Leninist apologists that Soviet totalitarianism cannot be considered fascist because of the absence of private ownership. In future years Sakharov would have more to say on the fascist character of Soviet society, that the Stalinist structure is still prevalant, despite some restraints on police terror thriving under the aegis of a military-industrial-KGB-party-complex. While the apparatus is prospering, the economy and the people are not.

Thus by 1973 Sakharov had turned from a believer in the Soviet system–he had previously sought only a measure of liberalization–to an outspoken opponent of the ideology of Soviet Marxism. "Our extreme state socialism," he said to his Swedish radio audience, "has led to the disappearance of private initiative in areas in which it would be most effective, just as it has been eliminated in industry and transport. In those areas the state system of administration perhaps makes more sense."

Particularly stultifying is the party monopoly in the country's administration. "Even under the conditions of a socialist economic system," he insisted, "the one-party system is not necessary." It is particularly harmful as it saps the energy and creativity of the artist and thinker. The suppression of intelligence, both economically and ideologically, has resulted in a general anti-intellectualism. Most intellectual workers have retreated into a "narrow professionalism." The damage is especially severe in the humanities, producing a state-sponsored literature that is "terribly conventional and boring."

Despite his unequivocal indictment of the Soviet system and its ideology, Sakharov has consistently opposed violent or abrupt change. Radical reorganization of the state, he said, is "unthinkable." "There must be some kind of gradualness and continuity, otherwise there would again be the terrible destruction through which we have passed several times and also total collapse." In this fateful interview he summed up his stand: "I am a liberal or a 'gradualist.' "

Sakharov's transformation from faithful searcher for Soviet thermonuclear might to the conscience of beleaguered humanity constitutes a story almost too improbable to be believed–except by those millions of unpraised men and women who, without fanfare or public appreciation, have also quietly chosen decency and personal integrity at a price they alone can know. But in Sakharov the world witnesses the rare example of a prince of the realm stepping down from lofty privilege to material insecurity, moral abuse, and physical danger, both to himself and to his family. Like the Buddha, he renounced kingdom and palace, stealing away into the night to search the kingdom of the heart for the secret of its cure. For Sakharov that cure required him to take his place at the side of the despised "dissidents" who challenge the injustice and oppression of the modern totalitarian state.

Andrei Sakharov speaks with authority of the arrogance and corruption of the princely elite of the Soviet state and their technological and cultural retainers. He knows also the millions who must subsist in rural serfdom or forced-labor camps in order to serve the aims and appetites of the autocrats of this "classless" society which boasts its superiority over all other social systems. Yet coming to understand the nature of the totalitarian state, so contrary to its claimed character and goals, could not have been easy for one who enjoyed the highest honors and privileges of Soviet society.

On June 22, 1941, as a student of twenty, Andrei had huddled with his classmates around the radio to hear Premier Molotov announced Hitler's surprise invasion of the Soviet Union. Most of Andrei's friends immediately volunteered or were promptly conscripted for service on the most devastated and bloody battlefield of all history. But Stalin's government declined to put at risk the life of so gifted a student as the young Sakharov, then in his third year of physics. Graduating in 1942, he served for the remainder of the war as an engineer in military production.

Returning to graduate studies at the war's end he received his science degree at the Lebedev Institute of Physics for theoretical work on cosmic rays. A member of a research team headed by Igor E. Tamm, one of the USSR's most brilliant physicists and a future Nobel Laureate, Sakharov was already a key figure in Soviet thermonuclear research. A few theoretical papers followed in scientific journals, and then Sakharov disappeared from sight. Less brilliant colleagues began to be discussed and to establish reputations, but for years it was as if Sakharov no longer existed. Nothing more was heard of him until long after the Soviets had exploded the world's first thermonuclear device (H-bomb). Eventually it came to be known that it was he who had created the bomb. For his achievement, he was given the Stalin Prize and three Orders of Socialist Labor, the Soviet Union's highest civilian decoration, all awarded in strict secrecy.

Material perquisities for high technological achievements were not wanting: a salary of two thousand rubles per month, special housing including a dacha in the country, the right to shop at special stores with choice and scarce commodities reserved for the elite, and a chauffeured limousine–all these were provided to Sakharov as a newly elected member (at thirty-two, the youngest ever) of the Soviet Academy of Science. And, of course, such a valued national resource had to be protected around the clock by personal bodyguards.

From this precocious elevation, Sakharov descended, not by a precipitous fall, but by a succession of uncertain, irregular steps, like a stone tumbling down a terraced pyramid. As early as 1955, enjoying the recognition of his recent accomplishment, Sakharov approached Marshal Nedelin to voice apprehension about the possible use of the deadly new thermonuclear weapon. The marshal brusquely dismissed his reservations, expressing the obedient soldier's view that the authorities were capable of deciding such matters without such advice. Two years later Sakharov appeared in print with an article, widely reprinted in the Soviet Union and elsewhere, on the dangers of nuclear testing. Although he believed that all further research and testing was perilous and should be halted by international agreement, his ideas, officially rejected at first, were finally accepted by Khrushchev as the basis for the limited 1963 agreement banning the testing of nuclear weapons in the atmosphere, the oceans, and outer space.

In a foray beyond his special field in 1958, Sakharov appealed to M. A. Suslov, politburo member and leading theoretician of the Soviet Communist Party, to protest the ideological control of biological theory. Soviet biology had decayed as a science because of Stalin's patronage of the agronomist Trofin Lysenko, a charlatan and confidence man whose touted Marxist-Leninist "science" had dominated Soviet biology for a generation. Among Lysenko's victims was N. I. Vavilov, the USSR's greatest geneticist, denounced by Lysenko for fostering "bourgeois" science. Vavilov was imprisoned by Stalin as an ideological offender and died in disgrace, in what is grimly recalled as one of the most bizarre chapters in the history of science. After Stalin's death Lysenko lost his ascendancy, except for a short revival during Khrushchev's regime–short, thanks largely to Sakharov and other academicians who opposed a revival of the Stalinist mentality in Soviet science.

Entering the controversy afresh in 1964, Sakharov delivered a speech at the Soviet Academy of Science in which he objected to the acceptance into membership of an associate of Lysenko, and he prevailed. The Lysenkoist was rejected. Having escaped its pseudo-Marxist straitjacket, Soviet biology rejoined the world of science and Sakharov and his colleagues had the satisfaction of having demolished the most grotesque idol of Stalinist pseudoscience.

Even before fighting Soviet leaders who supported ideological hacks in preference to genuine scientists, Sakharov had aroused Khrushchev's ire when he introduced his plan to require all students, including the most gifted, to do "practical" labor before undertaking higher education. Arguing the most productive theoretical work in science is done by researchers before the age of thirty–with the mid-twenties regarded as the peak years–Sakharov urged the reverse of the Khrushchev proposal: Gifted students, he pleaded, should be excused from labor in order to accelerate their studies by one or two years to prepare them for an earlier entrance into their specialities.

For this and other initiatives that challenged official policy, Sakharov began to lose standing, although his position as a member of the Academy and his reputation as father of the H-Bomb gave him substantial immunity from the harassments and penalties inflicted on lesser "dissidents." Sakharov saw this difference, which only intensified his rejection of the Soviet "new class." He shared and further refined the insightful criticism of the Communist system that had been made by the Yugoslav, Milovan Djilas.

In the mid-sixties Sakharov drew closer to the circle of dissidents and was soon propelled into a leadership position. He joined with a group of eminent figures in the arts and sciences to petition the Twenty-third Congress of the Soviet Communist Party to reject the rehabilitation of Stalin, a move then feared by many. The petition was successful. Sakharov turned to other issues, especially to the protection of the environment, which he recognized as being of lesser concern in the Soviet Union than in the industrialized West.

In 1968 he finally crossed the Rubicon, publishing in *samizdat* (the typewritten prohibited tracts that pass from hand to hand) a treatise that was to become almost a bible to the Russian human-rights movement. His personal manifesto, entitled, *Thoughts on Progress, Coexistence, and Intellectual Freedom*, appeared in June, just a few weeks before Soviet tanks crushed the "Prague spring," ending the liberalization introduced by the reform-minded Czechoslovak Communist Party and government of Alexander Dubcek. "Socialism with a human face"–the slogan of the Marxist reformers–was not to be permitted by the Kremlin. Freedom, even carefully circumscribed under Communist leadership, was heresy to the authoritarians in Moscow.

Dubcek's many admirers and well-wishers in the Soviet Union were not to escape notice and retribution from the Kremlin. In that hopeful, anxious spring the widespread fear that the Soviet leadership would destroy the Prague experiment in socialist humanism prompted Sakharov to publish his manifesto calling, for human rights and democratization. Within one month of its appearance in *samizdat* it was widely translated and reprinted throughout the world. Sakharov could not now turn back. The dissidents had a leader, who still desperately tried to believe that Soviet Communism could be liberalized, and still hoped to reconcile the social and political systems of East and West. A major thesis of his monograph *Thoughts* held that the two social systems are "converging," and would produce a democratic socialist system with universal peace, and save human rights. Sakharov had arrived at a halfway house that gave him shelter–temporarily–as a professing "socialist."

Official reprisal was not slow in coming. Although he had for some time not been given access to the most sensitive secret information, he had continued to be a nominal employee of the nuclear weapons program. Arriving one morning for work in his chauffeured car, he was brusquely denied entry into the laboratory with the blunt announcement that his security clearance had been canceled. He was given no information about the status of his position until much later, when finally he learned he had been fired. For a year he remained without a post, until the scandal of leaving a most celebrated physicist unemployed induced the government to give him a low-ranking faculty position at his alma mater, the Lebedev Physical Institute of the Soviet Academy of Science in Moscow. He had completed the circle from graduate student to decorated physicist in thermonuclear weapons production and back to teacher in his old school in little more than twenty years.

At the same time he suffered the personal tragedy of his first wife's death. For his political activities he was thereafter ostracized by his two grown daughters and teenage son. Many old friends and colleagues shunned him. But others drew closer. A year after his wife's death he married a physician with whom he was working to assist dissidents who were facing trial or imprisonment or were being held for "treatment" in KGB-directed psychiatric hospitals.

Elena Bonner is a spouse to match the courage of her husband. The daughter of a mother who spent years in Stalin's slave-labor camps, Elena made human rights and the defense of dissenters the major cause of her life long before she and Sakharov had met. Since their marriage, she has been the target of repeated efforts to silence him by intimidation, including an "Arab" terrorist invasion of their apartment, warning her of their destruction if Sakharov did not refrain from criticizing Soviet involvement in radical Arab politics. Like many other ruses of the KGB to scare and occasionally harm human-rights activists, the "Arab" terrorists were apparently agents delivering a warning from Andropov's ministry of secret police.

The years that followed publication of *Thoughts* witnessed a steady evolution in Sakharov's moral and political philosophy away from state socialism and in the direction of economic pluralism. He began to recognize, as Western liberals have long argued, that a tightly centralized state economy must inevitably lead to the stifling of individual freedom and social diversity. Monopolistic state "socialism," as avowed and practiced in the Soviet Union, is incompatible with freedom. It has to be, Sakharov concluded, as he now analyzed the relationship between one-party dictatorship and the suppression of human rights. Democracy and humanism flourish where the means to make decisions are widely distributed. To speak of democracy and socialism where absolute economic and political power are concentrated in the hands of a highly centralized party hierarchy is a mockery.

Marxist-Leninists have forced the march of human liberation into a cul-de-sac from which the only possible escape is a retracing of steps back to a polycentric political and economic order. A mixed system that provides for individual exceptions and differences must be preserved, as Bertrand Russell contended, if the best in humanity is not to be crushed.

A mixed economic system, combining the strengths of a private and a public sector, mediates the one-sidedness of both extreme state socialism and unbridled capitalism. It provides a balance of private and public energies that exists in pragmatic combination in the social democracies and "New Deal" economies of Western Europe and North America. Beyond this, Sakharov offers no blueprint. He has seen enough of utopian schemers who amputate humanity to fit a procrustean bed.

This turn away from the Soviet structure and theory, however reasoned and moderate, was a course that many of Sakharov's fellow dissidents refused to follow. His courageous comrade in the human-rights struggle, Soviet historian Roy A. Medvedev, who in 1970 was a cosigner with Sakharov and their friend, V. F. Turchin, of a second major treatise, known as "Manifesto II," continued to argue persuasively for a thoroughgoing democratic reform of the Communist system. In his book, *Socialist Democracy*, sent to the West for publication, Medvedev pressed the case for a reformed socialist humanism, incorporating many of the ideals and principles of the ill-fated Czechoslovakian experiment. Marxism, according to Medvedev, had been corrupted and dehumanized, but the essence of the Marxist thesis is still valid and should be restored by a democratized party and state. (Roy's brother Zores, an eminent biologist also active in the human rights movement, had his passport lifted by Soviet embassy officials while lecturing in England, a means of expelling an unwanted dissident from the USSR–a lesson not lost on Sakharov and others.)

Sakharov expressed satisfaction in the differences of opinion that exist within the so-called dissident movement. In a 1979 article written for *Trialogue*, publication of the Trilateral Commission, he wrote: "The use of the word 'movement' . . . should not bring to mind any sort of organization or association, much less the concept of a party. We are simply speaking of people who are united by a largely common point of view and method of action." It is this formless stratum of opinion and individual initiative that has given the movement resiliency in the face of government-sponsored disruption and harassment. By resorting to illegal KGB activities, including arrest of dissidents on fabricated charges and the confinement of many in bogus psychiatric wards (on the possibly apparent principle that those who reject such a beneficent regime must be mad), the authorities have managed to decimate and paralyze considerable sections of the movement, but the truths it represent continue to circulate in *samizdat* and to be expressed by those who remain at large.

Elena Bonner and Andrei Sakharov have helped to make the spirit of resistance invincible. In January 1980 Sakharov was arrested and taken to the Procurator's Office, where he was informed that by action of the Presidium of the Supreme Soviet he had been stripped of his awards. Having lost the protection of his favored status, he was forcibly exiled to a house in Gorki, where he has since lived under strict surveillance. A special transmitter was installed on the roof of his residence to jam foreign radio broadcasts. The few friends allowed to call were required to undergo secret-police interrogation after each visit. On Elena, suffering from a serious medical problem, fell the burden of many train trips between Moscow and Gorki to bring medicines and other needed goods–and to supply whatever news of the outside world she could learn.

In 1981 after a final desperate appeal to Brezhnev to allow Lisa Alekseyeva, Elena's daughter-in-law, to join her emigrant husband in the United States (the couple having been married by proxy in Montana), Andrei and Elena began a life-threatening fast from November 22 until December 8. It ended only after the assurance was given to Sakharov that his stepdaughter-in-law would be permitted to leave. Lisa's case was crucial, the Sakharovs recognized, since the government's obstinacy was one of many vain pressures applied to the Sakharov family and friends to deter Andrei and Elena from their human-rights efforts.

Suffering a weak heart–Elena has severe diabetes–Sakharov lives quietly in his exile, refusing to capitulate to a tyranny that he believes menaces the future of all humanity. The struggle for the mind is urgent, he insists. Without the flexibility and tolerance of the open society there can be no social progress. "I am convinced that ideologies based on dogmas or metaphysical precepts, or that those who rely too heavily on the contemporary make up of their societies cannot be responsive to the complexity, sudden changes, and the unpredictability of human development."

Unlike the exiled Aleksandr Solzhenitsyn whose civil liberties he defended, Sakharov does not yearn to reestablish conservatve Russian traditions or Eastern Orthodox Christianity. An avowed liberal and humanist–the sole Soviet signer of *Humanist Manifesto II*, a 1973 consensus statement of humanist philosophy and ethics circulated by American humanists–Sakharov holds to the Enlightenment faith in free inquiry, application of the scientific method for human benefit, and a society open to diverse opinions. "The ideology of human rights is essentially pluralistic," he wrote in his 1979 article in *Trialogue*. "It also offers the individual a maximum freedom of choice."

He has defended the rights of Soviet religious minorities–Seventh Day Adventists, noncomplying Baptists, Pentacostalists, Old Orthodox Believers, and Jews seeking the right to emigrate to Israel–and also the rights of oppressed "national" minorities as well as those of ethnic Germans who for generations have sought permission to join their Western kinsmen, of Crimean Tartars brutally uprooted by Stalin for their Siberian resettlement and who now yearn to return to the Crimea, and the rights of other displaced and disadvantaged groups and individuals. The list of persons and minorities on whose behalf the Sakharovs have raised their voices is long.

He has expressed his moral and intellectual faith succinctly:

> I am convinced that under contemporary conditions it is precisely civil and political rights–the right to freedom of conscience and the dissemination of information, the right to choose one's country of residence and to live wherever one chooses within that country, freedom of religion, the right to strike, the right to form associations, and the absence of forced labor–which are the guarantees of individual liberty and give life to the social and economic rights of man as well as to international trust and security.

If Thomas Jefferson had written in twentieth-century

idiom describing the social conditions of our time, these could be his words as well as the credo of every man and woman on earth who loves liberty and reverences the free mind. Pondered soberly, Sakharov's moral testament summarizes the essence of human liberty and underscores the conviction that totalitarianism, for all its might, will not necessarily have the last word.

Surveying the barbarities of the twentieth century, he counsels both caution and hope: "The future may be even more tragic. Or it may be more worthy of human beings–better and more intelligent. Or, again, it may not be at all."

Whatever the fates hold, Andrei Sakharov and Elena Bonner have done their part to give the future a chance–and a human face. Those who follow have their own work to do and their own sacrifices to make. There can be no other way for freedom to survive.